DEVELOPMENTS IN SEDIMENTOLOGY   14

DESERT SEDIMENTARY ENVIRONMENTS

FURTHER TITLES IN THIS SERIES

1. *L. M. J. U. VAN STRAATEN, Editor*
DELTAIC AND SHALLOW MARINE DEPOSITS

2. *G. C. AMSTUTZ, Editor*
SEDIMENTOLOGY AND ORE GENESIS

3. *A. H. BOUMA and A. BROUWER, Editors*
TURBIDITES

4. *F. G. TICKELL*
THE TECHNIQUES OF SEDIMENTARY MINERALOGY

5. *J. C. INGLE Jr.*
THE MOVEMENT OF BEACH SAND

6. *L. VAN DER PLAS Jr.*
THE IDENTIFICATION OF DETRITAL FELDSPARS

7. *S. DZULYNSKI and E. K. WALTON*
SEDIMENTARY FEATURES OF FLYSCH AND GREYWACKES

8. *G. LARSEN and G. V. CHILINGAR, Editors*
DIAGENESIS IN SEDIMENTS

9. *G. V. CHILINGAR, H. J. BISSELL and R. W. FAIRBRIDGE, Editors*
CARBONATE ROCKS

10. *P. McL. D. DUFF, A. HALLAM and E. K. WALTON*
CYCLIC SEDIMENTATION

11. *C. C. REEVES Jr.*
INTRODUCTION TO PALEOLIMNOLOGY

12. *R. G. C. BATHURST*
CARBONATE SEDIMENTS AND THEIR DIAGENESIS

13. *A. A. MANTEN*
SILURIAN REEFS OF GOTLAND

DEVELOPMENTS IN SEDIMENTOLOGY 14

DESERT SEDIMENTARY ENVIRONMENTS

BY

K. W. GLENNIE

Koninklijke/Shell Exploration and Production Laboratory, Rijswijk, The Netherlands

ELSEVIER PUBLISHING COMPANY Amsterdam London New York, 1970

ELSEVIER PUBLISHING COMPANY
335 JAN VAN GALENSTRAAT, P.O. BOX 211, AMSTERDAM, THE NETHERLANDS

ELSEVIER PUBLISHING CO. LTD.
BARKING, ESSEX, ENGLAND

AMERICAN ELSEVIER PUBLISHING COMPANY, INC.
52 VANDERBILT AVENUE, NEW YORK, NEW YORK 10017

LIBRARY OF CONGRESS CARD NUMBER: 76-118253
ISBN 0-444-40850-9

WITH 147 ILLUSTRATIONS, 4 TABLES AND 4 MAP ENCLOSURES

PRINTED IN THE NETHERLANDS

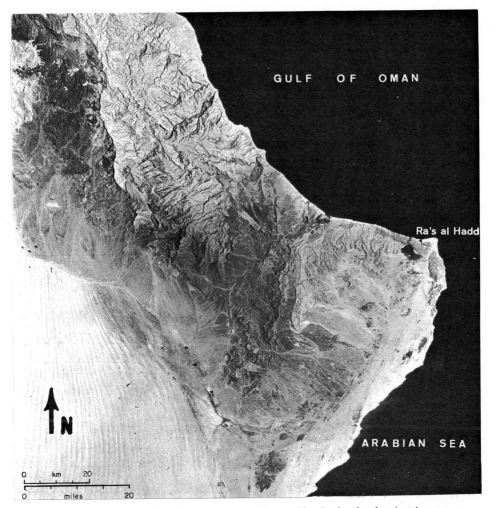

GULF OF OMAN

Ra's al Hadd

ARABIAN SEA

0 km 20

0 miles 20

Frontispiece: Space photograph of the eastern part of the Arabian Peninsula, showing the eastern Oman Mountains, Wahiba Sands, wadi gravel fans and the Arabian Sea. (Taken from the Gemini IV spacecraft during its June 3–7, 1965 orbital mission. Photo credit: National Aeronautics and Space Administration.)

PREFACE

About one fifth of the world's land surface is desert[1] but, contrary to the popular "Lawrence of Arabia" concept, only one fifth of the desert areas is covered with sand (HOLMES, 1965, p.760; see also Fig.1). Fossil desert sediments (mostly dune sands) have been recognised in various periods from the Cambrian to the present. The desert origin of many of such formations has been in dispute, however, for various reasons; sometimes it was because authors were discussing sediments of the same age but of different facies and locations, the one in a desert facies, and the other closely associated with marine fossils (McKEE, 1962, p.558). In other cases it is apparent that the authors did not know what factors were significant in deciding between desert and non-desert sediments, or the differences between aeolian and water-laid sands.

Widespread desert conditions are known to have occurred during the Permo-Trias and continental formations of this age, often referred to in Europe as the New Red Sandstone, contain important oil and gas reservoirs in North Africa (Algeria), Europe (Germany and The Netherlands), and in the United States. It follows that, since little is known about desert sediments, an increased knowledge of them and their inter-relationship with sediments deposited in other environments is of prime importance to the oil industry. Geologists in other walks of life, whether they be concerned with palaeontology or palaeobotany, sedimentology or stratigraphy, will wish to relate their observations to a particular environment within a palaeogeographic setting, and in all these branches of geology, the environment in question could be that of a desert. To them also, then, a knowledge of deserts and their sediments could be of importance.

Deserts were first described for the specific benefit of the geologist by WALTHER in his paper of 1888. He subsequently published several more papers and a text book, *Das Gesetz der Wüstenbildung*, which ran to four editions and is still the most complete authority on the subject for German students.

Since Walther's classic papers and book, much has been published on desert travel and life in the desert by such authors as LAWRENCE (1935), THESIGER (1948, 1959), GAUTIER (1935) and GERSTER (1960). While of geographical and ethnological interest, their works do not help greatly in the geological interpretation of desert

---

[1] Of the world's total land area of about $145 \cdot 10^6$ km², MEIGS (1953) classifies $5.8 \cdot 10^6$ very arid (4%), $21.7 \cdot 10^6$ (15%) as arid and $21.2 \cdot 10^6$ (14.6%) as semi-arid.

sediments. BAGNOLD (1941) in his classic work *The Physics of Blown Sand and Desert Dunes* tells how sand is transported in air and suggests the process by which dunes are formed. Several other authors have written on deserts, but their theme has usually been concerned with the morphology of dunes (CAPOT-REY, 1949; HOLM, 1953, 1960; SMITH, 1965), or with granulometric detail (ALIMEN and FENET, 1954; TRICART and MAINGUET, 1965).

Perhaps of greater use to the field geologist are the interpretations made of fossil desert environments by SHERLOCK (1947), SHOTTON (1937, 1956) and LAMING (1966) in Europe, and in North America by McKEE (1934, 1945, 1954). These authors, however, tend to confine their environmental analyses to the more obvious dune, coastal and wadi sediments. The shortage of literature from outside North America prior to about 1960 that covers all geological aspects of deserts and their sediments can be attributed to the past difficulties and cost of travelling over many of these inhospitable areas. A few years ago, however, the search for oil was intensified in desert areas. This led to an invasion by nomadic technicians, and the difficulties of travel were eased by the use of mechanical transport that could cover in a day distances that still take a week by camel. Those geologists who entered the desert were, however, usually too busy studying older non-desert rocks to have much time to spare for the recent desert environment. The subject remained more or less neglected outside North America and the "French" Sahara until the need for agricultural development of modern deserts and the finding of hydrocarbons in ancient desert rocks led to the economic necessity of understanding them. This need also resulted in the recent surveys by the writer. The recent geological interest in deserts and their sediments can also be seen from the great increase in literature on deserts during the 1960's.

By presenting pictorially a wide range of recent desert sedimentary structures and environments in relation to their geographic setting, the writer hopes to add to the knowledge of the geological aspects of present-day deserts. The examples are based on a personal knowledge of modern deserts in Libya, southeast Arabia and India. The geographic distribution of desert sediments of parts of Libya and southeast Arabia are given in Enclosures 1–4. Comparative fossil occurrences from the Permo-Triassic sediments of northwest Europe and the Tertiary to sub-Recent deserts of Arabia and Libya are used to indicate the appearance of the sedimentary structure when seen in outcrop or core. Although proof of the mechanism is normally lacking, tentative explanations are given to account for the process by which many of the sedimentary structures are formed.

Although the principles outlined in this book are thought to apply to deserts in general, it is realised that other, so far unrecognised, sedimentary processes may occur—both in deserts of which the writer has a personal knowledge and those of which he has not. Others, no doubt, will remedy this deficiency.

Deserts occurring in other environments such as the high altitude and moderate latitude (45° N) Gobi Desert, which is a very long way from the sea, or the polar areas of low precipitation, have no place in this book except, perhaps occasionally, for purposes of contrast with the hot deserts of more tropical latitudes.

Explanations for many of the more unusual terms used in describing deserts and their sediments are given in the glossary at the end of the book.

Provided that the reader can acquire sufficient data from the book to enable him to interpret a group of ancient rocks as having been deposited in a desert environment, and can interpret particular beds as "probably water-laid" or "probably aeolian" from cores and drill cuttings as well as in outcrop, then the book will have served its initial purpose. If it has assisted in making more precise palaeogeographic interpretations, so much the better.

This book is the outcome of research undertaken at the Koninklijke/Shell Exploratie en Productie Laboratorium (K.S.E.P.L.), Rijswijk, The Netherlands, with the addition of facilities for field work provided by the Royal Dutch/Shell Group of companies in Europe, Libya, eastern Arabia and India. In the latter country, Mr. S. Biswas and Mr. R. Mahotra, geologists of India's Oil and Natural Gas Commission, acted as guides in, respectively, the Ranns of Kutch and the Rajasthan Desert; without their help, much less of this interesting area would have been seen. In Libya and on three visits to Germany, the writer was accompanied by E. Oomkens. In Arabia, his companion was B. D. Evamy whose particular interest on the trip was the diagenesis of carbonate rocks. In India, G. Evans of Imperial College, London, accompanied the writer and was able to make valuable comparisons between the sediments of the Ranns of Kutch and those of the Persian Gulf. Many of the writer's ideas have been discussed with his field companions and other colleagues both in The Netherlands and elsewhere; this has proved invaluable as an aid to clear presentation. In addition, the writer was able to draw upon his colleagues' wide range of experience in many branches of geology. The field study was completed in under three years. It is natural, therefore, that gaps should remain in our knowledge and questions be left unanswered. It is hoped that there are no errors in interpretation.

The bulk of this book was prepared as a K.S.E.P.L. report in 1966. Since then, the writer has spent two winters in Oman and the Trucial States studying an entirely different geological problem. The opportunity to revisit this desert region has enabled him to recheck some of his ideas. Two short visits to Iran have added to his understanding of deserts in basins of inland drainage.

This book is published by permission of Shell Research N.V., The Hague, The Netherlands, to whom thanks are given. The maps and figures were prepared under the direction of Mr. R. R. J. Davilar, Head of the K.S.E.P.L. Exploration Draughting Department, whose assistance is gratefully acknowledged. Thanks are extended to Professor K. H. Wolf of Oregon State University and Dr. E. D. McKee of the United States Department of the Interior for advice and constructive criticism after reading a draft of the book. The writer remains, however, solely responsible for any errors or defects in style.

Acknowledgement is made to the undermentioned journals and other authorities for permission to use previously published illustrations or to adapt illustrations for this book. Acknowledgement to the authors and to their sources are made in the captions.

The United States National Aeronautics and Space Administration for the frontispiece; Methuen Co. Ltd. (R. A. BAGNOLD, 1941, *Physics of Blown Sand and Desert Dunes;* 2nd od., 1954) for Fig. 12; Elsevier Publishing Company, Amsterdam (E. OOMKENS, 1966. *Sedimentology*, 7) for Fig. 54 and 56; The Controller, H. M. Stationary Office (W. MYKURA, 1960 *Geological Survey Bull.*, 16) for Fig. 140; Ministry of Defence (Air Force Department) for Fig. 19, 74, and 76.

CONTENTS

PREFACE. VII

CHAPTER 1. SOME GENERALISATIONS CONCERNING DESERTS 1
Aridity leads to desert formation 1
Meteorological reasons for deserts . . ' 3
Trade-wind deserts 4
Monsoon deserts 5
Polar deserts 6
Desert rain. 6
Desert erosion 7
Aeolian transport 7
Sources of dune sand 7
Aeolian sedimentation 8
Basins of inland drainage 8
Preservation of fossil dune sands 10

CHAPTER 2. SOME CRITERIA FOR IDENTIFYING ANCIENT DESERT SEDI-
MENTS 11
Identification of wind-deposited sands in a desert environment 11
Identification of water-laid sediments in a desert evironment 12
Recognition of sub-aerial exposure of water-laid sediments in a desert environment . . . 12

CHAPTER 3. DESERT EROSION AND DEFLATION 15
General 15
Exfoliation and insolation 15
Deflation surfaces 16
Desert varnish 19
Ventifacts 20
Sand removal by wind 21
Sand accumulation 23
Differential deflation 23
Deflation hollows 24

CHAPTER 4. WADIS AND DESERT FLUVIATILE SEDIMENTS 29
Wadis in general 29
Braided pattern of wadi channels 30
Deflation of wadi sediments 32
Early cementation of wadi sediments 33
Relation between erosional highlands and wadi sediments 36
Relation between wadis and dune fields 37
Desert sedimentation in areas of low relief 39
The resistance of aeolian sand to erosion by water 39
Ancient wadi sediments 42
Wadi sediments as a source of aeolian sand 45
Interbedded wadi gravels and aeolian sand 48
Clay lags in wadis and mud cracks 49

Permo-Triassic mud cracks 49
Preservation of sun-curled clay flakes by aeolian sand 52
Clay flakes in ancient sediments 54
Interplay between wind and water in wadi sediments 55

CHAPTER 5. DESERT LAKES AND INLAND SEBKHAS 57
Salinity of lakes in basins of inland drainage 57
Wadi-flood-water origin of some desert lakes 58
Ground-water origin of some desert lakes 58
Inland sebkhas 60
The inland sebkha Um as Samim 61
Some sedimentary structures in inland sebkhas 64
Sand dykes in inland sebkhas 65
Sedimentation versus deflation in inland sebkhas 69
Horizontal bedding in inland sebkhas 69
Near-coast inland sebkhas 69
Adhesion ripples 71
Oases 73

CHAPTER 6. AEOLIAN SANDS 77
Sand ridges 77
Aeolian sand ripples 79
Sand dunes 81
Barchan dunes 81
Distribution of sand dunes 84
Dune complexes 86
Opposing wind directions 88
Seif dunes 89
Transverse dunes 95
Ancient dune sands and palaeo-wind directions 99
Forest laminae in dune sands 106
Horizontal laminae in dune sands 106
Horizontal laminae of sheet sands and interdune areas 106
Contorted bedding in dune sand versus temporary wadi deltas 108
Dikaka 113
Loess 118

CHAPTER 7. DESERT COASTAL SEDIMENTS 121
Development of coastal sebkhas behind longshore bars 121
Preservation of dunes behind protection of spit/coastal-sebkha complexes 122
Absence of fluvial deltas along desert coast lines 124
Tidal deltas 124
Prograding desert coasts 124
Coastal carbonate dunes 126
Carbonate dunes as barrier between wadi and sea 128
Cemented carbonate dunes 128
Time of cementation of carbonate dunes 132
Difficulties of recognising ancient carbonate dunes 133
The salts of coastal evaporitic lagoons 133
Recent anhydrite and contorted bedding 134
Gypsum dunes 136
The ranns of Kutch 136

CHAPTER 8. SUBSURFACE RECOGNITION OF DESERT SEDIMENTS 141
General 141
Sun-dried sediment 141

Evaporite environment 142
Recognition of dune sands in cores 143
Difficulties of deducing palaeo-wind directions from cores 150
A three-dimensional model of barchan bedding 150
Palaeo-wind direction deduced from core of barchan dune 152
Cores from seif dunes 153
Permeability in dune sands 156
Drill cuttings 156
Bedding and sorting in dune sands 157
Thin sections of carbonate dune sands 159
Dolomitised carbonate dune sands 159
Dune sand and roundness of quartz grains 165
Frosting of quartz grains in a desert 165
Frosting and calcite corrosion of quartz grains 166
Frost-free conchoidal fractures on desert quartz sand and relict desert soils 167
Dune sand from deflation to top of dune 167
Possible preservation of environmental history on a quartz grain 170
The significance of red-stained quartz grains 172

CHAPTER 9. THE RELATION BETWEEN RED BEDS AND DESERTS 173
Introduction 173
Hot, wet tropical origin for red sediments 173
Red sediments in tropical climate having seasonal rainfall 177
In-situ formation of red beds 179
Are red beds red throughout? 180
The "Barren Red Measures" 181
Recent desert sands 183
Permian red beds of Britain 185
The apparent anomaly of yellow ancient dune sands 188
The necessity for water in the formation of red desert sediments 190
Criteria for the recognition of a desert palaeoclimate 191
Conclusions 193

GLOSSARY 195

REFERENCES 199

CROSS REFERENCES TO FIGURES, TABLES AND ENCLOSURES 209

INDEX 211

Chapter 1

SOME GENERALISATIONS CONCERNING DESERTS

ARIDITY LEADS TO DESERT FORMATION

Essentially, a desert, in the sense that we are concerned with of a hot tropical desert, is a land area on which there is little or no plant cover because of an insufficiency of regular rainfall; a place where the potential rate of evaporation exceeds the annual precipitation. This may be the result of several factors such as the presence of a mountain barrier in the path of the prevailing wind and the creation of a rain shadow beyond, prevailing off-shore winds, insufficient relief to induce rainfall from temporary onshore winds or wind systems of natural low humidity (Fig.1).

The upper limit for average annual rainfall in a desert is 10 inches (25 cm) according to HOLMES (1965, p.769) and this is reached only near the desert margins, with the adjoining semi-arid regions averaging between 10 and 20 inches (25–50 cm) annually. This obviously applies only to "hot deserts" where the potential rate of evaporation[1] is much greater than the rainfall because of the high average temperature and low humidity.

In some of the arctic regions of North America and Eurasia, the annual precipitation (including the snow equivalent) is less than 10 inches, but the annual rate of evaporation does not exceed the rainfall. Plants have difficulty in maintaining an existence in these polar areas because of the problems of absorbing water into the plant tissues at sub-freezing temperatures. In the hot deserts, on the other hand, there is often little moisture to absorb and the xerophytic plants that inhabit these regions are adapted to reduce evaporation from their surfaces to a minimum.

Whether near a coastline or in the interior of a sand sea, it is rarely so arid in a desert that no plant life can exist. In the few areas where no plants occur, their absence is usually the result of continually shifting sands that prevent the plants from obtaining a firm hold with their roots, or of a salt concentration that is too great to permit plants to exist.

---

[1] For example, KENDALL and SKIPWITH (1969) quote Privett (1959) as estimating that evaporation rates in the southern Persian Gulf can be as high as 124 cm per annum. This is more than thirty times the annual precipitation recorded at Tarif on the coast of AbuDha bi (average of 3.7 cm per annum) from 1958 to 1964, with a maximum of 6.73 cm and a minimum of 0.33 cm (KENDALL and SKIPWITH, 1969, table I).

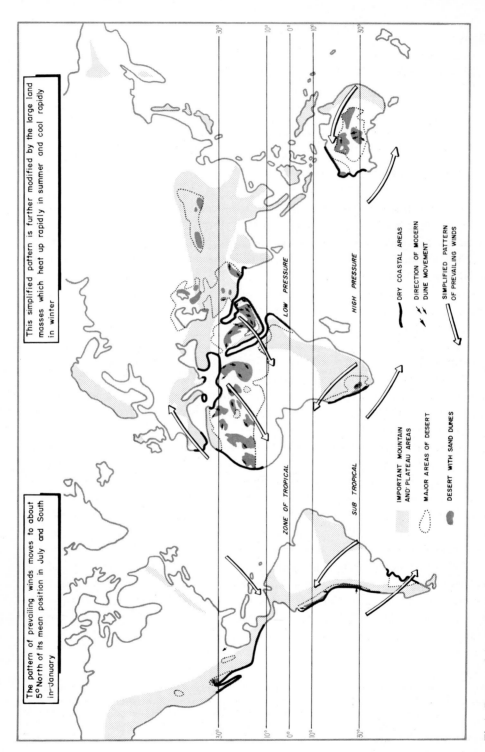

The pattern of prevailing winds moves to about 5° North of its mean position in July and South in January

This simplified pattern is further modified by the large land masses which heat up rapidly in summer and cool rapidly in winter

30°
10°
0°
10°
30°

ZONE OF TROPICAL

SUB TROPICAL

LOW PRESSURE

HIGH PRESSURE

IMPORTANT MOUNTAIN AND PLATEAU AREAS

MAJOR AREAS OF DESERT

DESERT WITH SAND DUNES

DRY COASTAL AREAS

DIRECTION OF MODERN DUNE MOVEMENT

SIMPLIFIED PATTERN OF PREVAILING WINDS

Fig.1. Deserts of the world.

METEOROLOGICAL REASONS FOR DESERTS

The atmospheric conditions that aid the initiation, growth and maintenance of deserts result from the planetary system of high and low air-pressure belts (Fig.2). These air-pressure belts are caused by the circulation of air between the hot equatorial belt and the cold polar regions. If the earth were stationary with the sun revolving around it, a simple convection system would exist with hot air rising over the equator and cold air descending over the poles so that there would be a surface wind blowing towards the equator. The earth, however, rotates, and the winds of the convection system are consequently deflected by the Coriolis force, which is associated with the difference in the earth's rotational velocity at the equator and at the poles. In the equatorial regions, winds tend to be left behind by the earth, so that the convection pattern is deflected towards the west. A further complication is due to the build-up of other high-pressure belts between the equator and the poles. They are formed by hot equatorial air passing into latitudes that are shorter than the equator. These high-pressure belts, known as the Horse Latitudes,

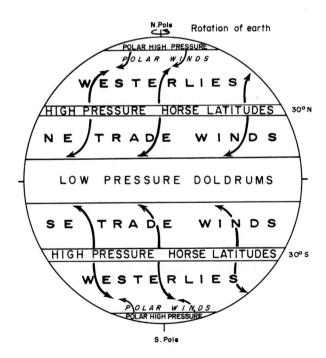

Fig.2. Ideal planetary distribution of high- and low-air pressure belts and associated pattern of prevailing winds.

occur roughly 30° N and 30° S of the equator although, because of the unequal distribution of land and sea, the northern one is slightly further from the equator than the other. The descending high-pressure air of the Horse Latitudes gives rise to clear skies that are not conducive to rainfall. The outflowing air that is directed towards the equator—the "trade winds"—is deflected to the west. The winds that blow towards the poles from the Horse Latitudes are deflected to the east and are known as the "westerlies".

The sun appears directly overhead at the equator only at the two equinoxes. At the solstices, the sun is vertically overhead at either the Tropic of Cancer or the Tropic of Capricorn. As a result of these seasonal changes in the declination of the sun, the wind systems move about 5° north of their mean positions in the Northern Hemisphere summer and an equivalent distance south in its winter.

TRADE-WIND DESERTS

When the trade winds blow across continental areas such as North Africa and Arabia, they usually do so under an almost clear blue sky and no rain falls on the desert landscape across which they pass. In fact the air heats up over the barren desert surface as it moves towards the equator and tends to dessicate still further the land beneath because of its ability to absorb more moisture. This is the reason why the hot and very dry Harmattan, blowing from east or northeast from the Sahara Desert, brings such welcome relief to the inhabitants of the hot and very humid Guinea Coast of West Africa. It is also, no doubt, a factor that gives rise to occasional reports that certain deserts are extending down wind.

Most of the major deserts of the world lie in areas where the trade winds originate in, or pass over, extensive land masses (Fig.1). This is especially true of the Arabian and North African deserts.

Over the sea, the trade winds have a shallow moist layer capped by a stable inversion layer above which the air is very dry (HARE, 1961). When, however, there is a mountain barrier in their path, rain can be precipitated as the surface air is forced to rise over the mountains and a desert can occur in the rainshadow region beyond. This appears to be the reason for the existence of the deserts of central and western Australia. The Southeast Trades lose their moisture on the mountains of the Great Divide in eastern Australia, and although there are other ranges in central Australia, the air is already too hot and relatively dry for them to induce further rainfall (Fig.1). Similarly in South Africa, the trades lose much of their moisture over the Drakensberg and Cape ranges; the Kalahari Desert is beyond.

In the region of South America, the Horse Latitudes are virtually split into two by the Andes, with one high-pressure system centred over the southern Pacific and a second high-pressure system centred over the southern Atlantic. The anti-clockwise winds associated with the South Pacific high-pressure system, blow across the Atacama Desert from the southwest and swing north parallel to the Andes without normally precipitating rain.

In the very narrow southern part of the Atacama Desert, the effect of strong onshore winds—possibly accentuated by convection currents over the Andes foothills—causes sand transport towards the east, that is towards the Andes. Further north, sand is transported to the north by trade winds that here blow roughly parallel to the Andes (Fig.1). The stabilising effect on the atmosphere of the cold Humboldt current that rises along this coastline, is an added factor that prevents rain (WALLÉN, 1966, p.34). Similar conditions exist along the west coast of South Africa where the Benguela current in the South Atlantic flows north. As a consequence, much of the coastal area of southwestern Africa (Namib Desert) ranges from semi-arid to intensely arid[1] (FLINT, 1959).

Drought-inducing rain shadows exist also in the lee of the westerlies for both the arid plains of Patagonia and the intermontane Mojave and Sonoran deserts of the U.S.A. and Mexico. They are to the east of the Andes and Coast Ranges, respectively. The Gobi Desert represents an extreme case of a rain-shadow desert. It lies far from the sea in a great continental basin that is ringed by high mountain ranges.

MONSOON DESERTS

The existence of large land masses and the presence of high mountain ranges can strongly modify the ideal wind patterns shown in Fig.2. The Southwest Monsoon has its origins in the southern part of the Indian Ocean as the Southeast Trade Winds. It is drawn north of the equator by a low-pressure area over northwest India. As it crosses peninsular India, part of it swings north and then west over the Ganges Plain, to lose the last of its moisture on the eastern slopes of the Aravalli Range. The Rajasthan Desert lies beyond, to the west. The moist air that forms the major part of the airstream that crosses Rajasthan during the monsoon blows over the desert from the southwest and is confined to the near-surface layers.

In order to produce rain, moist air must be cooled. This is often achieved by an increase in altitude. PRAMANIK (1952) and RAMANATHAN (1952) have both pointed out, however, that over Rajasthan the near-surface air of the Southwest Monsoon is overlain by relatively warm, dry, anticyclonic air centred over Baluchistan. This will absorb any moist air that may rise and results in the dissipation of any cloud and decreases the likelihood of rain over the desert. The Southwest Monsoon is replaced in the autumn by light winds of the Northeast Monsoon. These, having had a long continental route before reaching Rajasthan, have little chance of bringing rain to the area.

---

[1] Although very arid, mist keeps the surface air over coastal parts of the desert saturated with moisture during much of the year; it rarely rains, however (LOGAN, 1960).

POLAR DESERTS

Like the Horse Latitudes, the poles also are regions of high atmospheric pressure. This is because of the weight of cold, relatively dry, descending air. As the air flows away from the poles it is deflected to the west in response to the higher rotational velocity of lower latitudes. The high-pressure polar air system is characterised by clear skies and low precipitation, whether it be in the form of rain or snow. Because of this relative aridity, Late Pleistocene winds were able to pick up the dry, unconsolidated sands deposited by glacial rivers during spring floods or left behind by retreating ice sheets, and build them into sand dunes such as can now be seen on the northern plains of the United States (SMITH, 1965), Germany and The Netherlands. The morphology of these dunes appears to have much in common with that of dunes in hot deserts.

It is apparent that deserts occur in continental areas of clear skies associated with high atmospheric pressure. The presence of a desert may modify the distribution of the high-pressure belt, but it is not the reason for its occurrence. As many a torpedoed seaman knew during the early 1940's, the trade winds might help him to sail to safety, but they did not always provide him with drinking water. "Water, water everywhere, nor any drop to drink." (*The Rime of the Ancient Mariner*, Coleridge.)

DESERT RAIN

As a result of temporary meteorological disturbances—often initiated outside the desert—rain does occur in desert areas. The frequency of rainfall may vary from several times annually to once in ten or even fifty or more years. Areas such as mountain ranges bordering deserts, or deserts bordering the sea usually receive annual though sparse rainfall. Away from the coast, it becomes increasingly insufficient to overcome the evaporation which takes place during the rest of the year.

Torrential rain can fall in a desert for a matter of hours, or even days. Since there is little soil or vegetation to hold the water in hilly areas, this results in rapid run-off; floods ensue on the plains with little warning and transport sediment over great distances. With no more rain to maintain the flow, the waters may subside almost as rapidly (McGEE, 1897). The sporadically flowing watercourses that form as a result of desert rain are known to the Arabs as wadis. Deposits of thin clay form films, which dry out, crack, curl up, and may be preserved in the geological record if covered by a protective layer of wind-blown sand. If not protected in this manner, then they are either fragmented to dust and blown away, or washed away by a succeeding flood and again deposited as a layer of clay, or as clay pebbles.

DESERT EROSION

In the desert, erosion of the rock surface is brought about by many causes. These include slow chemical weathering, exfoliation due to insolation and the abrading action of wind-blown sand. The products of desert erosion may be removed and redeposited elsewhere by the action of both wind and water.

AEOLIAN TRANSPORT

The wind is essentially only capable of transporting dry sediment. Because fine silt and clay particles take a relatively long time to settle even in air, the turbulent action of the wind tends to keep them in suspension over large distances, and the greater part is finally deposited in more humid areas outside the desert as loess, or over the sea.

The standard work on the physics of blown sand was written by Bagnold some 30 years ago, and would be difficult to improve upon. He made many important field observations on wind-blown sands; these were supported by experimental work. The more pertinent of Bagnold's findings are referred to a number of times in this book.

Referring to the movement of sand by the action of the wind, BAGNOLD (1941, p.11) states that sand-sized particles "having received a supply of energy from the forward pressure of the wind, their acquired horizontal velocity is converted into an upward one by impact with the ground... The pressure of the wind would drive them onward till, on sinking to the ground, they would bounce upwards once more". This gives to the sand grain a low parabolic trajectory. Its density is some 2,000 times greater than that of the air in which it is travelling (as compared with about two and a half times that of water), so the height it can rise above the ground is small. This type of motion is referred to as "saltation". On impact with the ground saltating sand grains, by virtue of their kinetic energy, "can move grains exceeding six times the size of those composing the saltation" (BAGNOLD, 1941, p.154); e.g., winds strong enough to cause grains of say 1 mm diameter (a common maximum diameter for some aeolian beds) to saltate would, in turn, lead to the movement by surface creep of pebbles up to some 6 mm diameter.

SOURCES OF DUNE SAND

The sand that wind transports comes, in part, from chemical weathering and from the fracturing of rock surfaces by rapid temperature changes and the abrasive action of wind-blown sand. This desert weathering and erosion occurs not only over the broad expanses of outcrop, but applies also to areas where aquatic sedimentation is predominant. Any breakdown of older rock or recently cemented sediment gives rise to a supply of sand that the wind is capable of transporting.

A second and possibly equally important source of sand is the sediments that are deposited in alluvial fans by the wadis. The loose sand is picked up and removed by the wind, leaving a lag of coarser pebbles and boulders.

A third and more restricted source of sand is the coastal beaches bordering the deserts. With a tropical sea, this sand often consists almost entirely of shell fragments, ooliths and Foraminifera. Under near-coastal conditions, this carbonate-rich sand can cement rapidly and form a protective barrier against the incursion of the sea. The shell fragments tend to abrade more rapidly than quartz, however, and are not usually recognisable in quantity more than 50 or 100 km from the coast.

AEOLIAN SEDIMENTATION

Whatever their derivation, sand grains are transported over the desert by the wind, until the surface wind velocity is reduced sufficiently for them to come to rest. On the large scale, this occurs in sinking continental basins or topographic traps formed by the uplift of a range of hills of mountains. On the small scale, the sand grains may come to rest in the comparative protection of the lee side of boulders or vegetation where sand drifts form, or in the shelter of a wadi bank where the aeolian sands cover fluviatile sediments. With greater quantities of sand, sand dunes develop, with deposition taking place, in the case of the simple crescent or barchan dune, on the lee slope. Because loose sand is readily transported by the wind, most major accumulations of sand dunes—the sand seas of desert regions—occur in depressions. These depressions may be structural, in the form of grabens or basins, or they may be lowland areas, surrounded by hills on two or more sides, that were eroded or peneplaned before the onset of desert conditions.

BASINS OF INLAND DRAINAGE

Many basins of inland drainage form the sites of deserts (Gobi Desert in Central Asia, Great Kavir of central Iran, Mohave Desert of California). This is very much the case with some of those basins that are situated within or near to the Tropics and have formed as the result of Tertiary mountain building. Since the river water of such regions never reaches the sea, evaporation from the surface of the terminal lake or swamp results in a steady increase in the concentration of salts that were carried in solution. Most plants are unable to live in saline soils; a decreasing cover of vegetation encourages more rapid evaporation from the surface of the soil and desert conditions ensue.

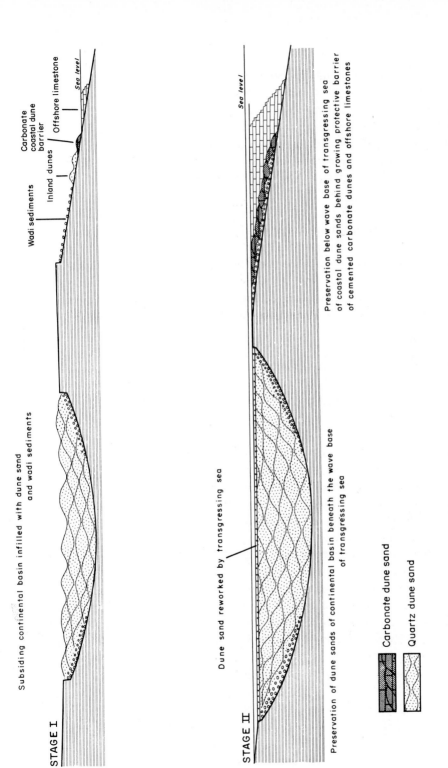

Fig.3. Schematic cross-sections to illustrate how unconsolidated dune sands may be preserved beneath the wave base of a transgressing sea.

Within a basin of inland drainage, the type of sediment fill will partly depend upon relief and climate. Provided there is sufficient rainfall, a lake will form at the lowest point in the basin and fluvial sediments will be deposited in channels leading to the lake. As the central part of the basin fills with sediment, the local base level will slowly rise (DAVIS, 1936). With a decrease in rainfall, rivers may flow only seasonally. Much sediment will be deposited on alluvial fans at the foot of the surrounding hills, but large amounts of gravel, sand, silt and clay can still be carried into local terminal basins by floodwater. After drying out, the wind can remove from the area the finer fractions of this fluvial sediment with sand-sized particles forming migrating dunes. Under increasingly more arid conditions, the base level in the central part of the basin may be lowered as sediment is removed by the wind more rapidly than it is replaced by stream flow. Occasional fluvial transport of sediment into these terminal basins results in sand, silt and clay settling between dunes. Interstratification of aeolian sand and water-laid sediment is characteristic of many areas of Central Asia (HÖRNER, 1936).

PRESERVATION OF FOSSIL DUNE SANDS

The question is sometimes posed: "How can unconsolidated dune sands survive the erosive action of a transgressing sea?" Fig.3 goes far to answer this. Dune sands of the coastal plain are protected behind cemented carbonate dunes and even lightly cemented quartz dunes of the coastal dune barrier. These coastal dunes can themselves be protected from strong wave action by the upward and seaward development of limestone reefs and coastal lagoons. Even in the case of completely unconsolidated dune sands, although the surface sand will be reworked as the relative sea level rises, it thereby forms a "buffer zone" preventing erosion of the aeolian sand beneath.

Inland, great thicknesses of unconsolidated dune sand may accumulate in subsiding continental basins. A transgressing sea will only be capable of reworking the dune sands down to the wave base. For example, in Libya, 120 m of unconsolidated sands overlies the Cretaceous in one basin, and 1,200 m overlies Palaeozoic formations in another (R. Jordi, personal communication, 1964; see also Enclosure 4). MCKEE and TIBBITTS (1964) refer to the presence of about 300 m of aeolian sand south of Bir Zelten in Cyrenaica. This places the base of the sand at this locality some 100 m below the present level of the Mediterranean Sea.

Chapter 2

SOME CRITERIA FOR IDENTIFYING ANCIENT DESERT SEDIMENTS

The following criteria are given as an aid to identifying fossil desert sedimentary environments by recognition of: (*a*) wind-deposited sands; (*b*) water-laid sediments; (*c*) sub-aerial exposure of water-laid sediments.

They are presented here as unsupported statements so that the reader may appreciate the significance of the various sedimentary patterns shown in the following chapters. That these statements are essentially correct will become apparent from the examples given. The numbers in brackets refer to figures in which these features are well shown. It is emphasised that no one criterion is sufficient to permit a positive identification of a desert environment to be made, but it may be enough to suggest it. Individually, many of the criteria can also be found in the sediments of non-desert environments. Criteria for the subsurface recognition of desert sedimentary rocks from cores and drill cuttings are given in Table I (p.144).

IDENTIFICATION OF WIND-DEPOSITED SANDS IN A DESERT ENVIRONMENT

(*1*) Sand laminae horizontal (Fig.88–90, 115, 122) or usually with either fine (centimetre) or large-scale (several metres) foresets having either: (*a*) constant orientation (crescent or barchan dune type) (Fig.84, 87, 102, 115, 117, 120, 121); (*b*) multiple orientation (linear or seif dune type) (Fig.79, 103, 122).

(*2*) Individual laminae well sorted especially in the finer grain sizes; sharp grain-size differences between laminae common (Fig.88, 90, 120–122, 124–128).

(*3*) Grain size commonly ranges from silt (60 μ) to coarse sand (2,000 μ). Maximum size for grains transported under the action of wind is in the order of 1 cm but grains over 5 mm are rare (Fig.6, 30–36, 43–48, 64–66, 124–129, 131–136, 138, 139).

(*4*) The larger sand grains (500–1,000 μ) tend to be well rounded (Fig.124–129, 131–139).

(*5*) Clay drapes very rare (Fig.62, 79, 87, 88, 90, 91, 102, 103).

(*6*) Sands free of clay[1] (Fig.66, 125–128).

---

[1] This criterion implies that the sand was free of clay at the time of deposition and does not preclude the possibility that authigenic clay may be present in ancient dune sands as a result of later diagenesis.

(7) Quartz grains that have not been cemented by calcite usually exhibit a frosted (pitted) surface under the microscope (Fig.124, 131–139).

(8) Mica generally absent.[1]

IDENTIFICATION OF WATER-LAID SEDIMENTS IN A DESERT ENVIRONMENT

(1) The bedding may be that of normal stream-flow sediments of both the upper and lower flow regimes (foresetted gravels, sand ripples, dunes, plane-bed, antidunes etc.) (Fig.18, 25, 27, 28, 33, 36, 42, 43).

(2) The bedding may also appear as unsorted mudflow conglomerates (Fig.118), sheet-flood sediments, horizontally laminated and steeply foresetted flood-plain deposits, and as contorted (recumbent) folds (Fig.94, 95).

(3) Channeling (Fig.27, 28) and accretion foresets common in stream-flow sediments.

(4) Clay laminae or clay drapes common (Fig.37, 38, 43, 56–60, 62).

(5) Many sands are not well sorted, being sometimes argillaceous and pebbly (Fig.31, 34, 45).

(6) Sediment commonly cemented by calcite.

(7) Sand and silt layers commonly missing from graded conglomerates (Fig.18, 27, 28).

(8) Majority of quartz grains that are not cemented by calcite exhibit frosted (pitted) surfaces under the microscope.

(9) Water-laid sediments that are deposited in a desert environment may also possess any of the features mentioned in the succeeding set of criteria.

RECOGNITION OF SUB-AERIAL EXPOSURE OF WATER-LAID SEDIMENTS IN A DESERT ENVIRONMENT

(1) Presence of curled (generally with concave side up) clay flakes (Fig.36, 41–48, 110).

(2) Common presence of clay pebbles (Fig.36, 43–48, 56).

(3) Presence of mud cracks with sandy infill (Fig.37–42, 110–113).

(4) Presence of sandstone dykes (Fig.42, 56–58, 110–113).

(5) Aeolian sand interbedded with beds of aquatic origin. The contacts may show evidence of fluvial erosion or deflation (Fig.24–27, 30–36, 43–48, 56–58, 61–62).

---

[1] So far, mica is only known from coastal dunes adjoining micaceous beach sand and in other wind-blown sands derived directly from mica-rich water-laid sediments, or nearby micaceous outcrops where the distance of aeolian transport from its source is assumed to be small. The absence of mica is not, by itself, indicative of dune sands but may rather be the result of provenance in water-laid sediments.

As a first approximation, the presence of red beds in an ancient sequence can be taken as an indication that they are of continental (although not necessarily desert) origin, were derived from nearby continental sediments or were secondarily reddened as the result, perhaps, of later desert conditions. Many ancient desert sands are often red, but many instances are known where they are grey, brown, yellow or even white. This subject will be dealt with in some detail in chapter 9, where additional criteria for the recognition of fossil desert sediments are given in Table IV (p.192).

The above criteria have been found useful in the identification of different desert environments of deposition in the Permo-Triassic sedimentary rocks of northwest Europe.

Chapter 3

DESERT EROSION AND DEFLATION[1]

GENERAL

In the arid environment of a desert, flowing water plays only a small part in processes of erosion. More important are the effects of changes in temperature, which help to bring about exfoliation of the rock surface and the breaking up of rock and rock fragments. Coupled with these effects of insolation, are those of crystal growth within the rock itself (WELLMAN and WILSON, 1965), micro-chemical corrosion (KUENEN and PERDOK, 1962) aided by wetting effects from rare rainfall and the frequent early-morning dews, and the abrasive action of wind-blown sand and dust.

EXFOLIATION AND INSOLATION

Rapid temperature changes in a desert environment as the means of splitting rocks was brought into disrepute by BLACKWELDER (1933, 1936). He pointed out that experimental work indicated that most rocks did not break at four times the temperature range of solar heating. Hobbs – in a discussion on BLACKWELDER's (1936) paper – opposed these arguments by pointing out that the presence in deserts of split rocks, large and small, called for an explanation. Morris (in the same discussion) pointed out that the rocks themselves had many inhomogeneities that predisposed the line along which it would fracture irrespective of the final "trigger" of splitting.

In another discussion on Blackwelder's paper, DE TERRA (1933) states "Insolation as a geologic process cannot be denied...". He supports this by pointing out that black surface gravel shows the effects of spalling more frequently than lighter rock fragments. He also quotes descriptions by KAISER (1925) of angular fragments from disintegrated quartz veins that fitted each other when pieced together.

More recently, SUGDEN (1964) suggested that the facets found on ventifacts originate by fracturing, "partly attributable to diurnal heating and cooling, but ordinarily following flaws initiated otherwise". BRÜCKNER (1966) attributes much

---

[1] See Glossary.

of the reason for breakdown of the rock surface to "exfoliation in the widest sense, that is to say, the result of release of internal stress in the bedrock at or near its surface, ascribed solely to removal of load by erosion, or to temperature variations, or to differential hydration, or a combination of these and other causes".

The writer has observed many boulders in the desert that can be seen to have split in situ, the pieces lying fractionally apart. Some have been seen on hillsides (where tumbling boulders could, of course, have caused them to crack by impact), but others have been noted on hilltops and open plains where no mechanical fracturing can be expected. Insolation seems the most likely reason for the splitting of larger boulders, and is also thought to play a part in the formation of much finer fragments (see p.167).

Fig.4 shows the south flank of the Fahud anticline in Oman. Beds of sub-rounded boulders of limestone cover the surface of the outcrop. However, on closer inspection, it is seen that these boulders are formed in situ by the exfoliation of bedded limestone (see also Fig.15). Whether this is caused solely by temperature changes, by differences in hydration, by chemical action, or a combination of all three, is uncertain.

The original bedding is still discernible in the layering of the boulders. No transport has taken place.

Fig.5 shows a limestone boulder which has fallen from a nearby cliff within the Fahud anticline. The way in which the surface layers are flaking off to produce a somewhat smaller, sub-rounded boulder is clearly seen[1].

The finer sand surrounding the boulder of Fig.5 is angular (Fig.6). Fragments of both limestone and associated chert are present up to a diameter of roughly 3 mm. Transport by the wind has been practically nil, although some grains may have been blown back and forth over a comparatively small area and become almost spherical in the process. A small percentage may have been derived from outside the area. As seen from Fig.7, the sorting is very poor, and cannot compare with that of an ideal dune sand (cf. Fig.66, 136).

DEFLATION SURFACES

Over areas of flat desert, the processes of deflation cause the removal of the finer fragments by the wind, leaving a lag of coarser pebbles and boulders composed of more resistant rock (Fig.8). Before sand grains can be removed by the wind, they must first, of course, be deposited there by another means such as flowing water, or be derived locally from larger rocks. Chemical corrosion and insolation bring about slow fragmentation of the solid rock beneath the desert surface lag. HÖRNER

---

[1] With a different lithology, insolation can result in angular pebbles formed by the splitting, rather than flaking, of boulders. BOBECK (1959, pp.36, 37) considers the widespread angular pebbles of the "dasht" in central Iran to have been formed by splitting.

Fig.4. Formation of boulders by exfoliation of limestone. Fahud, Oman.

(1936) and BEAUMONT (1968) believe that in areas of alternating wet and dry conditions of the ground, a high salt concentration in gravels can also play an important role in the breakdown of pebbles into finer fragments. COOKE and SMALLEY
(1968) consider that thermal expansion of salts as well as growth of crystals from
solution and hydration of anhydrous salts are also important factors in weathering
of desert areas. If these hypotheses are correct, then this form of weathering may

Fig.5. Detail of limestone boulder showing exfoliation layers. Fahud, Oman.

Fig.6. Aeolian sand grains from close to an area of deflation. Fahud, Oman.

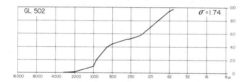

Fig.7. Grain-size distribution curve and sorting coefficient of aeolian sand grains from near t o an area of deflation. Fahud, Oman.

be important in certain coastal areas and in desert regions of inland drainage. It is possible that gypsum acts in this way since it has been seen associated with highly fragmented sandstones east of the Umm as Samim in Oman (Enclosure 1).

Areas which are more resistant to these forms of erosion stand slightly proud of the surface and break into rock slabs that are often the nearest thing to an outcrop for many miles around. When these lag deposits of pebbles and boulders cover large areas they are sometimes called "stony desert". They are referred to by the Arabs of North Africa as "serir" (Libya) or "reg" (Algerian Sahara), and as "gibber plains" in Australia.

A serir, then, is a more or less horizontal deflation lag resulting from the erosion of an older rock surface. The term applies equally well to the deflation surface of older alluvial sediments provided that it is not deeply dissected by erosion gullies. Because of the lack of a covering of pebbles, the term "serir" is not normally extended to include the deflated surface of peneplaned aeolian sediments.

Fig.8. Desert deflation surface. Hamada al Hamra, Libya.

DESERT VARNISH

Outcrops, and the pebble lags of deflation surfaces in desert areas, develop with
time a shiny dark mineral coating known as desert varnish. According to ENGEL
and SHARP (1958), desert varnish forms as the result of a weathering process that
involves solution, transportation and deposition of manganese, iron and a variety
of trace elements. They believe that the elements are derived from within the rock
or, in the case of pebbles of a deflation lag, from the underlying weathered rock
material. Moisture is almost certainly required for the varnish to form. Since rain
is an infrequent visitor to the desert, it is thought that dew, which is fairly common
in the desert after dusk, is important in providing a moist film along which ionic
diffusion can take place. OPDYKE (1961) assumes that the moisture is brought to
the surface by capillary action.

The undersurfaces of pebbles do not receive a desert varnish but possess,
rather, an orange, yellow or brown matt surface. Desert varnish does not form
on soft friable rock, and can be destroyed by abrasion with wind-blown sand,
burial, and presumably also by a climatic change to a wetter climate. Because
desert varnish is destroyed as a result of burial, it is unlikely to be a factor that
can be used for the recognition of arid conditions in ancient sediments.

The dark surfaces of the outcrops seen in Fig.15 are the result of desert varnish. In the deflation hollow below (see p.27), desert varnish has darkened areas of wadi gravel that have probably not been reworked by water for several decades. In the lighter-coloured areas, sediment has been transported in recent years and the varnish has not had time to form.

VENTIFACTS

Sand-blast abrasion of pebbles of a deflation lag is considered to cause facets to form on the windward surface of the pebbles and thereby forms ventifacts. If there are two dominant winds, facets will be cut on two surfaces. A pebble with one sharp edge forming the intersection between the two facets is known in Germany as an "Einkanter", one with two such edges, a "Zweikanter", and with three edges, a "Dreikanter". An analysis of the trends of such edges on some ventifact pebbles, and the apparent direction of the sand-laden wind that is presumed to have formed them has been made by HIGGINS (1956). Deflation of the surrounding sediment undermines the pebbles and they topple over to expose another surface to the wind. In this way, a Dreikanter may be formed. WALTHER mentions having seen Dreikanters in his 1888 article, and described them at some length in his book *Das Gesetz der Wüstenbildung* (1900). Ventifacts have also been recorded by BIGARELLA and SALAMUNI (1964) from the Early Mesozoic Botucatú Sandstone of Brazil and Uruguay.

Ventifacts that have been formed solely by the action of the wind are probably not so common as is generally believed, however. So far, the writer has not found any preferred orientation of the facets of angular pebbles on a desert surface, and certainly none that could be referred to known prevailing winds either existing at present or inferred for earlier times.

Sand-blast abrasion undoubtedly occurs in the desert, but within the writer's experience, most of the angular pebbles found as a lag on the desert surface were probably formed by splitting as a result of the effects of insolation (see also the references to Sugden and Bobek on p.15 and 16). The polished surfaces that have also been associated in the past with ventifacts (e.g., HOLMES, 1965, p.755) are almost certainly formed of desert varnish and, as has been mentioned above, desert varnish is destroyed by abrasion with wind-blown sand; this does not, however, preclude the possibility of earlier shaping by this means.

The writer has examples of pebbles from deflation surfaces whose exteriors show typical desert varnish but whose shapes appear to depend upon an earlier history (such as rounding by transport in a wadi) and the lithology of the rock from which it was derived; siliceous rocks seem to have broken with sharp edges as the result of insolation; argillaceous rocks have flaked surfaces formed by exfoliation, whilst calcareous rocks show a typical intricate pattern of surface grooves and ridges that could well be related to slow chemical solution resulting from dew or rare rain. Similar grooved and ridged limestones are mentioned by MAXSON (1940).

The widespread presence of angular pebbles can, in many cases, be considered as indicative of desert conditions, but their universal origin by sandblasting must be held to be in doubt: splitting by the effects of insolation followed by the formation of desert varnish would appear to be a more likely mechanism for the formation of many "ventifacts".

SAND REMOVAL BY WIND

When the wind blows with sufficient strength, it picks up the particles of sand and moves them, first by rolling, and then close to the surface in a low cloud of saltating grains. With a surface consisting of both fine and coarse sand grains, a certain wind velocity is capable of removing exposed fine grains, but is not capable of moving either the coarse grains or the fine grains they protect. With a greater velocity, both coarse and fine grains are set in motion by the wind. Some grains may still be too heavy to be moved by the direct force of the wind, but creep over the desert surface under the force of impact of the bombardment by smaller saltating grains.

At low wind velocities there is a tendency for selective transport of particles of low sphericity (WILLIAMS, 1964). This is well seen in the sands of many coastal dunes, where angular shell fragments derived from the adjoining beach have a greater sieve-size than quartz grains from the same lamina (GIBBONS, 1967; YAALON, 1967). Although not visible in the photo, this is also the case in the dune sands from near the coast of the Persian Gulf seen in Fig.122. This difference in grain size is less apparent farther from the coast. At greater wind velocities, on the other hand, transport of more spherical grains predominates and these grains reach a greater height during saltation than the more angular grains (WILLIAMS, 1964). This latter character is presumably a reflection of the greater elasticity of a rounded grain.

Fig.9 was taken during a sandstorm in Libya. Most of the sand was seen to move very close to the ground. Saltating grains of 1 mm diameter were collected about 1 m from the ground. Grains of about 5 mm diameter, too heavy to be moved by the direct action of the wind, were slowly creeping along the surface under the force of impact of saltating grains while grains of 2 mm diameter were rolling continuously over the ground. For sands of more uniform size, BAGNOLD (1941, p.34) tells us that between 20 and 25% of the total sand movement is by surface creep. Although the 5-mm grains will represent nothing like that percentage when the total weight of sand moved is considered, in some cases surface creep can result in sizeable sedimentary structures (see p.77 and Fig.64). Since no dust was available in the area for the wind to transport, the sky was clear when Fig.9 was

Fig.9. Dust-free air during a sandstorm. North of Edri, Libya.

taken. Sand grains are too heavy to go into suspension in any normal wind.

Even in areas essentially of sand accumulation, if the supply of sand is insufficient to cover the interdune areas as well as the dunes, then deflation of the interdune areas continues. Fig.10 from the eastern edge of the Rub al Khali, Arabia, shows low areas of chalkified Eocene limestone outcrop, a deflation lag of angular limestone pebbles, sand drifts on the protected leeward side of outcrops, and, in the distance, a line of sand dunes to which much of the deflated limestone is blown.

Fig.10. Deflation surface of interdune outcrop area. Near Barik, Oman.

SAND ACCUMULATION

On p.72 of his book, Bagnold states that "a given wind can drive sand over a hard immobile surface at a considerably greater rate than is allowed by the loose sand covered surface" (BAGNOLD, 1941). This means that sand tends to accumulate on areas that are already sand covered, in preference to the bare surrounding areas (see Fig.10 and also Fig.69–71).

Pressure gradients also occur between the interdune and dune areas, caused by the resistance to the wind of the dunes themselves. This also means that sand will tend to be transported from the sand-free interdune areas towards the dunes. A combination of these two factors explains why sand concentrates into individual dunes and groups of dunes where there is an insufficiency of sand to cover the whole area. With an excess of sand, the dunes grow in height and the interdune areas also become sand covered. The transport of sand from interdune to dune is then solely the result of eddies caused by the pressure gradient between the two areas. This subject will be discussed more fully in chapter 6.

DIFFERENTIAL DEFLATION

In desert areas of horizontal strata, variations in lithology or types and degree of cementation result in differing rates of deflation. In this way, considerable relief can develop without the necessity for fluvial erosion. Fig.11 shows such an area in the Jabal Uaddan, Libya, where hard limestone beds alternate with softer marls. The harder limestones tend to act as a protective "cap", but, as the underlying marls weather and are blown away, so boulders of limestone, helped by insolation, become unsupported, break off and tumble down the slope. Further wind-scouring of the soft marl beneath the boulder causes the latter to tip over and move further

Fig.11. Differential rates of deflation. Jebel Uaddan, Libya.

down the slope away from the outcrop. In this way, a limited amount of spreading of a lag gravel is obtained.

Layers that are more resistant to erosion can result from caliche cementation of the desert surface. Such calcite-cemented layers of sediment, a metre or so thick, are common in some desert areas as the result of evaporation of carbonate-rich flood or ground water. If this protective layer is broken through by processes of erosion for any reason, then removal of the softer more poorly cemented sediment beneath can proceed at a faster rate and can give rise to an erosional form that is similar to that seen in Fig.11. In some cases the protective caliche-cemented cap may overhang the softer sediment beneath to give the outcrop a "mushroom" shape (see DI CESARE et al., 1963, photo 3). Another example of differences in the rate of deflation between well and less-well cemented sediment is mentioned on p.34 and illustrated in Fig.19 and 20.

Concerning deflation of the clay and fine silt-sized particles produced by weathering of the marl, BAGNOLD (1941) has made a most important observation. For any given size of grain, there is a certain velocity of wind (named by Bagnold the "threshold velocity") at which the grains are set in motion. Fig.12 is a reproduction of two of Bagnold's graphs. Fig.12A shows that particles below about $80\,\mu$ have a higher threshold velocity than rather larger particles: below this limit, the finer the grain size, the greater is the threshold velocity, so that a wind which is strong enough to move pebbles 4.6 mm in diameter is unable to move finely scattered portland cement. He explains this by pointing out that there is a wind velocity gradient which reaches zero close to the ground, so that "once fine solid particles smaller than about $30\,\mu$ have settled on the ground after carriage in suspension by a wind, they cannot be swept up again individually, because they sink into a viscid surface layer of air and are out of reach of the disturbing influence of the eddies of turbulence". The same principle applies whether the dust has settled out of the air, or has been derived in situ by processes of weathering. The only way in which these fine particles can be moved—apart from scouring with water—is for them to be attacked by a storm of larger saltating sand grains which eject the dust particles above the viscid surface layer of air and thus force them into suspension in the turbulent air above. Once airborne, silt and clay-sized particles can be readily kept in suspension by virtue of their small size and weight, so that if the wind persists for long enough, this fine material may be carried great distances and be deposited as loess far beyond the desert margins.

DEFLATION HOLLOWS

An extreme case of differential deflation can result in the wind scooping out a hole in what is otherwise a horizontal stony desert surface, such as occurred at Al Fugaha, Libya (Fig.13). Here, there is an almost circular hole some 2 or 3 km

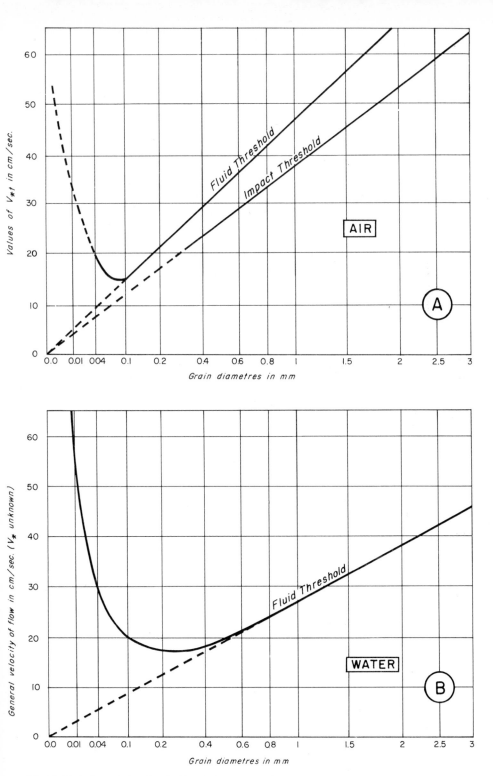

Fig.12. Variation of the threshold velocity with grain size for air and water. From BAGNOLD (1941, 1954, 2nd ed., pp.88, 89).

Fig.13. Deflation hollow in flat desert. Al Fugaha, Libya.

across and 60 to 70 m deep. The few short wadis all drain into the hollow but, nevertheless, it is believed by the author to have been formed primarily by wind erosion, aided possibly by the presence of strata which weather to a fine dust and can therefore be carried out in suspension by a strong wind. The depth to which deflation can penetrate is limited by the level of the water table. This is the case at Al Fugaha which, since the water there is not too saline, is also an oasis (see also p.74). The largest known depression thought to have been formed solely by deflation is the Qattara Depression (Fig.14) in northwest Egypt, which covers an area of some 18,000 km² and reaches a depth of 134 m below sea level. The sediment removed from the Qattara Depression by the wind is now found as part of a dune field extending away to the south (BALL, 1927, 1933).

     Evaporation at the level of the water table in the base of such depressions often causes precipitation of gypsum and rock salt (cf. Fig.59). Salt marshes occur at several levels near the bottom of the Qattara Depression. They are by no means horizontal, and the lowest point in the depression is actually dry clay. Although evaporation of the groundwater has undoubtedly increased the salt content of the marshes, BALL (1933, p.292) points out that as the depression is approached there is an increase in the salinity of the water found in wells that tap the same aquifer. He suggests that solution of salt from these Tertiary rocks is reponsible for this after the water has left its original Nubian Sandstone aquifer. An alternative possi-

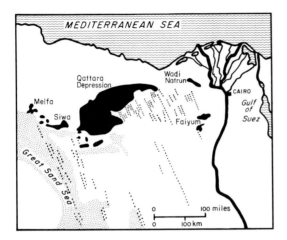

Fig.14. Map of large deflation hollow. Qattara Depression, Egypt. (After HOLMES, 1965.)

bility is that the aquifer that supplies the water to the marshes becomes enriched in salt because of the semi-permeable nature of the overlying Tertiary shales. Deflation brings the aquifer relatively nearer to the surface. Upward percolation of water through this semi-permeable barrier to the bottom of the depression brings about an increase in the salt content of the water still within the aquifer. Although part of the salt is retained in the aquifer, a percentage will pass through the shales and be precipitated at the surface as a salt crust. This process is discussed at greater length on p.60 in connection with other areas of salt precipitation.

At Fahud, Oman (Fig.15), a flat elongate plain forming the centre of a dissected anticline is surrounded by an escarpment whose beds dip away from the plain. Although there is now a thin partial covering of braided wadi sediments, the whole area is suspected of having been formed partly by deflation. At one point

Fig.15. Deflation hollow with thin veneer of water-laid sediment. Fahud, Oman.

there is a small gap in the escarpment on the southern side of the structure (Fig.4), but this is at a level which is a few metres higher than the lowest portion of the plain. Although Tertiary gypsum was plentiful, this lowest part of the plain consisted only of marl and occasional bands of limestone undergoing deflation. Even though there had been some fluvial drainage, it was not sufficient in volume to carry sediment to the lowest part of the basin and much of the evidence of its presence might yet be removed by deflation before the next rainfall. It is apparent that the wind is a very effective agent of sediment removal during the process of deflation in a desert environment.

Most of these deep deflation hollows (Qattara, Fahud, Al Fugaha and others) are known to be associated with calcareous rocks. ANDERSON (1947) has suggested that in these cases the process of deflation is assisted by fragmentation of the rock by solution and collapse associated with ground-water movement. He may well be right.

Chapter 4

WADIS AND DESERT FLUVIATILE SEDIMENTS

As has already been stated, some rain does fall in the desert. In hilly areas this can result in wadis becoming flooded and, especially in the lower reaches where aeolian sediment is common, the flowing water in a wadi can transport considerable amounts of sediment for a short period such as a day or two. With a low water/ sediment ratio, the wadi may be filled with a flowing slurry of sand or mud which can support boulders of considerable size which are then deposited as an unsorted muddy gravel—the mudflow conglomerates of BLACKWELDER (1928) and BLUCK (1965, 1967). A higher water/sediment ratio gives normal stream sorting with some grading of the sediment.

Because the flow of water is not maintained in a wadi, permanent channels, such as occur with rivers are not found. As the water velocity in the wadi drops and water is absorbed into the dry sediment over which it flows, so the sediment, whether it was transported in suspension or by traction, is deposited. In this way, the wadi channel may become partly filled with its own sediment or, later, by wind-blown sand. Since deposition often takes place over a more or less planar deflated surface, the next flood finds its old route partially or completely blocked. It must then seek alternative routes and, in so doing, builds up a braided alluvial fan.

The use of the word "wadi" in the title of this chapter is significant. It immediately indicates a form of fluviatile transport which is sporadic and abrupt. This particular means of intermittent transport of sediment has many implications which are discussed in the following pages.

Many of the landforms in modern deserts have been partly inherited from a wetter past. Thus, many wadis now occupy erosional channels in areas of outcrop, which were cut at a time of greatly increased water flow (e.g., during Pleistocene "pluvial" periods). This is well seen on the southern edge of the Rub al Khali (Enclosure 1). Here, the wadi channels are partly filled with sediment, but at present the flow of water is not sufficient to carry sediment beyond the areas of outcrop. The existence of a more extensive system of rivers or wadis in former times can be inferred from the fluviatile gravels now occupying the long sand-free interdune corridors (or feidjs) along the southern edge of the Rub al Khali.

Much of the sediment found in wadi channels is deposited under normal stream-flow conditions of deposition. The bed forms that result from different regimes of stream-flow have been described in some detail by such workers as SIMONS and RICHARDSON (1963, 1966), JOPLING (1963, 1965), ALLEN (1963, 1968a, b) and MIDDLETON (1965). At lower stream velocities small ripples form that are transverse to the flow direction. At a higher velocity of flow, the small ripples are abruptly replaced by larger ripples (dunes, or sand waves) that are also arranged transversely to flow. A further substantial increase in flow strength will commonly lead to the destruction of the large ripples and the formation of an apparently flat bed over which there is intense sand transport (ALLEN, 1968a). At still larger flow velocities (the upper flow regime of SIMONS and RICHARDSON, 1966) the plane bed is replaced by standing waves (antidunes) that are roughly in phase with the waves of the water surface. Irregularities in the flow strength may result in scouring of the underlying sediments.

When water in flood breaks the banks of its containing channel, it may spread out over the surrounding countryside in a broad sheet. The sediments that are deposited during such a phenomenon have been described by McKEE et al. (1967). They consist of a combination of steeply forsetted sands, horizontally laminated sands and sets of climbing ripples. The foresetted sands are interpreted as being the result of the formation of a sediment front where the water became deeper and was unable to maintain massive sand transport over a flat surface. The formation of foresets with relatively low angles is attributed, however, to current movement that was still strong at the time of deposition; the horizontally laminated sands are thought to have been deposited under conditions of the upper flow regime; the climbing ripples are considered to indicate overloading of the water with sediment as the water velocity falls (ALLEN, 1963; McKEE, 1966b).

When sediment-laden flood water flows across sand that is saturated with water, the laminae of underlying cross-strata can be dragged forward into a recumbent fold (McKEE et al., 1962; McKEE, 1962). This, apparently, can occur when flood water flows into a standing body of water such as a shallow lake or the sea (see Fig.94, 95).

BRAIDED PATTERN OF WADI CHANNELS

Wadis usually exhibit a braided-stream pattern of sedimentation. Braided streams[1] develop in the continuously flowing rivers of non-desert areas when they are heavily laden with sediment and there is a rapid fall in stream velocity. This often occurs where rivers emerge from mountainous regions and flow out over gently sloping alluvial plains (see also BLISSENBACH, 1954).

The same principle applies to wadis. They, however, suffer from additional factors peculiar to their desert environment. The water in a wadi does not flow

---

[1] See Glossary.

continuously all the year round. Normally, after rain, the water in the wadi will soak into the ground only a few hours, or at the most a few days, after it first starts to flow following rain. All the sediment carried in the water—and this may, in some instances, have almost the consistency of a mud flow—has to be deposited. Much of this sedimentation occurs in the vicinity of the downstream limit of water flow, so that locally, the wadi channels become clogged with gravel and sand. During the succeeding dry period of several months or even years, deflation will result in the removal of the finer sediment from the more exposed parts of the wadi channels and wind-transported sand may be deposited in the more sheltered parts. In some places, the channels may be partly, or even completely, blocked by wind-blown sand. The next time that the wadi again flows with water, it may flood too rapidly for the water to immediately remove all the aeolian sand blocking its path. The water in the wadi overflows its bank and scours new, or modifies old, channels.

HÖRNER (1936) describes similar processes of deflation and deposition in Central Asia that result in the strange phenomenon of wandering lakes, some of which, such as Lop Nor, migrate over wide areas.

Any tendency for the channel of a wadi to be filled with sediment is counteracted during the next flood by the cutting of new channels that spread out fanlike. This spreading of alluvial sediments is possibly also helped by deflation of the pre-existing sediments on either side of the wadi.

The structure of the sediments of braided streams in deserts is, in general, similar to that described by DOEGLAS (1962) for two tributaries of the Rhone in southern France. An important exception, however, is the change brought about by the wind; removal of the finer sediment from some areas and deposition of aeolian sand over others.

Fig.16 is a photo of an alluvial fan occupying the area of a narrow coastal plain between the Oman Mountains and the shores of the Persian Gulf. It measures roughly 2.5 km from its apex to the coast. The braided pattern of the channels is clearly visible. Because the flow of water in a wadi is only sporadic, there is no continuous supply of sediment into the sea. Marine longshore currents rapidly destroy any small delta which may have built up during a flood, and the sediment of this temporary delta is redeposited as marine gravels, sands and clays. Beach sands are often blown inland to form a low dune covering of, in this case, largely carbonate sand.

Many of the large alluvial fans seen around the edge of the Oman Mountains had their origins, like the wadis of the southern edge of the Rub al Khali, during the Pleistocene (or even earlier?), when at times rainfall must have been considerably greater than now. The present rainfall is rarely heavy enough to account for the great volume of coarse sediment contained in them. The alluvial fan shown in Fig.16 must have extended much farther from the mountains during the last Pleistocene Glacial period. The post-Glacial sea-level rise has resulted in the sea cutting a low cliff that reaches a height, in some places, of 3 to 4 m above sea level.

Fig.16. Wadi fan between Oman Mountains and Persian Gulf. North of Ras al Khaimah, Trucial Coast.

It is reasonable to assume that this fan extends westwards beneath the younger marine sediments of the sea floor in the same way as the conglomerates of the alluvial fan east of Ras al Khaimah extend down beneath the coastal sebkha sediments that are now being deposited (see also Fig.98, p.60 and 121).

With a decrease in rainfall, sediment is transported over shorter distances and in smaller amounts, and the wadi tends to cut deeper into its own channels rather than extending the limits of the fan. The dissected remnants of older alluvial fans are quite a common sight around the flanks of the Oman Mountains.

Along the northern side of the Oman Mountains, these deeply dissected fans are not necessarily the result only of a decrease in rainfall. Arguments are presented on p.94 in support of the hypothesis that in this part of the world, Pleistocene "pluvials" coincided with interglacial periods of high sea level. A later lowering of the sea level as ice caps again extended would result in considerable lowering of the base level of the wadis and consequently increased downward erosion. On the other side of the mountains where such changes in base level did not occur, downward erosion is much less apparent.

DEFLATION OF WADI SEDIMENTS

Over the bulk of the fan seen in Fig.16, deflation has caused the removal of the exposed wadi sands, silts and clays to leave a boulder-strewn surface (Fig.17). The boulders on this surface are continually broken down by insolation and other forms of weathering and the fine fragments removed by the wind.

Fig.17. Boulder-strewn deflation surface of wadi fan. North of Ras al Khaimah, Trucial Coast.

Fig.18 illustrates the imbrication[1] of pebbles and boulders seen in a channel cut by one of the braiding streams through a previously deposited conglomerate. There is a tendency for pebble size to decrease upwards; sand layers are usually missing. Above the hammer, a later flow is represented by a slight coarsening in the pebble size. Some of the boulders may have received part of their rounding as the result of exfoliation before transport occurred. Roundness is not a guaranteed criterion for indicating distance from source (cf. Fig.5).

EARLY CEMENTATION OF WADI SEDIMENTS

In areas where the mountains being eroded are rich in limestone, cementation of the wadi gravels can take place almost immediately after deposition. The water evaporates and calcium carbonate precipitates at the contact points of the boulders

---

[1] The pebbles and boulders dip upstream with their long-axes showing a marked preference for being aligned parallel to the direction of stream-flow, thus indicating, according to RUCHIN (1958, p.41), a fast current. The orientation of these pebbles may be contrasted with the orientation of pebbles in the gravel horizon seen in Fig.33, where the pebbles dip downstream parallel to the foreset planes. Other variations in the orientation of pebbles in wadi gravels (such as those caused by pebbles slipping down the side of an undercut pebble bank) conform closely to the descriptions given by RUCHIN (1958, pp.413–416, and Abb.161) for his "Gebirgsflüsse" and "Flüsse des Gebirgsvorlandes" (mountain rivers and rivers of mountain forelands). (See also LAMING, 1966, pp.945–947.)

Fig.18. Imbrication of boulders in wadi conglomerate. North of Ras al Khaimah, Trucial Coast.

and finer sediment.[1] Rapid cementation is an additional factor aiding the blocking of wadi channels and the formation of a braided distributary pattern and fan development. The cementation of gravels in an alluvial fan of a wadi system is uneven. The upper part of a bed is poorly cemented because the water soaks rapidly away rather than slowly evaporating to dryness. The strongest cementing action appears to be confined to the main wadi channels where the flow of underground water may continue for many months. Cementation takes place at the water–air interface as the level of the water flowing underground slowly falls.

In several instances in the Oman Mountains, the writer has noticed that the calcareous cement holding the limestone boulders together gave the rock such coherence that large pot holes, that were later cut into the conglomerate during a succession of floods, were formed in boulder and cement alike as if the conglomerate were completely homogeneous.

Examples are known of cemented wadi-channel systems resisting erosion by deflation more strongly than the more poorly cemented sediments on either side (differential deflation), with the result that they have later been exhumed and now stand proud of the desert floor (see, for example, STOKES, 1961, fig.15). One such system of probable Pleistocene age occurs to the west of the Wahiba Sands in

---

[1] It must not be assumed, however, that rapid cementation of fluvial sediments can only occur in a desert environment. It can take place in any area of hot climate where river waters are rich in dissolved carbonates and the water level falls slowly during the dry season to permit a long period of evaporation.

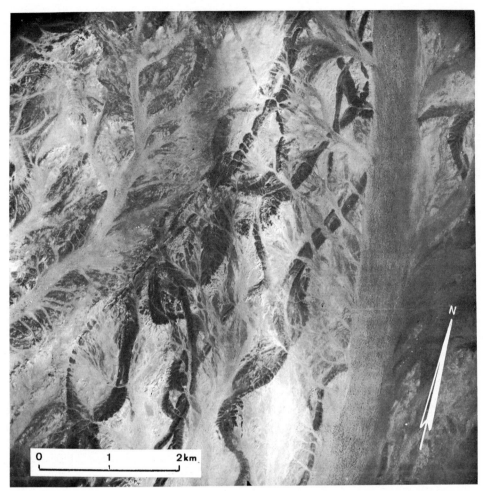

Fig.19. Aerial photo of ridges of exhumed cemented Pleistocene(?) wadi gravels showing the distribution of old wadi channels.

Fig.20. Simplified photogeological map showing the relation between ancient exhumed (dark coloured) and present (light coloured) wadi systems. West of Wahiba Sands, Oman.

Fig.21. Jebel Hafit encircled by interfingering wadi fans, that control the location of the dunes (*d*) at southern end of Jebel. Oman–Abu Dhabi border.

Oman (Fig.19, 20). The ridges of conglomerate occur at several different levels down to that of the present wadi system.[1] There is a striking similarity between the two patterns, ancient and modern. Even though the Oman Mountains to the north must have been higher at the time these old wadi sediments were deposited, the alluvial fans occupied sites in roughly the same localities as today.

Cementation of wadi sediments soon after deposition may result in an early loss of porosity and permeability. This could have an important bearing on the later availability of the sands to act as a reservoir for hydrocarbon accumulations. On the other hand, aeolian sands that are interbedded with wadi sediments seem to be relatively poorly cemented and often retain good reservoir characteristics (see also p.43). The widespread, poorly cemented aeolian sandstones of the Lower Triassic of northwestern Europe are gas reservoirs in northern Germany. Associated fluviatile sandstones do not appear to be reservoirs, possibly because of early cementation.

RELATION BETWEEN EROSIONAL HIGHLANDS AND WADI SEDIMENTS

Any highland area within a desert is likely to receive a higher rainfall than the adjacent lowland areas and hence to be surrounded by a fairly well-defined belt of wadi sediments. Since its elevation exposes it to the erosive action of the wind, it will not be covered with dune sand. In contrast, the surrounding plains may have a covering of dune sands which will compete with the water-borne wadi sediments for a site of deposition. This pattern of an erosional highland surrounded

---

[1] The pebbles of the exhumed conglomerates have acquired a dark patina of desert varnish in contrast to the light-coloured gravels of the present wadis.

Fig.21 (continued).

by wadi and dune sediments is well illustrated on a fairly small scale by Jebel Hafit
on the Oman–Abu Dhabi border (Fig.21). Jebel Hafit has a visible relief of over
1,000 m, is some 30 km long, about 5 km wide and is being actively eroded. The
relief may formerly have been considerably greater, since the lower parts are now
buried beneath an unknown thickness of wadi sediments. The encircling, interfingering alluvial fans coalesce with the distal ends of other fans which spread out
from the Oman Mountains some 25 km behind the viewer (Enclosure 2). When
the wadis are in flood, the combined water-flow divides to go round either end of
the Jebel, to become lost in the sand dunes of the eastern edge of the Rub al
Khali (Enclosure 2).

RELATION BETWEEN WADIS AND DUNE FIELDS

The routes followed by the wadis which intermittently flow with water around
Jebel Hafit are strongly controlled by the presence of dune sand, such as the linear
dune seen in the left background of Fig.21. The erosion caused by the short period
of flowing water is easily compensated for by the intermittent aeolian deposition
during the remainder of the year. In the left foreground of Fig.21, there is an ill-
defined patch of low sand hills occupying an area where the wadis are not active.
Their morphology appears not to be sharply defined, and possibly results from a
multi-directional interplay between the locally predominant west winds and those
associated with "updraughts" formed around the Jebel in the heat of summer.

The effects of updraughts associated with mountain ranges are perhaps part of
the reason why the Wahiba Sands are oriented north–south and not parallel to the
main track of the Southwest Monsoon (Enclosure 1).

The major dunes of the Wahiba Sands—so clearly seen in the frontispiece—

E   W

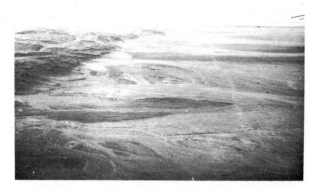

Fig.22. Belt of wadi fans along east side of Djofra Graben, Libya

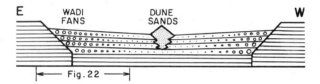

Fig.23. Schematic cross-section through Djofra Graben.

were probably formed during a Pleistocene Glacial period of very high winds. They were formed by winds that were possibly associated with a Pleistocene "Southwest Monsoon" and blew from south to north. Apart from a loose sand cover on the dunes, they, and the interdune areas, consist of cemented dune sand rich in carbonate grains.[1] At their fullest extent, the dunes probably extended across the present alluvial fan of Wadi Batha as far as the edge of the mountains to the north. Recently modified remnants of this dune system can be seen in the middle of the fan. Since that time, heavy rains must have caused floods of sufficient magnitude to erode and remove up to 25 km from the northern end of this magnificent system of dunes. Now, Wadi Batha is annually trying to remove further sand while winds of the present Southwest Monsoon try to extend the sand cover further to the north. Although at present the dune sands appear to be winning, one major flood, such as might happen once in a century, could remove much of this thin cover of small barchan and seif dunes. In the meantime, the supply of dune sand is more than sufficient to repair damage caused by mild intermittent flooding.

---

[1] These grains consist of detrital limestone, abraded Foraminifera and other organic calcareous fragments. See also p.127.

DESERT SEDIMENTATION IN AREAS OF LOW RELIEF

Desert sedimentation occurs in areas of relatively low relief. This may be on a coastal plain as with the wadi sediments seen on Fig.16 and 17, in continental basins formed by crustal downwarping, subsiding fault blocks or areas which have been earlier lowered by a period of intense deflation.

Fig.22 shows the eastern edge of the Djofra Graben in Libya (Enclosure 4). The highland area to the east is one of erosion and wind or wadi transport. At the escarpment edge, each wadi spreads its sediments out into an alluvial fan which coalesces at its margins with the neighbouring fans. The grain size of the sediment within a fan fines away from its apex. In the Djofra Graben this finer sediment is removed by the wind and accumulates in a belt of dune sands occupying a median position in the graben (Fig.23). These dunes effectively prevent the wadi waters from flowing any further, so that after rain, they are flanked by a series of temporary lakes (Fig.49) which remain until the water has either evaporated or soaked into the ground.

THE RESISTANCE OF AEOLIAN SAND TO EROSION BY WATER

Even though flowing water has considerable erosive power, desert wadis often do not flow for a sufficient length of time to allow them to remove all the wind-blown sand which may have filled their channels. This is well illustrated by Fig.24, where on the inner edge of a curve in the wadi, clean, well sorted horizontally laminated sand has resisted much of the scouring action of the flowing water. This sand is thought to have been deposited by the wind. The deeper channels (not seen in the photo) are filled with pebbles but apart from this the only other evidence of the recent presence of water is a thin lamina of clay covering the upper surface of the scoured aeolian sand.

Another example of the resistance shown by aeolian sand to fluvial erosion is given by Fig.25. Here, a clean aeolian sand, showing sharp differences in grain size between the horizontal laminae, had occupied the wadi channel prior to flooding. The flowing water had sculptured the sand into a ripple transverse to the direction of flow. As the water velocity dropped, the only sediment deposited by the flowing water at this locality was a thin covering of pebbles which, only two months later, at the time of the photo, was already being covered by wind-blown sand (cf. lower part of Fig.26).

Stream-flood deposits of the upper flow regime (SIMONS and RICHARDSON, 1963, 1966) are also horizontally laminated. Such deposits resulting from a major flood in Colorado have been described by MCKEE et al. (1967). The horizontal strata figured by McKee and his colleagues is often overlain by rippled, foresetted and convolutely laminated sands; scour and fill structures are also present. The

Fig.24. Wind-blown sand only partly removed by flowing water. East of Tripoli, Libya.

Fig.25. Thin pebble layer deposited by flowing water which only sculptured the previously deposited aeolian sand. Wadi Ouenine, Libya.

horizontal bedding is considered to be characteristic of rapid flow, whereas climbing ripple lamination, convolute structures, festoon bedding and scoured surfaces are thought to result from a decrease in velocity during the waning stages of the flood.

In the areas of the coarser gravels indicating high-energy stream flow, aeolian sands cannot withstand the erosive power of the flowing water (cf. Fig.18).

Fig.26. Interbedded wind- and water-transported sediment. Wadi Al Ayn, Oman. (For explanation see text.)

Further out into the plains where stream-flow is lower in energy, the wadi sediments continually show evidence of the presence of wind-blown sands which have not been completely removed by the flowing water. Fig.26 exemplifies this interplay between wind- and water-transported sands better than the examples given on the previous figure. It shows the edge of the present channel of Wadi Al Ayn, Oman, with, from the top downwards:

(a) Deflation lag of wadi pebbles plus the non-deflated remnant of a wadi conglomerate.

(b) Thin, horizontally-laminated wind-transported sand.

(c) Steeply dipping accretion foresets of pebbly aeolian sand. This sand overlies with angular contact in almost horizontally laminated, aeolian sand (d).

(d) Near the base of this sand, quite coarse clay flakes and granules have been incorporated by wind action. It, in turn, overlies a wadi gravel (not seen in photo).

Fig.27. Interbedded wind- and water-transported sediment of Permian age. Devon, England.

Unlike stream-flow sediments, the concentration of pebbles in horizon (*c*) increases upwards towards what is assumed to have been their source. These pebbles are thought to have rolled, or slid down, from a former bank of a wadi in whose protection the aeolian sands were being deposited. All evidence of the former existence of this bank is assumed to have been removed by deflation prior to deposition of the overlying horizontally laminated sand (*b*).

The aeolian sands of horizon (*c*) could have been deposited by a wind that blew upstream (towards the left) in the same manner as the aeolian sands that again covered the wadi bed at the time the photo was taken, about two months after the wadi had been in flood (see also Fig.116).

ANCIENT WADI SEDIMENTS

A rather similar sequence from the Lower Permian sediments of Roundham Head, Paignton, Devon, is interpreted as conglomeratic sands deposited in the braided stream of a wadi (Fig.27). The water in the wadi is thought to have scoured a channel through aeolian sands that initially were deposited with horizontal laminae. Flakes and small pebbles up to 1 cm were incorporated in these well-laminated wind-blown sands from nearby water-laid gravel. Upwards the gently dipping

Fig.28. Permian conglomerates of braided wadi channels. Devon, England.

foresets of a large wind-formed ripple indicate wind transport from right to left. Imbrication of the pebbles indicates water transport away from the viewer. The wadi conglomerate is much more firmly cemented than the well-laminated aeolian sand. This is possibly because the water in flood, which produced the later scouring, trapped air in the pore spaces of the aeolian sand instead of replacing the air by a potentially cementing fluid. A rather analogous situation has been described by STIEGLITZ and INDEN (1969) in which air-filled vesicles formed in the sediment of a dam spillway following heavy rain.

Fig.28 illustrates another Permian outcrop a few kilometres away in Maidencombe Bay, South Devon, and shows the braided nature of the wadi channels which were filled with angular pebbles set in a sandy matrix. Here, no aeolian sands were recognised. Imbrication of the pebbles suggests that the current flowed from N 320°E at this locality. A simplified geological map of this part of Devon is given in Fig.29. The diversity in transport directions for water-laid sediments shows a marked contrast to the uniform directions deduced for aeolian sediments. LAMING (1966) had described these Lower New Red Sandstone wadi sediments of South Devon in some detail. Apart from describing these sedimentary rocks in considerable detail, he also gives a very good "palaeoview" of the wadi fans as he imagines them to have been during the Permian (LAMING, 1966, p.950). Such a scene can be found in many modern deserts.

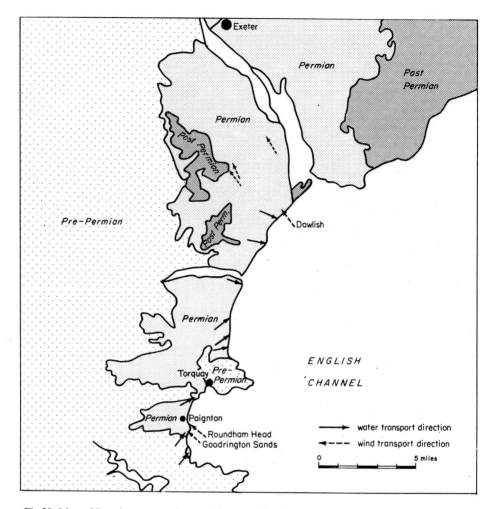

Fig.29. Map of Permian outcrops in south Devon with palaeo-wind and water transport directions.

It is generally accepted that the sandstones and conglomerates of the Upper
Old Red Sandstone of Scotland were deposited in the environments of fluvial and
lacustrine deposition (BARRELL, 1916; WATERSTON, 1965). BLUCK (1967) has recognised a sequence that starts with alluvial fan sedimentation (mud-flow conglomerates presumed to have been deposited by sheet floods), and is followed by
braided stream (stream-flow conglomerates and cross-bedded sands; sandy cross-
bedded conglomerates with numerous erosion surfaces; mud-cracks and shale
pebbles), and river-channel deposits of a floodplain. The development of this
sequence is related by Bluck to accumulation in the area of deposition on one side
of a fault, combined with downward and backward erosion of the source area on
the other side of the fault.

Significant colonisation of the land by plants did not occur before the Devonian Period, and until the end of the Palaeozoic Era was probably confined to near-shore and coastal-plain environments (SCHUMM, 1968). It seems likely that the presence of sedimentary characteristics in the Old Red Sandstone of Scotland that are also typical of some modern arid and semi-arid regions, is related to lack of vegetation rather than lack of rainfall. Prior to widespread terrestrial vegetation, SCHUMM (1968, p.1577) estimates that with more rapid erosion and uninhibited transport, the rate of sediment yield in areas of high rainfall could have been four times greater than at present. Rapid run-off after rain would have resulted in sheet floods; just as rapid a fall in the flow of water would have caused the formation of braided streams because of an overload of sediment, sub-aerial exposure of sediment, and the confinement of the reduced volume of flowing water to river channels of the flood plain. Out on the flood plain, evaporation from the surface of wet sediments that are close to the level of the water table is likely to have given rise to calcite cementation of sandstones; finer-grained rocks that have undergone a similar period of evaporation during a temporary dry period might be recognised by the presence of calcareous concretions similar to caliche. Such an interpretation is given for the Upper Old Red Sandstone in the Tweed Basin of southeast Scotland by WATERSTON (1965) and SMITH (1967). A similar interpretation of the formation of caliche by sub-aerial evaporation is given by NAGTEGAAL (1969) for parts of the Permian continental Peranera Formation of the Central Pyrenees. NAGTEGAAL (1969, p.163) believes that this formation was deposited in a semi-arid steppe environment that, like the Permo-Triassic rocks of the Vosges described by MILLOT et al. (1961) had seasonal rainfall. True desert conditions lay further north in Britain and Germany. NAGTEGAAL (1969) believes that the alluvial fans described by BRUCK et al. (1967) from the New Red Sandstone of Raasay and Scalpay on the west coast of Scotland, were deposited in an environment similar to that of the Peranera Formation.

WADI SEDIMENTS AS A SOURCE OF AEOLIAN SAND

Uncemented wadi sands are an excellent source of dune sand. There is often a high percentage of grains of a size suitable for immediate wind transport; indeed, many wadi sands are the result of fluvial reworking of aeolian sands which had choked the wadi bed before it came into flood. By natural fluvial grading of these sporadically water-transported sediments, the finer sand fractions tend to be the last to be deposited, and many dry out as a result of water-drainage rather than evaporation. This means that they are less likely to be cemented than the underlying coarser sediment, where the water slowly evaporates from stagnant scour channels.

NORRIS and NORRIS (1961) and McCOY et al. (1967) believe that the sands

Fig.30. Wind-sorted surface of wadi. Locality 39, Wadi Dhaid, Trucial Coast.

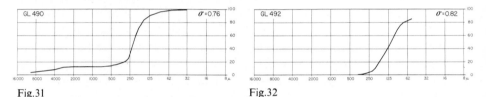

Fig.31   Fig.32

Fig.31. Grain-size distribution curve and sorting coefficient of sediments seen in Fig.30. Wadi gravel. Locality 39, Wadi Dhaid, Trucial Coast.
Fig.32. Grain-size distribution curve and sorting coefficient of sediments seen in Fig.30. Wind-formed ripples. Locality 39, Wadi Dhaid, Trucial Coast.

of the Algodones dunes of southern California were derived from the beach sediments of Lake Cahuilla, lying between the dunes and the Salton Sea. MERRIAM (1969), on the other hand, points to the similarity between the Algodones dunes and the Sonora dunes across the border in Mexico. He relates their content of volcanic fragments, feldspar types, calcite and dolomite grains and abraded Cretaceous Foraminifera to a source in the delta sediments of the Colorado River. Such sediment underlies the dunes and extends westward over hundreds of square miles.

With a continuously flowing river such as the Colorado, additional sediment is deposited over the delta annually, especially during periods of flood[1]; as the flood level subsides, this loose sediment is exposed to the action of the wind.

Fig.30 (Wadi Dhaid, Trucial Coast, Arabia), shows the wind-formed rippled surface of a wadi bed a few weeks after the wadi had been in flood. The ripple

[1] Little sediment now reaches the delta of the Colorado River since the building of the Boulder Dam and associated irrigation schemes.

Fig.33. Interbedded aeolian sands and wadi gravel. Locality 37, Wadi Dhaid, Trucial Coast.

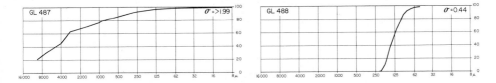

Fig.34   Fig.35

Fig.34. Grain-size distribution curve and sorting coefficient of sediments seen in Fig.33. Wadi gravel. Locality 37, Wadi Dhaid, Trucial Coast.
Fig.35. Grain-size distribution curve and sorting coefficient of sediments seen in Fig.33. Dune sand. Locality 37, Wadi Dhaid, Trucial Coast.

crests are dark because of wind-concentration of heavy minerals. Fig.31 gives the grain-size distribution of the wadi gravel, which here contained over 7% of heavy minerals. Fig.32 gives the grain-size distribution of the wind-formed ripples in which the heavy-mineral concentration had increased to over 22%. The high (14) percentage of grains smaller than 62μ in this sample from an aeolian ripple probably reflects the nearby presence of clay flakes on the surface of the wadi (see also remarks on pp.56 and 148 on laboratory techniques[1]). For comparison, Fig.35 shows the grain-size distribution of sand from a dune bordering the same wadi at a different locality (for sample localities, see Enclosure 2).

---

[1] Note that because the standard deviation is calculated at 16 and 84%, and the extreme grain sizes are ignored, the wadi gravel (Fig.31) would appear to be better sorted than wind-sorted ripples (Fig.32). This is obviously not the case, as a comparison of the two graphs shows.

Deflation gravel of some higher level of wadi.

Foresetted slightly pebbly wind-transported sand.

Horizontally bedded gravel with top portion deflated away.

Finely laminated wind-blown **sand.** Wind from left to right

Clay flakes, slightly curled.

Fine ripple lamination in wind-transported sand.

Fig.36. Interbedded wind- and water-transported sediment. Wadi Amayri, Oman.

INTERBEDDED WADI GRAVELS AND AEOLIAN SAND

Also in Wadi Dhaid, but farther downstream, the pebble content of the wadi sediments is reduced to fairly thin beds between wind- and water-transported sands. The accretion foresets in the gravel are up to 30° or more (Fig.33). Much of the aeolian bedding overlying the gravel has either been destroyed by plant-root burrows or prevented from developing clearly defined laminae as the sand was deposited around plant stems. The grain-size distribution diagrams of the gravel (Fig.34) and the sands from the dunes flanking the wadi (Fig.35) are given for comparison (cf. Fig.44–48).

A somewhat different association is illustrated in Fig.36. A predominantly wind-transported sequence is overlain by alternations of wind- and water-transported sediment, the highest bed of which is now represented by a deflation lag of pebbles. Since then, flowing water in the wadi has cut a new channel down through the previously deposited sediments. Note that the clay flakes about one third of the way up the section form a more or less continuous band. These flakes have been preserved by the overlying aeolian sand in the position where they formed. The coarse, slightly pebbly, foresetted sand in the upper part of these sequence becomes more pebbly to the left (beyond the photo) with the pebbles concentrated in the upper slopes of the laminae. To the right, the foresets continue at a steep angle and with a sharp angular contact with the underlying water-laid gravel before passing laterally into horizontally laminated sands that can be followed for at least 30 m. As with Fig.26, the pebbles in this aeolian sand are assumed to have been derived by rolling or sliding from a former wadi bank, all evidence of whose earlier existence having since been removed during a period of intense deflation.

CLAY LAGS IN WADIS AND MUD CRACKS

The presence of clay in water-transported sediments is very common, and the phenomenon of mud cracks has long been recognised as evidence of subaerial dessication of such clays. In Wadi Dhaid, Trucial Coast (Fig.37), a deep water-formed scour was cut into the previously deposited wadi and wind-blown sands. On drying out, it was lined with up to 10 cm of clay which was still damp in the deepest part of the channel at the time of photographing. Dessication caused broad clay polygons to form (Fig.38). The intervening cracks will probably become infilled with wind-blown sand; in fact whole polygons may be preserved from further destruction by a covering of aeolian sand. Note the sand dunes seen through the trees in the background of Fig.37. Small rain-drop pits can be seen on the surface of the clay (Fig.38). The deeper impressions seen in the photo were made by the paws of a dog while the clay was still soft. In spite of their thickness, the polygons are slightly curved concave-upwards.

Rather larger dessication polygons with fissures up to 5 m or more in depth are described by NEAL et al. (1968), but they are from clay playas in the southwest United States. They interpret them as having formed in thick clays as the result of dessication in the zone between the hard surface crust of the playa and a water table that had been lowered possibly as a result of man's activities.

PERMO-TRIASSIC MUD CRACKS

Mud polygons with an infilling of sand are known from the Permo-Triassic rocks of northwestern Europe. In Devon, England, examples have been seen which were of the same order of size as the recent case described above. Unfortunately, no good photographs are available. The example shown here (Fig.39) is from the Volpriehausen Sandstone of the Triassic Buntsandstein of north Germany, where water-laid sands and clays are associated with aeolian sands.

In southern Germany, although sandstones of doubtful aeolian origin are occasionally found interbedded with water-laid sedimentary rocks of the Buntsandstein, their occurrence is not thought to be widespread. Instead, cross-bedded sandstones and conglomerates showing no signs of deflation suggest rivers that flowed throughout the year. The presence of numerous clay-pebble conglomerates and mud-crack horizons, however, indicate considerable fluctuation in the water level of the rivers with sub-aerial exposure of the sediments. Presumably there was a marked dry season in the source area of these rivers further to the south.

Fig.37. Clay polygons on the surface of a water-scoured hollow. Wadi Dhaid, Trucial Coast.

Fig.38. Close-up of 10 cm thick clay polygons. Wadi Dhaid, Trucial Coast.

Fig.39. Clay polygons and sand infill. Volpriehausen Sandstone, Buntsandstein, northern Germany.

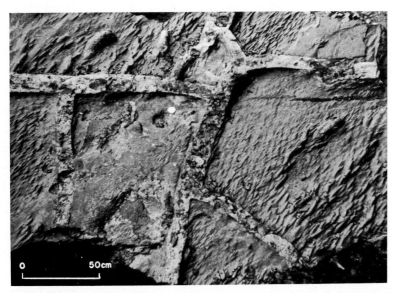

Fig.40. Mudcracks and superimposed flute casts in "Plattensandstein" of the Bunter. East of Eberbach on the Neckar, West Germany.

Fig.41. Preservation of curled clay flakes by wind-blown sand. Wadi Amayri, Oman.

Near Eberbach, on the banks of the river Neckar, there occurs a combination of mud-cracks with superimposed flute casts in the Plattensandstein. The latter were presumably cut during a sudden flood of water in the Triassic river not long after the mud-cracks had developed. The clay polygons were probably still damp and fairly soft when the flood took place (Fig.40).

PRESERVATION OF SUN-CURLED CLAY FLAKES BY AEOLIAN SAND

The mode of preservation of sun-dried clay flakes by wind-blown sand is well illustrated by Fig.41, taken in Wadi Amayri, Oman, about two months after the wadi had been in flood. The clay may have been deposited as a continuous sheet covering a large scour hollow such as is seen in Fig.37. In other instances, clay has been seen as a thin drape covering ripples that were formed in water. On drying, the clay cracks along the crests of the ripples and curls up, the degree of curling apparently being related to the thickness of the clay, with the thinnest clays curling most.

Fig.42. Curled clay flakes and sand dykes interbedded in aeolian sand of Permian age. Devon, England.

Unless the clay is very thin and fragile, it is capable of withstanding winds that are strong enough to transport quite large sand grains. This sand not only fills the hollows formed by the curled clay flakes, but also fills the spaces between the clay and the underlying water-transported sand. Such clay flakes, when incorporated into a dune sand. are likely to give a grain-size distribution curve and sorting coefficient similar to that shown by the dashed line in Fig.45.[1]

Had another wadi flood followed the formation of the curled clay flakes seen in Fig.41, instead of aeolian sand transport, then these clay flakes would almost certainly have been removed and destroyed by the action of the water. Water-laid pebbles of clay might have been preserved downstream provided that the original clay was thick and hard enough to withstand this form of transport.[2] If not, then the clay would have been redeposited elsewhere as part of another clay drape.

---

[1] For further comments on this particular grain-size analysis, see p.56.
[2] Although comparatively delicate curled clay flakes are normally only preserved in the place where the flakes formed by a covering of wind-blown sand, clay pebbles are a fairly common feature in the river sediments of areas that have a marked seasonal rainfall.

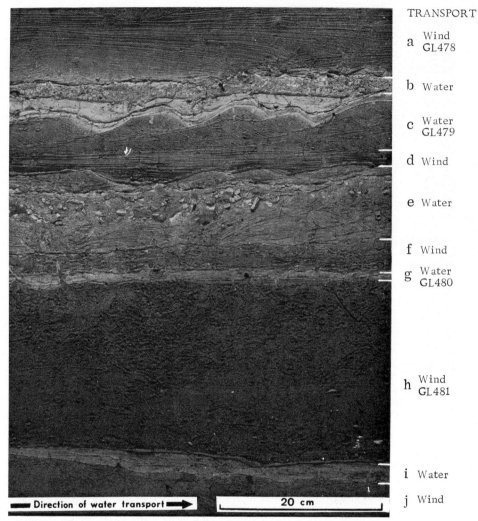

TRANSPORT

a Wind
   GL478

b Water

c Water
   GL479

d Wind

e Water

f Wind

g Water
   GL480

h Wind
   GL481

i Water

j Wind

Direction of water transport ➡   20 cm

Fig.43. Interbedded wind- and water-transported sediment. From lacquer peel. Locality 34, Wadi Dhaid, Trucial Coast.

a = a few rootlet burrows; b = clay flakes and pebbles; c = clay-filled troughs of ripples, moulds of plant roots, climbing ripples; d = sandfilled troughs of clay-covered ripples; e = clay-covered climbing ripples, clay flakes and burrows, moulds of plant roots, climbing ripples; f = laminae disturbed by moulds at plant roots; g = finely laminated sand with curled clay flakes; h = laminae disturbed by moulds of plant roots (sand possibly deposited around living plants—drifting sand—where laminae will not be well developed; i = laminated sands covered by clay film, moulds of plant roots; j = laminae disturbed by moulds of plant roots.

CLAY FLAKES IN ANCIENT SEDIMENTS

Similar features can be seen in the Permian sedimentary rocks of Devon, England (Fig.42). At the time of deposition, the upper part of the sequence shown was pre-

water-transported sediment   wind -transported sediment

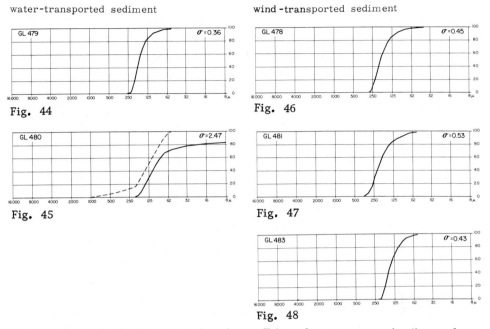

Fig. 44   Fig. 46

Fig. 45   Fig. 47

Fig. 48

Fig.44. Grain-size distribution curve and sorting coefficient of water-transported sediment of sample GL 479 seen in Fig.43.

Fig.45. Grain-size distribution curve and sorting coefficient of water-transported sediment of sample GL 480 seen in Fig.43.

Fig.46. Grain-size distribution curve and sorting coefficient of wind-transported sediment of sample GL 478 seen in Fig.43.

Fig.47. Grain-size distribution curve and sorting coefficient of wind-transported sediment of sample GL 481 seen in Fig.43

Fig.48. Grain-size distribution curve and sorting coefficient of dune sand of sample GL 483 taken from nearby the same locality as Fig.43.

dominantly sand with clay pebbles (water-borne?) and curled and cracked clay drapes (sun-dried and preserved by wind-blown sand?). The lower part of the sequence contains a higher proportion of clay with many thicker clay drapes. The clays have obviously for the most part been exposed to sub-aerial drying and are curled with the concave surface upwards. Wind-blown sand, incorporated from above, now occupies the space beneath the curled-up edges. In other parts of the exposure, especially with thicker clays, the waterlogged sand beneath may have flowed-up between the clay polygons as a wet "slurry" to form a "sand dyke". This possibility will be explained in greater detail on p.64.

INTERPLAY BETWEEN WIND AND WATER IN WADI SEDIMENTS

Fig.43 is a photo of a lacquer-peel section made on the banks of Wadi Dhaid, Trucial Coast. The close relationship between what are thought to be alternations of wind- and water-transported sediment is apparent. Features such as climbing ripples —which here suggest overloading of the water with sediment as the water velocity in the wadi falls (see ALLEN, 1963; McKEE, 1966a)—clay lags in ripple hollows, clay flakes and pebbles, all point to sediment transport by water, with the clay flakes and pebbles indicating sub-aerial exposure. The wind-transported zones are indicated by the clearly defined horizontal or low-angle laminae which generally show better sorting of the grains in the individual laminae than do those that are water-laid. This criterion does not apply to the water-formed climbing ripples, however, where the particular conditions of deposition have resulted in well-graded sets of laminae in which the sorting (Fig.44) is better than that found in the associated wind-blown sand (Fig.46, 47 and 48). All the graphs shown are for bulk samples comprising material from several laminae.

Fig.45 gives a more typical grain-size distribution and sorting coefficient for a wadi sediment. The continuous line on this graph shows some 16% of clay with a diameter less than $2\,\mu$. As sampled, this clay was in the form of clay flakes and pebbles. In other words, although the sorting coefficient is perhaps indicative of its origin as a water-transported sediment, if the laboratory techniques used had not involved the use of water which resulted in breaking down the larger clay fragments, the grain-size distribution curve would have looked more like the dashed line showing a higher percentage of coarse grains.

Fig.46 shows aeolian sorting with a coefficient of around 0.45, with slightly poorer sorting in Fig.47. That these results are caused by the close proximity and reworking of wadi sediments is suggested by Fig.48. This is of a bulk sample taken from a dune sand to windward of the wadi. It is, therefore, largely unaffected by admixture with wadi-transported sediment. As will be shown in the section on aeolian sands, bulk samples can give very misleading results on the sorting ability of wind. Fine-grained laminae will probably give a sorting coefficient in the range of 0.25–0.3.

Chapter 5

DESERT LAKES AND INLAND SEBKHAS

SALINITY OF LAKES IN BASINS OF INLAND DRAINAGE

As was pointed out on p.8, many basins of inland drainage are also the sites of deserts.

In regions of active mountain building, new ranges of hills may be raised across the path of previous drainage. If these hills are elevated more rapidly than the rate at which the rivers can cut down through them, then a basin of inland drainage is formed. When there is sufficient rainfall, a temporary lake will extend within the basin until such time as the water level reaches the lowest point in the barrier; a new drainage channel is then cut (see, for instance, GLENNIE and ZIEGLER, 1964), the lake reduces in size and any temporary increase in the salt concentration is reversed as the water again flows to the sea.

When the rate of evaporation equals or exceeds the supply of water to the basin, its centre of drainage will never acquire sufficient water to flow over the top of the newly formed barrier. The water level in the lake will fluctuate in response to rainfall on the surrounding hills. During dry periods, the lake shrinks in area leaving a thin salt crust over the exposed lake bed. In Iran, the salty and often seasonally marshy nature of such lakes is expressed in some of their names (Daryacheh-ye-Namak—lake of salt; Kavir-e-Namak—salt desert; Batlaq-e-Gav Khunt—marsh of Gav Khunt; Hamoun-e-Jaz Murian—ephemeral lake of Jaz Murian). With increasing accumulation of salts left behind by evaporation, vegetation in the areas surrounding the lakes becomes more sparse and a desert develops, such as around Jaz Murian in southeast Iran or Hamoun-i-Helmond on the Iran–Afghanistan border.

In some regions of Iran, the natural concentration of salts in the river water is increased by the addition of salt from exposed salt plugs. This is the case in the Great Kavir of north Central Iran, where Eocene salts are involved. Cambrian salts are added to the natural content of lakes Neyriz and Bakhtegan, east of Shiraz (see also space photo in WOBBER, 1967, plate I and fig.19) thus rendering the lake water increasingly unsuitable for irrigation. If it were not for the high concentration of salt in these lakes, the fertile region east of Shiraz would be much more widespread. But it is not only in basins of inland drainage that the Cambrian salt prevents the full use of water for irrigation. Many rivers that flow through the southeast Zagros Mountains to the sea acquire much of their salt content from the

Tertiary Fars Formation over which they partly flow, but they are also contaminated with dissolved Cambrian salt from salt plugs. As a result, the valleys through which these rivers flow are commonly vegetated only along their upper flanks.[1]

WADI-FLOOD-WATER ORIGIN OF SOME DESERT LAKES

In an earlier chapter, it was mentioned that temporary lakes may form when wadi flood waters fill a desert depression and further progress is barred by sand dunes. This has happened in the Djofra Graben, Libya, where sand dunes, occupying a median location in the graben, prevent the wadi waters from flowing beyond them (Fig.22, 23, and Enclosure 4). In the initial stages of the wadi flood, fluviatile erosion will occur. Later, however, additional influx of water to this area will result only in a rise in water level, so that the dune pattern is preserved as it slowly becomes drowned in the temporary lake (Fig.49). Since water velocity in these desert lakes becomes virtually zero, a graded bed, fining up to the clay which was held in suspension, will be deposited. Clay drapes cover the lake floor. As with wadi clays, they will break into polygons or crack and curl into flakes on drying out. They will be preserved if protected by a covering of aeolian sand. The writer has only identified one clay drape in ancient aeolian rocks which was thought to have such an origin. It was found at the lowest point of a set of dune laminae —i.e., an interdune area—in Permian dune sands at Gatelawbridge Quarry, Thornhill, southwest Scotland. The lack of mud-cracking suggested that this clay was rapidly covered by dune sand. The low boron content (89 p.p.m.)[2] of this Permian clay is similar to that found in recent non-saline desert wadis.

The calcareous shales that cover parts of the Late Stampian sandstones of the Paris Basin are compared by ALIMEN (1936, pp.187–218) to the clays deposited in the interdune "bahrs" found around Lake Chad on the southern edge of the Sahara. A bahr is an interdune area which in that region becomes flooded during seasonal rise in the level of the water in Lake Chad. These Stampian sandstones form ridges of very constant orientation and regular spacing. They have a relief of some 15 m and are considered to be ancient sand dunes. As is the case with the bahrs of Lake Chad, the calcareous shales cover only the interdune areas and lower slopes of the dunes.

GROUND-WATER ORIGIN OF SOME DESERT LAKES

Fig.50 shows a desert lake occupying an interdune area in the Ubari Sand Sea, Libya. There is no surface flow of water into the lake, and yet, judging from the concentration of date palms around its shores, it has existed for many years. It is

---

[1] For further discussion on the salt domes and salt deserts of Iran, see STÖCKLIN (1968).
[2] Analysis by D. H. Porrenga (K.S.E.P.L.).

Fig.49. Dune pattern preserved in a temporary lake formed by water that flowed down a wadi. Djofra Graben, Libya.

thought that the lake exists because the water table is higher than the surface of the interdune area. Further away (but visible in Fig.50) are some salt pans that presumably indicate that the ground-water level there is just too low to sustain a permanent lake. Clays are not likely to be found in these lakes unless deposited from occasional dust storms, but the salts precipitated from the evaporating ground water could be important in providing local cementation of the sands with resulting low porosity and the formation of permeability barriers.

Fig.50. Permanent inter-dune desert lake fed by ground water. Ubari Sand Sea, Libya.

INLAND SEBKHAS

The term "sebkha" (see Glossary) is used by the Arabs of North Africa and Arabia to denote flat areas of clay, silt and sand which are often encrusted with salt. Sebkhas fitting the above definition can be found in both inland continental and coastal environments, but since the reasons for their existence and the criteria for their recognition are different in the two environments, it is necessary to add the words "inland" or "coastal" to the word sebkha (see also SHEARMAN, 1966).

HOLM (1960, p.1378) wishes to restrict the use of the word sebkha (sabkhah) to coastal regions, for he says that in parts of Arabia the salt-covered flats of the interior are known by another arabic word "mamlahah". POWERS et al. (1966), however, use "sabkhah" in the sense described above and say that "mamlahah" refers to sebkhas that have been excavated for salt. Colleagues who have worked in the interior of Algeria, however, were well versed in the meaning of sebkha (sebkra) in its "inland" sense, but were surprised to learn that in Arabia it is also used in coastal regions. It is used to designate both inland and coastal salt-covered flats on published maps of Arabia (e.g., U.S.G.S., Miscellaneous Geological Investigations Map I-270A), and is used in this sense by the writer with the addition of the appropriate prefix "inland" or "coastal", because of the environmental situation implied by its use.

In North America, the words "playa" and "salina" have both been applied to sebkha-like areas in the interior of a desert. HOLM (1960, p.1379) states that "playa" is synonymous with "mamlahah" (inland sebkha). VON ENGELN(1942, p.412), on the other hand, says that if the percentage of salts in a playa is high enough for a salt crust to form when the flat is dry, it is then called a salina. Because of this lack of definition in the application of their meanings, the writer has avoided further use of "playa" and "salina".

Inland sebkhas develop where water flowing in wadis intermittently floods low-lying depressions to leave behind damp, salt-encrusted sediments. They are also found in depressions where, for one reason or another, the water table reaches, or almost reaches, the surface. The water table may reach the surface in the unconsolidated sands of a dune-filled depression as seen in Fig.50. Another way was explained to the writer by A.A.E.A. Coffinier (personal communication, 1966).

In a stable, clastic, sedimentary basin, water flows from the perifery of the basin towards its centre and returns to the surface mainly by percolating through the overlying shales and clays. Though these shales and clays are only slightly permeable to brines, their horizontal section is so large that considerable amounts of water may move upwards. In the aquifer itself, because the overlying shales and clays are semi-permeable, the water increases in salinity along its flow path. This relatively simple process was suggested by DE SITTER (1947), and has been shown to be responsible for subsurface water-salinity patterns in various areas by

BREDEHOEFT et al. (1963) for the Illinois Basin, and by A.A.E.A. Coffinier in an unpublished report on the Polignac area of Algeria.

Coffinier also mentioned the coincidence of interdune inland sebkhas overlying an anticline in the Great Eastern Erg of Algeria. These interdune sebkhas occupy sites that are topographically higher than other interdune areas in the neighbourhood, thus implying that the water and salt both came from an underground source. It is assumed that the aquifer that supplies the salt and water comes sufficiently near to the surface in the anticline for its water to percolate upwards to the surface and so create sebkha conditions. In some cases, this upward movement of artesian water may be aided by small crestal faults.

A similar relationship between inland sebkhas and anticlines has been noticed on aerial photographs by E. Th. van der Bent (personal communication, 1967) on the north flank of the Igma anticline, Algeria. In Tunisia, Sebkha el Kourzia is described by COQUE and JAUZEIN (1967, p.241) as occupying a hollow that is being deepened by wind erosion and which also overlies an anticline.

In inland sebkhas, the salt crust forms as the result of concentration of salts caused by evaporation of the water. Gypsum crystals are common in the sediments of inland sebkhas. Algae are known, but the algal mats so commonly associated with coastal sebkhas have not been recognised. At present, inland sebkhas cover a vastly greater area than do coastal sebkhas (see Enclosure 1).

A coastal sebkha, on the other hand, is characterised by marine flooding and evaporitic conditions. It is a diagenetic environment whose sediments are of continental and adjacent marine origin.

In the following sections, various features associated with inland sebkhas are described.

THE INLAND SEBKHA UMM AS SAMIM

Fig.51 is an aerial photo of a part of the surface of the giant Oman inland sebkha called Umm as Samim (mother of poisons) (see also Enclosures 1 and 3). The foreground is covered with salt polygons which appear large, even at a flying height of 500 ft. above the surface. The force of crystallisation of the salt probably causes the roughly polygonal shapes and result in their being surrounded by walls of salt up to 4 ft. high (as may be the case with the large polygons in the aerial photo).[1]

Fig.52 shows the surface of a road across the salt crust of the Umm as Samim about one year after it had been bulldozed smooth. Already the salt (mostly halite) has grown up about 5 cm at the polygon edges. Beyond the bulldozed area, the salt-polygon walls are between 10 and 20 cm high.

The salt has incorporated in it considerable amounts of wind-blown sand.

---

[1] See also BOBECK (1959, plates IV and VI) for similar salt polygons from Iranian inland sebkhas.

Fig.51. Pattern of giant salt polygons on surface of Umm as Samim, Oman.

Fig.52. Bulldozed area of salt-polygon surface. Umm as Samim, Oman.

Fig.53. Needle-like crystals of salt preserved in impervious clay. Umm as Samim, Oman.

Under normal circumstances, the salt is either deflated away or dissolved by rain or wadi-flood water, thus permitting the sand grains to sink into the sediment beneath. In desert areas, sodium chloride in solution in ground water is normally brought to the surface by capillary flow that is balanced by evaporation and formation of a halite crust. This means that when the halite is covered by a permeable sediment such as sand, the upward flow of less saline water from below causes solution of the salt and its recrystallisation at the surface. Water flows intermittently from wadis into the eastern end of the Umm as Samim, however, and carries considerable quantities of clay into the area both above and below the existing salt. This can result in salt lenses being permanently trapped in the impervious clay (Fig.53).

The salt crust is up to 30 cm or more thick. After a wet season, it may have between 6 and 8 m of salt water between it and the underlying sediment (H. van Deventer, personal communication, 1964). When visited by the writer, no free

water existed; the salt was in contact with the underlying gypsum-rich, rather
structureless sediment.

When the salt is dry, sand dunes migrate across its surface. It very seldom
rains over the Umm as Samim, but when it does, the surface may be pitted with
solution hollows which become the starting point for a new series of salt polygons.
The Umm as Samim exists essentially because its surface is at, or below, a fluctuating
ground-water level. Whether the original basin shape was caused by deflation or
structural warping is not known. The salts are probably derived from outcropping
Tertiary strata by solution in rare rain water or water-filled wadis, although there
is the possibility that the area also represents a relict arm of the sea left behind as
the result of relative sea-level changes; its surface is less than 70 m above the present
sea level.

SOME SEDIMENTARY STRUCTURES IN INLAND SEBKHAS

The temporary desert lake shown in Fig.49 is caused by water flowing down a
wadi and into a continental basin in which the water is prevented from flowing
farther by a barrier of dune sand. Similar conditions can give rise to inland sebkhas.
Salt-rich water slowly percolates into the ground and evaporates leaving a surface
crust of salt. Salt polygons may or may not grow, depending upon the relative
concentration of salt. Fig.54 shows the surface of such an inland sebkha on the
northern edge of the Ubari Sand Sea, Libya, where a heavy truck has broken through
the thin hard crust and sunk into the soft wet sediment below. Here, salt polygons are not well formed, because each year the local people remove the salt crust
in order to plant crops in the relatively salt-free sediment beneath. However, the
clayey sands beneath the salt crust are rich in gypsum crystals (the shiny spots in
Fig.55). The wavy lamination is typical of sedimentation in such sebkhas. It is not
certain whether the lamination results from deposition from flowing water, or
from deformation of horizontal laminae by growing gypsum crystals. Another, and
perhaps more likely possibility, is that they grow by the adhesion of wind-blown
sand and silt to the damp sebkha surface. Capillary flow of water between the
grains permits adhesion of additional laminae to the surface of the structure (see
Fig. 61, 62).

SAND DYKES IN INLAND SEBKHAS

In the environment of the inland sebkha one can also find the "sand dykes" encountered by OOMKENS (1966) at the northern edge of the Ubari Sand Sea. Water-
transported clay on the sebkha surface broke into polygons as it dried out; rifts
between the polygons either became filled with wind-blown sand, as would be the

Fig.54. 10-ton Fiat which broke through the thin hard crust of an inland sebkha. North edge of
the Ubari Sand Sea, Libya. (From OOMKENS, 1966.)

Fig.55. Wavy lamination in sediment of inland sebkha. North edge of the Ubari Sand Sea, Libya.

case in Fig.37, 38, or were injected from below with water-saturated sand which flowed out onto the edges of the polygons (Fig.56). This latter phenomenon seemed to occur where the clay rested on beds consisting mainly of aeolian sand.

In Fig.57, a slight up-arching of the sand laminae can be seen at the base of the dyke. The sand at the top of the dyke flowed over the edge of the dark clay; its pattern is outlined by the up-arched crust of salt (Fig.56, 57).

Oomkens gives alternative explanations for the mechanics of formation of these dykes as follows:

(1) When a hard, impermeable, clayey surface bed is fractured as a result of shrinkage, underlying sandy slurry might rise through the cracks and flow over the clay because of a difference in density between the dry and watery sediments.

(2) The weight of isolated dune bodies that migrate and locally load an impermeable hard crust will increase the pore pressure in the underlying mobile sediments, and thus facilitate upward injection through cracks.

(3) A slow downslope flow of soft sediment below an impermeable rigid crust, for instance towards the centre of a depression, will increase the pressure in the flowing sediments.

(4) Examples of mud and sand welling up from fissures during earthquakes have been observed (HOBBS, 1907). In such cases, the earthquakes, in addition to rupturing the thin hard surface bed, also increased the pressure of the formation water. Most ancient sand dykes so far described have been explained in this manner.

(5) Upwelling of sand from (man-made) fissures under the influence of large variations in atmospheric pressure during storms have been observed (BUHSE, 1892).

OOMKENS (1966) suggests that the first explanation is the most likely, but it is probable that explanation (3) also plays an important part.

Siltstone polygons that are bounded by walls of sandstone are described by HARSHBARGER et al. (1957) and TOMKINS (1965) from the Jurassic Carmel Formation of Utah. Tomkins believes that the mud polygons formed as the result of desiccation and were then infilled from above by aeolian sand. On the other hand, Harshbarger and his colleagues noted that the sandstone infill appeared to have flowed, and they postulated that the mudcracks may have formed under subaqueous conditions and were then filled by the upward flow of underlying quicksand. Although fossils were lacking to support their ideas, they thought that sedimentary structures within the Carmel Formation suggested an estuarine or lagoonal environment. However, associated regional features suggestive of an arid climate (dune sands, etc.) leave open the possibility that although some mud cracks may have been infilled from above by wind-blown sand, others may have been filled by injection of a quicksand from below in the manner inferred for the inland sebkhas of Libya.

In the Permian sediments of Devon, England, similar sand dykes were seen at several localities. One has already been referred to in Fig.42. Fig.58 shows

Fig.56. Polygonal sand-dyke pattern seen in salt crust of inland sebkha. North edge of Ubari Sand Sea, Libya. (From OOMKENS, 1966.)

Fig.57. Up-arched flow laminae of sand dyke. North edge of the Ubari Sand Sea, Libya.

Fig.58. Permian sandstone dyke. Roundham Head, Paignton, Devon, England.

another from Roundham Head, Paignton, in an environment where clay-pebble conglomerates with a sand matrix and possible aeolian sand are interbedded with polygonally cracked clay. The top of the sand dyke has probably been removed by deflation prior to the deposition of the succeeding aeolian sand. OOMKENS (1966) figures an excellent hand specimen of a sand dyke of similar age from Germany.

LAMING (1966, p.925) also refers to Permian sand dykes from south Devon and figures examples associated with conglomerates. These, however, are likely to have required some more violent mechanism, such as the shock-wave of an earthquake, to cause their formation. PETERSON (1966) describes sandstone dykes that are up to 8 ft. wide and several miles long. He relates their formation to strike-slip faulting in the underlying basement rocks. Even bigger sandstone dykes up to 300 ft. wide and 1,000 ft. in vertical extent penetrate Precambrian crystalline rocks in Colorado (HARMS, 1965). Their mode of origin has, in common with those described by OOMKENS (1966) from an inland sebkha, the necessity for tension in the intruded medium, and the presence of a sandy slurry that is capable of flowing into the tension gap.

SEDIMENTATION VERSUS DEFLATION IN INLAND SEBKHAS

It has already been mentioned in connection with the deflation hollows of Qattara, Fahud and Al Fugaha, that the depth to which deflation can penetrate is limited by the level of the water table. The presence of moisture inhibits deflation and encourages sedimentation. Deposition occurs in two main ways, by water-filled wadis bringing the sediment into the inland sebkha, and by the adhesion of wind-blown sediment to the damp surface of the sebkha. As soon as sedimentation brings the sebkha surface above the limit of permanent capillary flow from the water table, then deflation can become active and the surface is again lowered until the inhibiting effect of the ground water is met. Permanent sedimentation will occur when the rate of sediment supply exceeds the rate of deflation or when a rising water table (such as in a subsiding continental basin) permits the addition of further sediment by adhesion (see also p.71).

HORIZONTAL BEDDING IN INLAND SEBKHAS

Fig.59 shows a pit dug into the horizontally bedded sediments covering the floor of a wind-deflated basin of inland drainage in Libya similar to that at Al Fugaha (Fig.13). Erosion by deflation is assumed to have ceased once the ground-water level had been reached (if the impervious cap of an aquifer was breached, this may have produced a temporary lake). Thin horizontal beds of brown and green clays and streaks of red sand alternate with green gypsiferous clays and white bedded gypsum. They are overlain by about 25 cm of reddish-brown, non-laminated gypsiferous sandy clay. The former are thought to have been deposited during an early period as a temporary lake; the latter, in which no laminae were visible, are thought to have been deposited by adhesion of wind-blown sand and dust to the damp salt-encrusted surface. No algal mats were recognised. The salt crust had a very uneven surface and possibly played a part in preventing the formation of laminae in the sandy clay.

NEAR-COAST INLAND SEBKHAS

It will be shown later that wadis which once drained into the sea can have their exits blocked by longshore bars and coastal dune barriers. Under these circumstances, if there is an insufficient flow of wadi water to break through this barrier, tempo-

Fig. 59. Bedded sand, clay and evaporite covering floor of a basin previously hollowed out by wind deflation. Hamada al Hamra, Libya.

rary lakes and inland sebkhas, having no marine influence, may form near the coast (see Fig.62, 101).

Fig.60 shows laminated Quaternary gypsiferous clays and sands known to be pre-Roman as the foundation of a Roman dam cut through the clays. Nearer to the sea they interfinger with gypsum-cemented dunes. It is assumed that inland sebkha conditions developed in the lower reaches of Wadi Tareglat behind a coastal dune barrier in Late Quaternary time. By the time of the Roman occupation of this part of Libya, the wadi channel was again in connection with the sea. (In the photograph the holes in the clays are artefacts caused by the removal of

Fig.60. Laminated gypsiferous clay and sand of pre-Roman inland sebkha. East of Tripoli, Libya.

clusters of gypsum crystals when an attempt was made to smooth the cut surface with a knife.)

On the Gulf of Oman coast of Oman (Batinah Coast), a series of near-coast sebkhas occurs just above sea level behind the protection of the coastal dune barrier. Although wadis occasionally drain into these sebkhas, the salt water is usually, in this case, supplied by percolation of sea water through the coastal dunes. The surface of the sebkhas is dampened twice daily at high tide when water rises by capillary action and makes the salt surface of the road that crosses them exceedingly treacherous. At low tide, the salt dries out to make a good firm road surface. Although supplied with sea water, these sebkhas are cut off from direct access to the sea. No marine fauna lives in the sediment, but the tests of dead marine Foraminifera become incorporated from the nearby beach and coastal dunes by the action of onshore winds.

ADHESION RIPPLES[1]

Sedimentation by adhesion of wind-blown sand to a damp surface has already been referred to (Fig.55). Adhesion ripples were first described by REINECK (1955)

---

[1] See Glossary.

Fig.61. Adhesion ripples. Sebkha Matti, Trucial Coast.

Fig.62. Wind-blown carbonate sand forming possible adhesion ripples and wadi clays in an inland sebkha. West of Tripoli, Libya.

from the northern German coastal flats. Where the ground surface is so damp that deflation is inhibited, as in many sebkha environments, both coastal and inland, sedimentation by adhesion can become important.

Sebkha Matti, Trucial Coast (see Enclosure 1), is a large plain some 120 km long and 60 km wide. It slopes gently northwards to sea level from an altitude of 50 m or more at the southern end. Most of the area is at ground-water level. Dunes and outcrops above this level are subject to deflation, and sediment is carried south by the strong shamal winds. Towards the south, sand dunes begin to accumulate. At the windward end of the dune fields large ripples begin to form on the damp surface by adhesion (Fig.61), and so form the base for further dune accumulation. Still farther north, other adhesion ripples form the sites of temporary sand sedimentation. A balance between sedimentation and deflation probably coincides with the upper limit of capillary action, which is itself affected by seasonal changes in the level of the water table. Adhesion ripples will be preserved when overlain by a permanent accumulation of dune sand or fluvial sediment deposited from non-scouring water (e.g., temporary lake as in Fig.49). The base of the shallow pit seen in Fig.61 coincides with the start of gypsum-cemented sand—itself with a ripple-like surface. Surface relief, attributed to adhesion ripples, has been seen in the order of 30–40 cm.

West of Tripoli, Libya, inland sebkha conditions occur similar to those deduced for Fig.60. A wadi had its exit to the sea blocked-off by the formation of a longshore bar over which a coastal dune developed. Fig.62 shows the sediments seen in a pit dug into the sebkha that formed behind the coastal bar and dune. The dark bands consist of brown clay brought into the sebkha (annually?) by the wadi. The white laminae consist of both water-borne and wind-blown carbonate sand derived from the nearby coastal dunes (themselves formed from carbonate beach sand). The upper white surface consists of 2 cm of wind-blown carbonate sand in the form of fine adhesion ripples (the adhesion warts of Reineck, 1955). 30–40 m nearer to the coastal dunes, adhesion ripples were 5 cm or more in height. Many of the diapir-like sedimentary structures seen in the pit are thought to have been formed as large adhesion ripples.

Ripples, similar to those seen in Fig.55 and 62, and ascribed to a wind-blown origin by adhesion, have been recognised in Permian sandstones from North Sea cores.

OASES

By way of a slight digression from the geological aspects of deserts, this is, perhaps, the place to discuss one of its modern features, the oasis. It is not necessarily connected with either desert erosion or sedimentation, but it is intimately connected with the presence of water and vegetation.

An oasis can be defined as an area in the midst of a desert which is made fertile by the presence of water (MOORE, 1949). Its existence is dependent upon a continuous supply of water flowing at or near the surface. Apart from the rare occurrence of more or less permanent surface water in the form of a desert lake, spring, or restricted portion of a wadi, the water usually has to be brought to the surface from a well. Most oases are, therefore, artificial. The former existence of a natural oasis might be recognised in Cenozoic desert sediments by the widespread presence of dikaka (see p. 113) provided that the oasis was later covered by aeolian sand.

In Iran, and parts of Arabia and North Africa, water is commonly carried to an oasis from its mountain source in tunnels dug into the wadi sediments. In Iran, where the system is thought to have originated, each tunnel is known as a qanat; in Oman and Libya each is referred to as a falaj. They form a very important means of providing a local permanent supply of water to an area that would otherwise have none within reach of the surface.

Qanats became widely developed in Iran during the 6th century A.D. and may have been introduced into southern Arabia at about the same time. Their importance today as a means of providing fresh water to an otherwise arid area can be imagined from the numbers seen from the air around the ancient Iranian city of Isfahan which is only about 50 miles from the edge of the Great Kavir. The Buraimi oasis at the northern end of Jebel Hafit (Enclosure 2) is irrigated, and gets its supply of drinking water from such a source.

There is also evidence of the former use of qanats (falajes) on the southern edge of the Ubari Sand Sea in northern Fezzan, and in Morocco, where they are known as foggara. The introduction of qanats to North Africa probably followed the advent of Islam and the spread of the Arab Empire, with Persian slave labour and skill utilised for their construction. The Libyan qanats appear now to have fallen into disrepair and many of the oases that they used to supply with water have ceased to exist. In Oman, some of the tribes still maintain their qanats (falajes) and even occasionally build new ones.

Some examples of natural oases, together with the probable geological reasons for their presence, are given below:

(a) Deflation hollows: As already explained on p.26, the depth to which deflation can cause removal of sediment from a hollow is limited by the water table. Provided that the ground water so exposed is not too saline, an oases such as that at Al Fugaha (Fig.13) can exist. Famous Egyptian oases of this type such as that at Kharga, derive their water from the underlying Nubian Sandstone.

(b) Wadis: Permanently flowing water often exists in gravels below the surface of large wadis. In areas of considerable annual fluctuation in the level of the water table, wells have only seasonal value and permanent irrigation is impossible. Within and flanking the Oman Mountains, the presence of cemented wadi gravels coupled with the cutting of new channels and the redistribution of uncemented gravel sometimes leaves natural pools of flowing water. These are invariably the sites of oases. provided that there is sufficient flat ground nearby on which to grow palms or other plants. If not, then a falaj, or a surface irrigation canal, is constructed to carry the water downstream to the nearest place that can be cultivated— often a gravel and sand terrace. In other cases, unevenly cemented wadi gravels may act as a natural barrier that dams back the water to form a natural shallow reservoir.

(c) Ground water associated with wadis is less saline, and therefore less dense, than the salt water found in coastal sediments. When fresh water within the gravels of an alluvial fan flows towards a coastal sebkha, it may be forced to the surface by the denser ground water of the sebkha. This appears to have happened where a large oasis fringes the lower perimeter of a wadi fan between the Oman Mountains and the coastal sebkha at Ras al Khaimah (Fig.98, and Enclosure 2). On the other hand, such natural oases do not normally occur where ground water associated with a wadi flows towards an inland sebkha such as the Umm as Samim. This, presumably, is because the ground water is already too saline by the time it reaches the Umm as Samim to support cultivated plants.

A high proportion of the water that flows in a wadi eventually seeps into the ground. With modern drilling and pumping methods, much of this water can be utilised for agriculture, and so the creation of further oases.

Chapter 6

AEOLIAN SANDS

Some important aspects of the mechanics of transporting sand by the medium of the wind were mentioned briefly in chapter 1. Unsupported criteria for the identification of wind-blown sand were given in chapter 2, and in the succeeding chapters the importance of wind as a deflating and transporting agent and the almost universal presence of aeolian sand in a wide variety of sedimentary environments were made obvious. We must now consider some of the factors that control the accumulation of aeolian sand into drifts and ripples, individual sand dunes and sand seas with a continuous sand cover. We must also provide more evidence for the criteria by which aeolian sands may be recognised.

SAND RIDGES

When a source of sediment has a very wide range in grain size, as in a deflation plain, the finer grains will be blown away at a certain wind velocity leaving a lag of coarser grains. As the wind velocity increases, so coarser and coarser grains are removed until finally even the coarsest may move either by saltation or surface creep. It was in this way, by a combination of deflation and surface creep, that the dark ridges, seen below the dune in Fig.63, grew up. BAGNOLD (1941, p.149) states that the wavelength of such ridges may increase in time, as the surface grading grows coarser with removal of the finer sand. This ridge has formed on an interdune deflation plain which, as can be seen from the foreground, has a cover of pebbles left behind as a lag during earlier deflation. The lag is underlain by weathered outcrop containing a wide variety of grain sizes. Beneath the pebbles covering the ridge is similar weathered outcrop. The ridges—there are several of them—are transverse to the prevailing wind direction. The ridges are not a simple product of deflation, but rather the result of a balance between deflation and sedimentation. Surface creep carries the largest grains up the windward slope to occupy the exposed crestal position. These large grains need to be in the order of 3 to 7 times the diameter of those in saltation according to BAGNOLD (1956, p.141). As long as the wind is not so strong that it dislodges the crestal grains, and as long as deflation is predominant over sedimentation, the ridge can continue to "grow" in size, partly by surface accretion of coarse grains and partly by deflation of the inter-ridge hollows. The average size of the grains covering this ridge is about 1 cm.

Fig.63. Pebble deflation lag (*a*), pebble ridges (*b*), sand ripples (*c*) and dunes (*d*). Barik, Oman.

Fig.64 illustrates the grain-size distribution in a section cut through a large sand ridge about 50 cm high. It has an accretion covering of coarse grains of up to 5 mm diameter, which move by surface creep under the impact of smaller grains in saltation. Note how the grains in the laminae become progressively finer to the right, representing deposition on the then lee slope of the ridge. The sharp crest line is better seen in the continuation of the ridge into the distance with fine sand deposited in its protection on the lee slope. That the ridge has been in process of migration can be seen from the way the windward accretion layer overlaps the eroded, gently sloping foresets. The grain-size distribution for a bulk sample from the middle of this ridge is given in Fig.65. The same phenomenon can occasionally be seen in sand-covered inter-dune areas in a sand sea. The maximum grain size, which controls the relative height of the ridge, will be that of the coarsest available sand.

The sand ridges described above occurred as individual features, or in groups of two or three ridges on the desert surface. SHARP (1963) figures a sequence of smaller ridges that are regularly spaced which he names "granule ripples". He considers them to be a coarse equivalent of sand ripples that form where lag concentrates of larger particles are subjected to deflation and surface creep by strong winds.

Because of the size of the grains that cover and protect these large ridges from wind erosion they probably move very slowly, and may be preserved by burial under finer-grained wind-blown sand. Note the scattered vegetation.

Fig.64. ½-cm pebbles in large wind-formed sand ridge. Locality 213, Sebkha Matti, Trucial Coast.

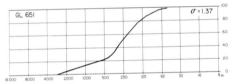

Fig.65. Grain-size distribution curve and sorting coefficient of sand from large wind-formed sand ridge. Locality 213, Sebkha Matti, Trucial Coast.

AEOLIAN SAND RIPPLES

Ripple formation appears to result from a natural tendency for the surface of a bed of sand grains to pucker into raised features. BAGNOLD (1956) has shown that during the formation of ripples, a tangential stress is applied to the surface of a bed of grains, and some grains are eroded. Since these grains cannot be supported in suspension without an increase in the applied stress, they are redeposited again. The conditions at the surface of the bed are unstable. "An ultimate steady state can, however, be achieved if the eroded grains are redeposited in such a way that some new and additional tangential resistance is created" (BAGNOLD, 1956, p.256). This additional tangential resistance is provided by the drag caused by vorticity created in the hollows between newly deposited ripple crests.[1] The principle applies

_____

[1] On the other hand, SHARP (1963, p.624) points out that an eddy forms on the lee side of a ripple only at low wind velocities. At higher velocities no such eddy occurs and if grains on the upper part of the steep lee slope are dislodged, they merely roll down the slope.

equally to sand ripples formed in water or in air.

Aeolian sand ripples develop with the axes of their crests transverse to the wind that formed them. BAGNOLD (1941, p.149) has defined wind-formed sand ripples as "those surface forms whose wavelength depends on the wind strength and remains constant as time goes on". He explains that in ripples, as in sand ridges, the coarsest grains collect at the crest and allow it to rise into the region of stronger wind. The troughs tend to fill up, but "if deposition is not too rapid, a balance is achieved between height of crest and trough" (see foreground of Fig.26). With an increase in the rate of deposition, balance is achieved at lower ripple heights until it finally disappears. This can be seen on the ripple-free accretion slopes of a growing dune. Ripples also flatten out and disappear when the wind rises above a certain strength.

The ratio of wavelength to height is known as the ripple index. For aeolian sand, the ripple index is commonly between 15 and 20, but when ripples flatten out at high winds, the index may be as high as 50 or 60. The index for the granule ripples measured by SHARP (1963) in the Kelso Dunes of the Mojave Desert ranged from 12 to 20 with a mean index of 15. He believes that the ripple index varies inversely with the grain size and directly with the wind velocity.

For sand ridges, the wind strength is below that required to remove the largest grains from the crest. Transport of the coarse grains is by surface creep. For ripples, an intercrest wavelength is developed which is proportional to the characteristic path of the grains in saltation; the variation in the distribution of the descending saltation causes a corresponding variation in the rate of surface creep. For a given grain size, wavelength increases with wind strength until a point is reached when the ripple has virtually flattened out. The height of the ripple also depends on the range in size of the grains forming the ripple, and the ability of the coarsest grains to remain in their crestal position for a given wind strength. As with sand ridges, a wide variation in grain size is necessary to produce large ripples, which are always asymmetrical. According to SHARP (1963) the degree of asymmetry varies directly with grain size.

Asymmetric ripples are well seen in Fig.26 of Wadi Al Ayn, where the asymmetry of the recently formed ripples shows that the wind that formed them blew upstream towards the Oman Mountains. Ripples are, in fact, an approach to the sand ridge. With uniform grain size, only low ripples are possible (BAGNOLD, 1941, p.151).

Although the accretion slopes of some dunes may be free from ripples because of strong winds or a sand supply of uniform grain size, other dunes may have their windward slopes and their flanks covered with ripples, and these ripples may be preserved (see Fig.120, 121). Ripples also develop on the steep avalanche slope of a dune when the wind temporarily blows across that slope. These ripples are preserved when an avalanche of sand covers them from above after the wind has reverted to its prevailing direction.

Wind-formed sand ripples of Permian age have been seen in dune sands in both the quarries shown in Fig.79 and 80, at Houghton-le-Spring, Durham, and at Locharbriggs, Dumfriesshire, and have also been described by MCKEE (1934, 1945) from the Permian Coconino Sandstone of northern Arizona. ALMEIDA (1953) refers to the preservation of ripples in Triassic aeolian sands from South America, and aeolian ripples of Jurassic age have been described from the Navajo Sandstone of Utah by KIERSCH (1950).

SAND DUNES

In contrast to the upward coarsening of the grain size seen in the sand ridges and ripples of Fig.63, the dune in the background shows a progressively finer grain size from the level of the deflation plain to its crest. At the same time, there is an upward improvement in the degree of sorting. This can be seen from the grain-size distribution graphs given in Fig.66.

The size of a ripple is controlled by the strength of the wind and the coarseness of the grains occupying the crestal position. The size of a dune is dependent upon the supply of sand and the ability of the wind to carry grains of any size up to its crest—and keep them there.

BARCHAN DUNES

It was stated on p.23, that sand tends to accumulate on areas that are already sand covered. Such an accumulation of sand is commonly either in the form of long strips or low, oval, ripple-covered mounds, depending on the velocity of the wind that formed them.

Under conditions of constant wind direction and accretion of sand, the highest point in an oval-shaped mound is found towards the down-wind end. As the patch of sand increases in height, so the angle of the lee slope increases until it reaches the angle of repose which, for dry sand, is about 34°, and a slip face (or avalanche slope) forms. This situation appears to be reached at a minimum height, for what may now be called a dune, of about 30 cm. The lee slope of the dune is fed with new material blown over the crest and the whole dune advances down wind. Any tendency to exceed the angle of repose causes sand to avalanche down the slip-face until the slope of 34° is regained. The largest and roundest grains are found at the bottom of the slope.

BAGNOLD (1954) has shown that this sorting on the avalanche slope is the result of an internal dispersive pressure within the flowing sand that varies with the diameter of the grains for any given shear stress. The largest grains tend to drift towards the zone of least shear strain which is found at the surface of the

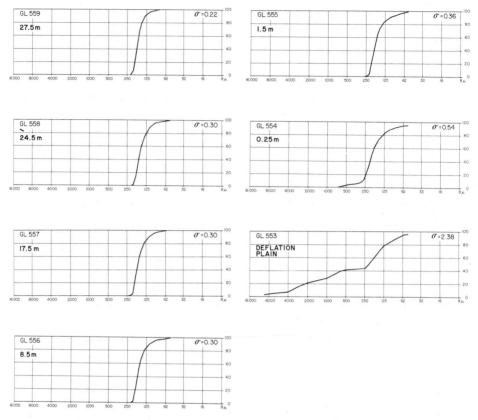

Fig.66. Grain-size distribution curves and sorting coefficients of dune sand in relation to dune height above deflation plain (taken from bulk samples). Locality 92 near Barik, Oman.

flow; these grains therefore travel farthest. The smaller grains move towards the zone of greatest shear strain which is found at the contact with the sand beneath the flow.

The individual grains on an avalanche slope come to rest with a preferred orientation of their longest and shortest axes roughly parallel to the azimuth of maximum dip, but they are imbricated in such a way that their long axes lie between the horizontal and the maximum dip of the bedding (REES, 1968). Relative to the avalanche slope, this angle of imbrication is about 25° for dry sand and 35° for sand deposited in still water (HAMILTON et al., 1968).

The small barchan dune seen in Fig.67 is migrating across a road east of Barik, Oman. It is about 60 cm high and its slip-face is about half that height. The process of migration can be seen from the arrangement of bedding laminae within a barchan (Fig.68). Sand is blown up the windward slope of the dune in saltation and by surface creep. When it is carried beyond the crest, it passes into a zone of relatively calm air where it accumulates on the slip face. As the barchan

Fig.67. Small barchan dune migrating across road. East of Barik, Oman.

migrates, so older slip-face slopes become covered at the leeward end of the dune and are exposed to erosion to windward.

With a growing barchan, rather more sand is deposited on it than is removed. Since there is a greater bulk of sand to be moved in the centre of the barchan than at its "horns", the latter migrate more rapidly, and it is from here that the greatest sand loss occurs. On the horns, there are no slip-faces. The laminae will all have dips of less than 34° in directions up to 90° to that of the wind, although a spread of less than 150° is normal. McKEE (1966a) gives excellent cross-sections and photos of dune-bedding relationships not only through barchans, but also through other dune types. The cross-sections were prepared by cutting trenches with a bulldozer right through dunes composed of lightly cemented gypsum dune sands. Barchans are known from most deserts, but for some reason do not appear to occur in the Kalahari or Australia (HILLS et al., 1966). They do, however, occur in the Namib Desert of Southwest Africa (KAISER, 1925). Detailed studies of the barchans of southern Peru have been made by both FINKEL (1959) and HASTENRATH (1967).

When the attitude of the preserved bedding of barchan dunes is plotted on a polar net (Fig.68), the resulting scatter of points can be used to indicate approximate palaeo-wind directions. This method has given the writer reasonably consistent palaeo-wind directions for Permo-Triassic dune sands in Britain and the Pliocene to Recent cemented dunes from eastern Arabia. The subject is discussed more extensively on p.100.

DISTRIBUTION OF SAND DUNES

Aeolian sand will be deposited in any location where there is a reduction in the velocity of a sand-laden wind. A wind of reduced velocity is no longer capable of transporting the larger grains that were previously in saltation. These grains therefore fall to the ground where, by increasing its roughness, apply a further drag resistance to the wind and so further reduce the effective velocity at ground level. We have already seen how wind-blown sand accumulates in the lee of the bank of a wadi. Given a sufficient supply of sand, dunes may fill the wadi bed. Dunes may also form as the result of a simple reduction in wind velocity: "Aeolian sand tends to accumulate on areas already sand covered. . ." (p.23 and Fig.10). Once started, dune build-up is often self propagating.

Most dune fields appear to form in areas where there is an adequate windward supply of sand and where the wind velocity is not so great that only deflation can take place. Dunes do not, as a rule, form on elevated landscapes where wind velocities are generally higher than on the planes below. The supply of sand is sufficient for dune formation along many low coastlines of prevailing onshore winds such as parts of the Pacific coast of North America (COOPER, 1958, 1967), The Netherlands coast (VAN STRAATEN, 1961) or the Trucial Coast of the Persian Gulf. As we have already seen, areas of sporadic fluvial or lacustrine sedimentation in a region of arid or semi-arid climate provide an abundant supply of sediment for incorporation into sand dunes further down wind. Two such examples are the Simpson Desert in Australia (MADIGAN, 1946) and the dune fields of the Great Kavir in Iran (BOBEK, 1959).

Sand transport is more effective over a hard immobile surface than over a sand-covered surface (p.23). Sand is therefore transported over and away from regions where active erosion of outcrop is taking place; it accumulates in areas where the surface roughness is greater and where wind velocities are lower. Erosion over the Hamada al Hamra and Harug el Hasued in Libya is compensated by deposition in the depressions or the Ubari and Murzuk Sand Seas (Enclosure 4). Erosion and transport of sediment over the highlands of northeast Arabia are followed by deposition to the southeast in linear depressions such as the Dahna of Saudi Arabia (HOLM, 1960).

Fig.69 shows the leeward edge of a barchan in a small dune field in Qatar, Persian Gulf. The windward end of this dune field starts as isolated barchans near the centre of the peninsula. As the dunes travel to the southeast under the action of the Shamal wind, they combine into more complex barchanoid forms which, on the east coast of Qatar, slowly migrate into the sea. At this coast, however, over much of the year there is an opposing daily onshore wind caused by the fact that

---

Fig.68. The bedding of ideal barchan and seif dunes and their relationship to the predominant wind direction.

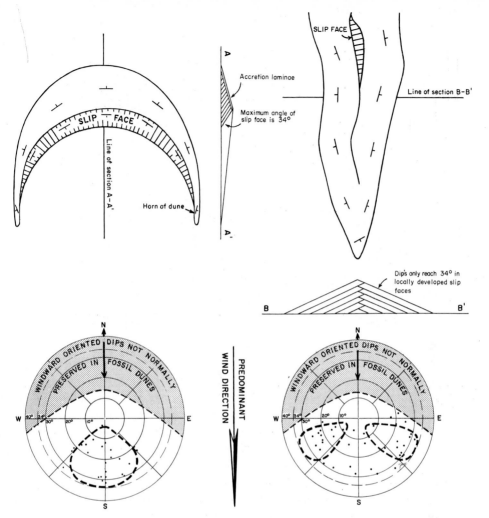

Polar nets of the distribution of dip attitudes in ideal barchan and seif dunes and their characteristic areas of point concentration. Taken from well-exposed fossil dune examples, they illustrate the use to which the nets may be put for deducing palaeo-wind directions.

BARCHAN DUNES

1. 'Horns' of dune directed down-wind.

2. Bulk of dune foresets dip down-wind at angles of up to 34°.

3. A small proportion of low-angle dips will be oriented at almost 90° to the predominant wind direction but with a component in the direction of the wind. They represent the bedding on the horns of the dune and are very similar to that seen in a seif dune.

4. Low-angle dips oriented up-wind may be preserved when a barchan climbs onto the windward accretion slope of a more slowly moving dune of similar type.

SEIF DUNES

1. Axis of dune parallel to the dominant wind direction.

2. The bulk of the dune will have dips of up to 34° oriented almost at right angles to the predominant wind direction but with a component in the direction of the wind.

3. Seif dune bedding may be complicated by the migration of small local barchans over their surface.

4. The frictional effect of the bulk of a seif dune is thought to give the wind a 'corkscrew' rotational component directed towards the dune. Localised 34° laterally dipping slip-faces may result.

5. The slight sinuosity of the dune may result in the preservation of low-angle dips which have an up-wind component.

Fig.69. Large barchan on rough deflation surface of limestone. Northeast of Umm Said, Qatar.

the air over Qatar heats up more rapidly than over the water of the Persian Gulf. This daytime wind is strongest during the late morning and early afternoon and is far more effective in moving sand grains than the nightly offshore winds. INMAN et al. (1966) have noticed a similar variation in wind strengths and directions along the coast of Baja California, Mexico. The result is that south of Umm Said (Enclosure 1) the dunes tend to build up along the coastline with only relatively small quantities of sand being carried out to sea.

    The source of the sand that is found in a dune field such as that just described on Qatar, is not always obvious. The sand grains consist predominantly of quartz and yet the surface of the Qatar peninsula is composed essentially of limestone and dolomite. It is believed that the quartz sand was supplied to the peninsula from Saudi Arabia during the last Pleistocene glaciation when the shallow Gulf of Salwa (Enclosure 1) would have been above sea level. Since the post-Glacial rise in sea level, the supply of quartz sand has been cut off and the dunes are now concentrated near the southeast coast of Qatar.

DUNE COMPLEXES

Not all dunes are simple barchans. In Fig.70, from the eastern edge of the Rub al Khali, Arabia, small barchan-like complexes oriented transverse to the wind, are being slowly added to the larger stellate dune forms. These latter, by virtue of their size, provide considerable resistance to the wind with an accompanying increase in the wind gradient. As a result, the wind tends to veer towards the larger

Fig.70. Small transverse dunes migrate over a deflation surface and add their bulk to almost static larger stellate dunes. South of Umm as Samim, Oman.

dunes and so deposits additional sand on and around them. In Fig.71, from the southern edge of the Umm as Samim, it can be readily imagined that the high stellate complex originally formed as the result of smaller barchans overtaking a larger one during migration from left to right. This description is, however, over-simplified; it applies only to the relationship between the large stellate and small

Fig.71. Barchans migrate over the salt encrusted surface of the Umm as Samim and add to almost static stellate dunes. Oman.

barchan dunes as seen at the time the photograph was taken. According to HOLM
(1960, p.1371), pyramidal (stellate) dunes form as the result of winds that "beat
around the compass". MCKEE (1966, p.68) also assumes that alternating winds
from several directions are required to build a stellate dune. Dune complexes, such
as those shown in Fig.70 and 71, can migrate over the salt surface of the Umm as
Samim.

Fig.72. Giant barchan complex. The Liwa, Trucial States.

OPPOSING WIND DIRECTIONS

Barchans can continue to multiply until they merge with one another and the
substrate is completely covered, as seen in Fig.72 of the Liwa Sand Sea, Abu Dhabi,
Trucial Coast. The major slip-faces of these barchan-like dunes are formed by one
dominant wind and are reported to be in the order of 500 ft. high. In Fig.72, a
small crestal "lip" occurs at the top of each of these giant slip-faces, with its avalanche slope (see Glossary) facing the opposite direction. This is assumed to result
from a temporary wind directly opposed to the prevailing direction. A similar
occurrence was observed in the Rajasthan Desert, India (GLENNIE and EVAMY,
1968, plate 3D). There, the major foreset slopes result from the Southwest Monsoon
but two months after the monsoon, a milder wind blows from the northeast and
forms small crestal lips whose foresets are directed towards the southwest.

SEIF DUNES

Not all dunes are of the barchan type. Many are roughly linear, with the line of elongation apparently parallel to the prevailing wind direction. They are referred to by BAGNOLD (1941) as "seif" dunes, from the Arab word for a sword. Bagnold (on p.223) has suggested that one type of seif dune may be formed by the elongation of one horn of a barchan which then fuses with the next dune en echelon with it. This, he claims, is caused by winds which are oblique to the prevailing transport direction. He is supported in his interpretation by McKEE (1966a) and McKEE and TIBBITS (1964) who consider that the seif-dune structure seen by them near Sebha, in the Ubari Sand Sea, Libya (see Enclosure 4), is largely controlled by winds from two directions about 90° apart. The present writer is not convinced by their arguments. Although the general pattern of wind directions over most desert areas is now known, there is little information available on the strengths and directions of wind at ground level and virtually no continuous (24 h/day) records are kept outside North America. It seems, therefore, that we can only speculate on the effect that a wind of varying strength and direction may have on dune formation.

McKEE and TIBBITTS (1964, pp.6, 7) quote wind records for the Sebha oasis in support of their interpretation. The figures given are of readings of wind directions and velocities that were recorded daily for several years at 6 a.m. and 6 p.m. The morning wind is dominantly from the southeast and shifts during the day to give an evening wind from the northeast. These times, and especially the earlier hour, are, however, often the calmest moments of daylight. In the desert, wind velocities normally increase during the day and die away again in the evening. From personal observation, winds often appear to be stronger in the afternoon than at any other time during the day or night. This may be the result of convection effects associated with the heat produced by the sun in the middle of the day. It is during the heat of the afternoon, when winds are assumed to be at their strongest and capable of transporting the greatest volume of sand, that they will probably blow from about north-northeast in the region of Sebha, or roughly parallel to the dune axes. This direction would appear to agree well with the sand distribution given by McKEE and TIBBITS (1964, fig.2).

Linear dunes can also undoubtedly form parallel to one wind direction, as can be seen from the results of a single storm in the dunes of the coastal areas of The Netherlands. BAGNOLD (1941, p.171) says "a strong wind causes an accretion of sand on an existing sand patch together with an extension up-wind of the border... this action lasts only as long as there is a plentiful supply of sand..." He goes on to say (p.178), "in a strong sand-laden wind a uniform drift of sand over a uniform rough surface has a transverse instability, so that sand tends to deposit in longitudinal strips". It is here suggested that the combination of these two factors, related essentially to a strong wind of uniform direction, causes the formation of many seif dunes.

In a region of seif dunes, pressure gradients exist between the axes of the interdune areas and the crests of the dunes; these pressure gradients are caused by the resistance to the wind of the dune itself. This results in the formation of "wind cells" in the inter-dune areas, which give the wind an overall spiral motion directed outwards at ground level towards the dunes (Fig.73).

Support for this hypothesis comes from a study of linear sand ridges in the North Sea that are parallel to the marine currents that formed them (HOUBOLT, 1968). From the distribution of lines of flotsam over the axes of the inter-ridge areas and the absence of flotsam over the crests of the ridges, Houbolt deduced that these ridges were built as the result of a spiral motion superimposed upon a tidal current that had an overall linear direction of movement. Unlike the winds in areas of seif dunes, the direction of these tidal currents is reversed four times each day.

Additional support for this hypothesis can be found in Fig.74, a vertical aerial photograph of part of the northern end of the Wahiba Sands in Oman. The major linear dunes are a part of the same pattern as that seen in the frontispiece, only a little further to the west. As was mentioned on p.38, they are thought to have been formed by Pleistocene winds that blew from roughly south to north (from about N180°E to N200°E). Since the Pleistocene, there has been a shift of about 20° to the east in the predominant sand-transporting wind direction (now from about N160°E to N180°E) so that these large dunes are no longer in equilibrium with the wind. The crests of the dunes are now being eroded and the sand is being redeposited in the old broad interdune areas as similar, but much smaller and more closely spaced linear dunes. The active dominant sand-transporting wind—the Southwest Monsoon—is here blowing parallel to the small linear dunes seen spreading over the sands and gravels of Wadi Batha. It is also sub-parallel to many of the small linear dunes that cross obliquely from the interdune areas up the eastern flanks of the large Pleistocene seifs. Many of them, however, show a distinct curvature westwards towards the crest of the large dunes. This curvature is even more pronounced, only this time towards the east, in those small dunes that stretch from the interdune areas towards the steeper western side of the Pleistocene seifs. This distribution of large and small dunes is thought to be in conformity with the idea that seif dunes are built by spiral eddies associated with a strong wind from one dominant direction, as outlined in Fig.73.[1]

Had the Pleistocene seifs been parallel to the present dominant sand-transporting wind, the dune pattern of smaller seifs could not have existed. It is because the dune orientation is out of equilibrium with the sand-transporting wind, that erosion of the crests provides sand in the interdune areas that can be used to

---

[1] The formation of seif dunes in a similar way by means of one strong dominant wind is proposed for the Sahara by DUBIEF (1952) and for the Simpson Desert (Australia) by MADIGAN (1946, pp. 57–62). Madigan (on p. 61) also has noticed that eddies can carry sand grains obliquely up the side of a seif.

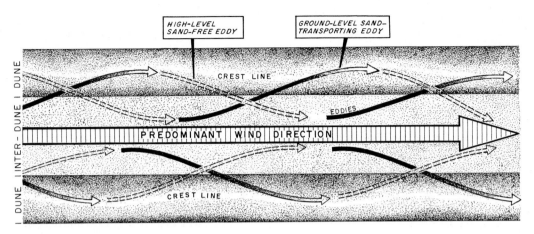

(A) WIND-GRADIENT EDDIES DIRECTED FROM THE INTER-DUNE TO DUNE AREAS.CAUSED BY THE GREATER RESISTANCE OF THE BULK OF THE DUNE.

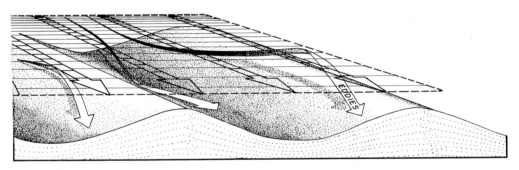

(B) SCHEMATIC REPRESENTATION OF THE SPIRAL PATH FOLLOWED BY THE WIND EDDIES.THEY MAY GIVE RISE TO CRESTAL SLIP FACES. A DEVIATION OF THE WIND FROM THE PREDOMINANT DIRECTION WILL ACCENTUATE THE DEVELOPMENT OF SLIP FACES ON ONE SIDE OF THE DUNE.

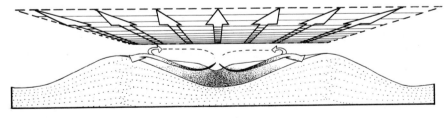

(C) INTERDUNE WIND-CELL PATTERN SHOWN SCHEMATICALLY

Fig.73. Suggested mechanism whereby a seif dune is formed by one predominant wind.

trace the path of the major dune-building eddies. Because the Pleistocene dune orientation is only slightly out of equilibrium with the present sand-transporting wind, these large seifs still affect the winds in much the same manner as a seif orientation that is in equilibrium with the wind. The large, moderately dipping surfaces of seif dunes will consist of tightly packed accretion bedding—in contrast to the loosely packed avalanche bedding of the foresets of barchan dunes. The accretion bedding is deposited by saltation and surface creep of sand grains moving over the surface of the dune at an angle only slightly oblique to that of. the predominant wind, and sub-parallel to the long axis of the dune. Some characteristics of the bedding associated with seif dunes are given in Fig.68 and MCKEE and TIBBITS (1964) figure the style of cross-bedding found in seif dunes as seen in test pits.

BAGNOLD (1941, p.69) states that sand movement is proportional to the cube of the excess wind velocity "above that at which sand begins to move. For a given sand, a wind of 16 m/sec will move as much sand in 24 hours as would be moved by a wind of 8 m/sec in 3 weeks." This fact lays great stress on the transporting power of strong winds which will control the shape and distribution of sand dunes. Gentle winds, on the other hand, are only capable of slight modification of the surface laminae of dunes.

Fig.75 is an aerial photograph, taken in the month of February, of a number of recently formed seif dunes in the central Wahiba Sands. They all have well developed slip-faces on their western flanks in response to a light easterly wind that blows throughout much of the winter. Further to the south, dunes occur as north–south rows of small barchans migrating slowly towards the west. A few hours of a strong wind blowing occasionally from the north in winter, or more regularly from the south in the summer, is sufficient to obliterate these slip-faces and convert the barchans into long seif dunes parallel to the path of the wind. The steep western flanks of both the large dunes seen in Fig.74 and the smaller ones that are superimposed on their surfaces have also been formed by the same light easterly winter wind.

It is thought that although the present southwest monsoon is strong enough to build small seif dunes with a crestal spacing of 100–500 m, it is not strong enough to have built large dunes of the size seen in Fig.74. To form dunes of this size it is probably necessary to have much stronger winds than exist at present. The occurrence of very strong winds would have been possible during glacial periods when the large areas of polar high pressure would bring about a concentration of the other air-pressure belts towards the equator (LAMB, 1961). HARE (1961) believes that the easterly winds of the desert belts would probably also be more strongly developed during glaciations.

The coincidence of active dune formation in desert areas with polar glaciation is proposed by FAIRBRIDGE (1964, p.128). He states that vegetated sand-dune ridges of the seif type can be observed disappearing below sea level in North Australia, Arabia and West Africa. FRIEDMAN (1964) has sampled cemented dune

Fig.74. Large seif dunes at the northern end of the Wahiba Sands, Oman. (Outcrops of Mesozoic sediments show through the sands of the interdune areas.) Ministry of Defence (Air Force Department) photograph. British Crown copyright reserved.

sand from below the high-tide zone off the Yucatan Peninsula in Mexico, KENDALL and SKIPWITH (1969) report the presence of Quaternary dune sand below sea level off the coast of Abu Dhabi, Trucial Coast, and the writer has traced cemented dune sand to below low-tide level near Muscat, Oman. The correlation of the formation of West African desert dunes with a time of lower sea level is also proposed by TRICART et al. (1957).

Traces of linear dunes of probable Pleistocene age occur within what is now the zone of tropical low pressure (roughly 10°N–10°S; see Fig.1). They have been

Fig.75. Seif dunes with barchan-like slip faces developed on their western flanks as a result of gentle eastern winter winds. Central Wahiba Sands, Oman.

mentioned by FLINT (1959) and FAIRBRIDGE (1964) as occurring in the Congo (4°S) and southern Sudan (5°N). Other old systems of linear dunes in Africa are found further from the equator, but their orientations are not compatible with the present prevailing winds (FLINT, 1959; FAIRBRIDGE, 1964; FLINT and BOND, 1968). These occurrences provide evidence of the shifting of air-pressure belts since these old dunes were formed.

The shorter distances involved between areas of high and low pressure during a Pleistocene glaciation would give rise to a much stronger global air circulation. Evidence of this can be seen in other areas of large seif dunes such as in the central Rub al Khali or the Rajasthan Desert, and in dunes that have already undergone or are now undergoing some modification of their original orientation because of shifting air-pressure belts. These latter can be seen in the dunes of the northern Trucial States (Enclosure 2) and possibly also in the periglacial dunes of Nebraska (SMITH, 1965).

Conversely, during the short "warm" interglacials, the areas of polar high pressure would be reduced to a minimum. All global air-pressure zones would spread out towards the poles and the earth's air-circulatory systems would be weaker than at present. In mountainous areas in a desert, winds caused by convection would probably be dominant over any trade-wind pattern. When these "convection winds" pass over a sea such as the Gulf of Oman, thunderstorms and heavy rain over the mountains are likely to follow; this, indeed, can occasionally be seen on the Batinah coast of Oman today. In the past, it could have been a common occurrence and might account for the widespread distribution of gravels that now flank the Oman Mountains.

This over-simplified explanation of "pluvials" is given a slightly different interpretation by BUTZER (1961, 1963). He points out (1963, p.212) that in the Mediterranean area, the "Würm pluvial *par excellence*" (italics in original version by Butzer) coincided with the period of glacial advance; the later period of maximum glaciation was dry. From this, he concludes that subtropical pluvials cannot be interpreted as secondary effects of the presence of polar ice sheets, but rather that they are associated with a primary change in the atmospheric circulation that is coincident with polar extension.

In its simplest form, therefore, it is suggested that, other conditions being equal, barchans (or transverse dunes, depending upon the supply of sand) will tend to develop at lower wind velocities, and seif dunes will form when the wind velocities are higher. The higher the wind velocity, the larger the seif dune and the greater the interdune spacing, is a statement that may well explain the distribution of the large and small seif dunes of the Wahiba Sands in time and space.[1] The wind velocities experienced today are probably incapable of causing the formation of the large seif dunes found in many deserts.

In the southern Rub al Khali, seif dunes may be 150 m high (BEYDOUN, 1966). In the Ubari Sand Sea, Libya, they attain a height estimated at around 100 m and a length of 100 km or more and are often covered by small migrating barchan-like dunes. In the conditions under which these large seifs were formed, barchans are unlikely to have been able to survive. These barchans are, therefore, indicative only of the present wind regime that bears little relation—apart, perhaps, from direction—to the older and stronger winds that almost certainly formed the large seifs.

TRANSVERSE DUNES

In the eastern part of the Rub al Khali, there exists a large area of dunes known as Uıuq al Mu'taridah (Enclosure 1). The long axes of these dunes are roughly perpendicular to those of the north–south oriented seif dunes found further to the west. These transverse dunes are separated by inland sebkhas. Although they have not been visited in the field, their morphology, as seen in aerial photographs (see Fig.76), suggests that they are formed by a wind blowing approximately from the

[1] This statement may be taken a stage further. For a given particle size, the strength of the wind is a factor that controls the character and spacing of aeolian sediments from transverse sand ripples and barchan dunes at low wind velocities to linear sand strips and seif dunes at high wind velocities. Similar relationships occur in an aquatic medium: low current velocities result in small transverse ripples: sand ridges form parallel to strong tidal currents on shallow continental shelves (ALLEN, 1968a).

north; they are probably built of more or less unidirectional foresets of barchan type dipping to the south. McKee (1966a) describes similar transverse dunes from New Mexico in which the axes of the dunes are at right angles to the dominant wind direction and the dune laminae dip down-wind. He does not, however, mention interdune sebkhas or playas.

The reason why these dunes have not developed as seifs, with an almost north–south axis parallel to the dominant sand-transporting wind, is probably concerned with the position of the area relative to the main path of the winds of Shamal origin. The Uruq al Mu'taridah lies to the east of the main Shamal track, and, as a result, the wind velocities may well be too low for seifs to develop.

If there had been a more limited supply of sand, it is thought that simple barchan dunes would have formed. With a more plentiful supply of sand, the barchans should grow in size, and coalesce. When this happens, the resulting morphology is commonly that of a complex sand body whose long axis is oblique to the wind but which still bears some resemblance to the barchan forms from which it was derived. Why then, should these transverse dunes posses such regular spacing at right angles to the predominant wind?

From observations aided by the use of black smoke, Cooper (1958) came to the conclusion that the path followed by the wind across a series of transverse dunes has a wave-like form. According to him, it climbs parallel to the windward surface of the dune and descends again to the windward edge of the succeeding dune, leaving a zone of dead air in the region of the slip face. Wind vortices occasionally develop in this zone of dead air and presumably account for the low velocity reversed wind directions measured close to the foot of a slip-face by Inman et al. (1966) in the coastal dunes of Baja California, Mexico. Cooper (1958) believes that no deflation takes place in the intervening interdune area. The writer, on the other hand, suggests that deflation of the interdune area does occur. He believes that over the transverse dunes that cover a flat desert surface, a wave-like path is followed by the wind that conforms closely to that sketched in Fig. 77; it causes successively, transport and then deposition of sand, followed by deflation of the interdune area.

Since such a wind path is unlikely to develop over a hard desert surface with only occasional barchan dunes, it seems possible that transverse dunes are derived from areas that are plentifully covered with sand. Once started, the wave path of the wind perpetuates the size and spacing of the dunes for any appropriate wind strength provided there is no gain or loss of sand. In the case of coastal dunes, the initial supply of sand is provided by the beach; with the dunes of the Uruq al Mu'taridah, the source of the sand is probably the southern edge of the Liwa Sand Sea (see Enclosure 1). As with the large seif dunes of the Wahiba Sands and Rub al Khali, the time of original formation of these large transverse dunes is thought to be during Pleistocene glaciations. The annual rate of sand transport is now probably much lower than formerly.

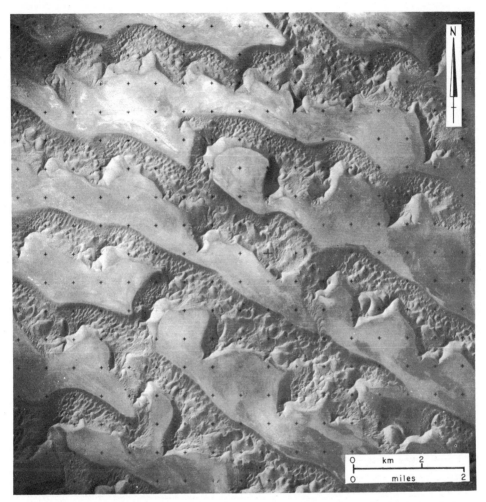

Fig.76. Aerial photo of a dune system whose long axes are at right angles to the dominant wind, which here blows from just east of north. The interdune areas are inland sebkhas. Uruq al Mu'tari-dah, southeastern Rub al Khali, Arabia. Ministry of Defence (Air Force Department) photograph. British Crown copyright reserved.

In Fig.77, the situation is depicted in which the almost planar surface of an inland sebkha is overlain by transverse dunes. Initially, the ground-water level is assumed to coincide with the sebkha surface. The transverse dunes that migrate across the surface of the sebkha will be regularly spaced because the near-surface path of the wind will follow a distorted wave pattern. The sand will be transported over the dune, deposited behind the dune and deflated from the interdune sebkha surface. If the wind is from the north, the dunes will slowly migrate to the south. The damp sebkha surface will inhibit growth of barchan-like horns and deflation will tend to lower any "dry-season" accumulations down to the level of the water

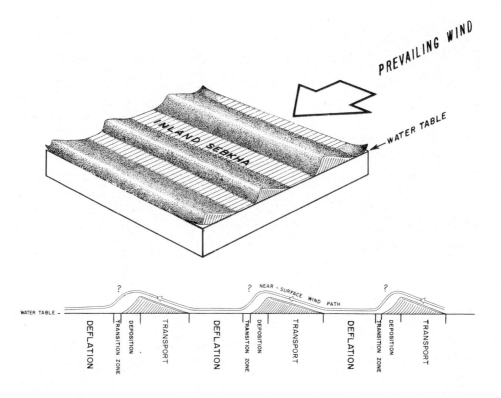

Fig.77. Transverse dunes and interdune inland sebkhas.

table. If sand supply exceeds sand removal, the dunes will grow in height and therefore in surface area. Given sufficient time, the interdune sebkhas will be reduced in size until eventually the area becomes a sand sea of transverse dunes. The final remoulding is that the transverse dunes of the sand sea may finish up with a complex barchan-like morphology resembling that seen at present in the Liwa (Fig.72).

With later burial and a rising water table, most of the salt and gypsum cement of the dune sands, at present seen in sebkhas, is likely to be dissolved by the comparatively fresh ground water brought in from below. An original association of transverse dunes and inland sebkhas may not be recognised in a fossil desert sequence.

The orientation of the almost linear dunes seen in the back half of Fig.78 does not appear to conform with the present wind direction as deduced from the small barchan dunes migrating over both them, and the large barchan-like structure in the foreground. This, perhaps, can be explained from a study of Enclosure 1.

The dunes are some 160 km south-southwest of Jebel Hafit. Their axes are aligned roughly west-northwest–east-southeast. They were probably formed by

Fig.78. Small barchans migrate over barchan-like complexes which are almost transverse to the present predominant wind. Southeast of Buraimi, Trucial States.

strong Pleistocene winds that blew parallel to the axes. They are assumed to have been originally formed as seif dunes but are now slowly undergoing modification under the influence of the present milder winds that blow from the north. This milder wind is not capable of building seif dunes, so that the large barchan-like structure is being modified into a crescent shape. Similar, large, distorted, barchan-like dunes are also being formed at present from the remnants of the Wahiba seifs now in the middle of the Wadi Batha alluvial plain a few kilometres due east of the locality seen in Fig.74. The foresets that have formed in recent time are all of barchan type and dip downwind. The dunes seen in Fig. 78 are seifs that are being modified into transverse forms because the wind velocities are now too low to build seifs. Without a complete analysis of the bedding of the sands in the core of the dunes, they may easily be confused with normal transverse dunes if the new wind blows at right angles to the old.

ANCIENT DUNE SANDS AND PALAEO-WIND DIRECTIONS

Dune bedding is preserved in the sediments of ancient deserts in many parts of the world, and excellent photographs have been given in many publications on the subject.

The bedding of these ancient dunes was laid down in a fairly regular pattern as the result of deposition of sand grains following aeolian transport. From a study of the orientation of the dune bedding, the approximate direction in which the wind was blowing at the time of deposition of these beds can be deduced. This has been done by many workers employing different statistical methods.

SHOTTON (1937) noted that in the Permo-Triassic dune sands of the west Midlands of England, the "false-bedding" with steeper slopes showed no more variation in attitude than that found on the down-wind side of a barchan. He extended this (SHOTTON, 1956) to show that barchan dunes should have a maximum in the direction of the wind that formed the dune when the measured azimuths were plotted on a rose diagram. By contrast, longitudinal (seif) dunes showed maxima that were almost opposed to each other, but with a small component in the direction of the prevalent wind (SHOTTON, 1956, fig.3E). WRIGHT (1956) measured the maximum angle of dip in each available sedimentary structure in an area of outcropping Tertiary Chuska Sandstone in Arizona and New Mexico. He found that the maximum percentage of recorded dips lay in the range $23°–27°$. The azimuths of these dips also gave an indication of the palaeo-wind direction when plotted onto a rose diagram. LAMING (1966) also used a rose diagram of the azimuths of dips for deducing the palaeo-wind direction of the Permian dune sands of Devon, England, and BIGARELLA and SALAMUNI (1961) used rose diagrams to show the overall palaeo-wind directions for extensive areas of the Early Mesozoic Botucatu Sandstone of Brazil and Uruguay.

When measuring the attitude of cross-stratification in aeolian sandstones, OPDYKE (1961, p.52) states that "in general the magnitude of the angle of dip is a reasonable guide to nearness of approach to the true (palaeowind) direction". In other words, low dip angles have little significance for palaeo-wind measurements. Opdyke then deduces the palaeo-wind direction from the statistical mean of a sufficient number of readings. RUNCORN (1961, 1964) carries this a stage farther. He ignores all values of dip less than say $15°$ and then plots the frequency of dip directions on a histogram. After smoothing out a curve through his histogram plot, he concludes that the mean direction of the wind that formed the dune bedding coincides with the maximum frequency percentage. Shotton, in a discussion on RUNCORN (1964), points out that if the bedding attitudes of longitudinal dunes were measured, two dominant dip directions would be recorded, each at right angles to the wind direction. If only one side of a longitudinal dune were exposed, then the deduced palaeo-wind direction would be almost $90°$ from the direction of the wind that actually formed the bedding. POOLE (1964) also plots his dip azimuths on histograms using 50 readings per histogram sheet.

Following the method of vector analysis described by CURRAY (1956), MACKENZIE (1964a) was able to reproduce remarkably consistent palaeo-wind directions for the Bermuda Pleistocene eolianites. He used between 2 and 11 dip measurements for each cross-bedded unit; the majority of dip angles measured were $30°$ or greater.

REICHE (1938) plots both the direction and the angle of dip of cross-bedded strata on a stereographic polar net. This has the advantage that the attitude of a bed can be represented by a point (the pole to the bedding plane). All dip attitudes may be shown but visual emphasis is still placed on the importance of the larger dip angles as indicators of the palaeo-wind direction. Polar nets have also been used by McKEE (1940, 1962) and KIERSCH (1950). The writer prefers to use the polar net for deducing palaeo-wind directions. In addition to direction, he believes that the distribution of the poles of dip planes can also indicate the type of dune that was formed (barchan-type or seif; see Fig.68) and may also suggest the local presence of more than one palaeo-wind direction.

Fig.79 illustrates large-scale dune bedding in the Permian "Yellow Sands" of Durham, England, possibly deposited as part of a linear or seif-like dune. The distribution of bedding attitudes and interpreted palaeo-wind direction is shown on the polar diagram, Fig.80. Dip attitudes from the other flank of the seif dune are poorly represented in this quarry.

Crests, probably associated with the "horns" of a barchan of similar age, are exposed in a quarry in southwest Scotland (Fig.81). They trend roughly N230°E and N250°E. The distribution of bedding attitudes for the crestal area and for the non-crestal remainder of the quarry are given in Fig.82 and 83, res-pectively. Note that the dip attitudes tend to be concentrated on either side of the wind trend in Fig.82, and that the additional points from the rest of the quarry, representing the centre portion of the barchan, fill in this gap in Fig.83. The distri-bution of dip attitudes on the horns of a barchan is rather similar to that found on the linear seif dunes (cf. Fig.80), but some of the dip attitudes found in the middle of the distribution seen in Fig. 82, perhaps more correctly belong to the central part of the barchan.

Fig.84 shows the planed-off festoons of a cemented barchan dune from locality 54, east of Abu Dhabi town, Arabia (see Enclosure 2). The distribution of dip attitudes (Fig.85), measured on a number of such dunes spread over a small area, does not show the gap seen in Fig.80. Some of the dip angles have been increased after deposition and cementation by the growth of gypsum crystals. Fairly steep dips almost normal to the prevailing wind have also been developed, possibly by wind-formed scours. This results in over-emphasis of the seif-like dip attitudes on the flanks of the barchan dune.

The distribution of the major seif-like sand dunes of the northern Trucial States is indicated on Enclosure 2 by crest lines. This pattern is emphasised by the presence of large feidjes. Together, they show trends that are roughly east–west in the south and progressively become more northerly to the north. This large-scale dune pattern is thought to have been formed by Pleistocene winds that blew from the west in the southern part of the area and that had a more northerly com-ponent further north. In the area covered by a broad strip bordering the coast and coastal sebkhas, the lower parts of these dunes have been cemented by calcite or gypsum cement. These cemented beds are occasionally exposed as the result of wind-removal of the overlying uncemented sands. At more than twenty localities,

Fig.79. Seif-like dune bedding. Permian Yellow Sands, Houghton-le-Spring, Durham, England.

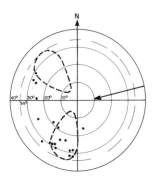

Fig.80. Distribution of dip attitudes and deduced palaeo-wind direction. Permian Yellow Sands. Durham, England.

palaeo-wind directions have been deduced from the bedding attitudes of outcropping cemented dune sands. They indicate that the wind that formed these dunes blew roughly parallel to the axes of the dunes in the directions suggested above.

The fine, closely spaced crest lines seen on Enclosure 2, east of Dubai and Sharjah, represent the axes of small seif dunes that are being formed today. They are roughly at right angles to the axes of the large Pleistocene seifs and are formed largely from sand derived from the Pleistocene seifs by wind action. They are now extending across the surface of many of the feidjes, thus indicating that here, the orientation of the Pleistocene seifs is no longer in equilibrium with the present dominant wind direction.

Fig.81. Crests of "horns" of barchan preserved in Permian dune sand. Locharbriggs, Dumfries-shire, southwest Scotland.

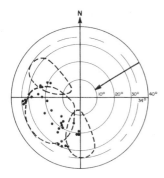

Fig.82   Fig.83

Fig.82. Distribution of dip attitudes and deduced palaeo-wind direction associated with horn of barchan dune. Locharbriggs, southwest Scotland.
Fig.83. Distribution of dip attitudes and deduced palaeo-wind direction associated with remainder of Permian barchan dune. Southwest Scotland.

Confirmation that the winds that formed the major seif dunes of the Wahiba Sands were parallel to the axes of these dunes (p.90), also comes from outcrops of cemented dune sand. The deduced palaeo-wind directions are consistently towards the north, ranging from about N360°E to N20°E (Fig.86).

Some of the polar diagrams shown in Fig.86 have concentrations of points that are indicative of barchan as well as seif dunes. Barchan-like characteristics are well seen at locality A, where high-angle dips (up to 30°) have developed directly down wind, and to a lesser extent at localities B and C.

Fig.84. Planed-off festoons of a Cenozoic barchan. East of Abu Dhabi, Trucial Coast.

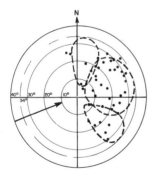

Fig.85. Distribution of dip attitudes and deduced palaeo-wind direction of Cenozoic barchan dune. East of Abu Dhabi, Trucial Coast.

Any temporary lowering of the wind velocity over an area where seif dunes are forming will result in modification of the surface of the seifs and the building and migration of superimposed barchan-like forms. This is happening over many areas of seif dunes today. Even though strong winds may later destroy the superimposed barchans, some of their foresets that are directed downwind will be locally preserved. In a case like this, the relative importance of the two types of dip concentration seen in the polar diagram can only be assessed correctly if the outcrop

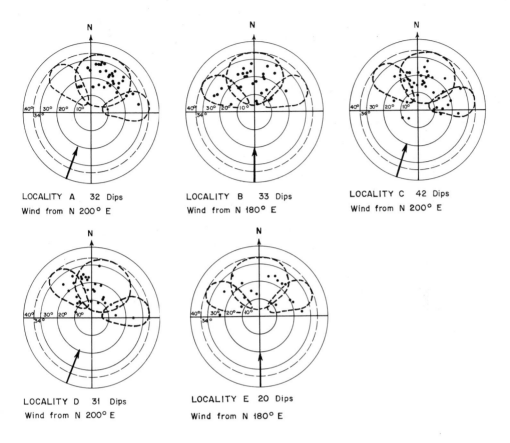

Fig.86. Palaeo-wind directions deduced from the bedding attitudes of cemented Pleistocene dune sands from five localities near the western edge of the Central Wahiba Sands, Oman.

areas are sufficiently well exposed. Apart from quarries and recently eroded dune sands in present desert areas, this is rarely possible.

OPDYKE and RUNCORN (1960), RUNCORN (1961), OPDYKE (1961) and POOLE (1964) point out the palaeoclimatological significance of desert sands, and show how the wind directions deduced from their bedding may be used to reconstruct the climatic conditions of the past. There is apparently, still sufficient evidence preserved in present day dune orientations to enable deductions to be made about deserts of probable Pleistocene age. By analogy, they point also to the possibility of local complexities in Permian desert dune orientation that reflect the influence of a Late Palaeozoic polar ice cap.

FORESET LAMINAE IN DUNE SANDS

As shown in Fig.68, the bulk of the bedding on a barchan dune dips at angles of up to 34° (the maximum angle of repose for dry sand) in the direction of the wind. In contrast, the bedding of linear seif dunes is oriented more nearly at right angles to the wind direction but with a variable component which is down wind.

From the arguments presented on the formation of seif dunes, it follows that bedding that is at the angle of repose should be confined to only a small percentage of the total volume of a seif dune. It is likely, however, that if an orientation study were made of the bedding attitudes found across the unconsolidated surface sands in the Wahiba (Fig.74, 75), the resulting plot of points on a polar diagram would be asymmetric. This asymmetry would result from formation of dunes by two winds of different character; the strong south winds of fairly short duration that give the overall linear shape to the system, and the more persistent but gentle east winds that add the transverse or barchan-like character of widespread avalanche slopes (see p.92).

The foreset bedding seen in Fig.87 from the northern edge of the Ubari Sand Sea, Libya, was "fixed" by soaking with water and then exposed by digging. The 34° foresets continue down, parallel to the visible slip-face, almost to the base of the dune some 8 m below. The thin low-angle accretion laminae on the surface were destroyed by the flow of water.

HORIZONTAL LAMINAE IN DUNE SANDS

Horizontal and low-angle accretion bedding is found on the tops, windward slopes and rounded flanks of dunes. The horizontal bedding seen in Fig.88 is in a pit dug on the flank of the same dune as that seen in Fig.87.

HORIZONTAL LAMINAE OF SHEET SANDS AND INTERDUNE AREAS

Similar-looking but much more widespread horizontal bedding may be found in interdune areas and also in some sheet sands, as is the case shown in Fig.89, also from the Ubari Sand Sea.

BAGNOLD (1941, pp.158, 244) suggests that horizontally laminated sheet sands develop as the result of the distribution of protective layers of pebbles by periodic flooding. The sheet sand seen in Fig.90, however, contains no pebbles; the grain sizes are similar to those found in nearby dunes; the well-sorted laminae are typical of wind-blown sands; there is little in either the sediment or its structures to suggest any fluviatile transport; all features point to an aeolian origin. An alternative explanation for the origin of some sheet sands can be derived from

Fig.87. 34° foreset dips of slip face of barchan dune. Northern edge of Ubari Sand Sea, Libya.

Fig.88. Horizontal laminae on the broad flank of a barchan dune. Northern edge of Ubari Sand Sea, Libya.

Bagnold's remarks (pp.151–153). He shows that ripples flatten out and disappear above a certain wind strength, that the ripple-forming tendency is reduced with sand grains of nearly uniform grain size, and that an increase in the rate of deposition lowers the ripple height so that with very rapid deposition the ripples disappear altogether.

This interpretation of the origin of horizontally-bedded aeolian sands is analogous to horizontally bedded fluvial sands. SIMONS and RICHARDSON (1966, p.311) state that "in the Upper Flow Regime, resistance to flow is small and sediment transport is large. The usual bed forms are plane bed or antidunes". ALLEN (1968a, p.174), after discussing large ripple forms at moderate water velocities, continues: "a further substantial increase in flow strength will commonly lead to the destruction of the large ripples and to the formation of an apparently flat bed over which there is intense sand transport." A similar conclusion for the origin of horizontally-bedded flood deposits was reached by McKEE et al. (1967).

Perhaps a combination of rapid deposition, high wind velocities and fairly uniform grain size of the transported sand may also result in sheet sand formation in deserts (see BAGNOLD, 1941, pp.149–153).

On the other hand, in the broad interdune areas, deflation tends to be dominant over deposition. The grain size at the surface will tend to be the largest which can withstand the interdune wind strength. Grains will be transported by both saltation and surface creep. Horizontal accretion laminae will form during periods of lesser wind strengths. Sorting may be expected to be poorer than in the adjoining dunes (see McKEE and TIBBITTS, 1964, fig.4).

McKEE and TIBBITTS (1964, p.8) suggest that the horizontally laminated sands of interdune areas, and the low-angle laminae of the lower slopes of seif dunes are both formed by saltating sand grains. Whatever the explanation used for their formation, horizontally bedded sheet-like sands occur over wide areas of the desert without the presence of interbedded pebble beds of fluviatile origin.

CONTORTED BEDDING IN DUNE SAND VERSUS TEMPORARY WADI DELTAS

The contorted bedding seen in Fig.91 is in the slightly damp sand of a dune photographed about 3 km from the Mediterranean coast in Libya. The low-angle accretion bedding which truncates the slumped beds is clearly seen. The light-coloured laminae consist of carbonate grains, including Foraminifera, and shell fragments, etc., blown in from the coast, while the darker laminae consist of quartz grains.

How the slumping occurred and became preserved is partly explained by Fig.92. The surface of this coastal dune in Libya had become damp and heavy after rain. Being relatively unstable on the steep flank of the dune because of its water content, it slipped down over the underlying less-cohesive dry sand and retained a record of this movement in the form of folds and fractures because the sand was

Fig.89. Horizontally bedded sheet sand and small buttes. Northern edge of Ubari Sand Sea, Libya.

Fig.90. Horizontally bedded sheet sand. Northern edge of Ubari Sand Sea, Libya.

still damp at the time of slumping. A pit dug into the dune on the line of fracture revealed broken and contorted bedding similar to that seen in Fig.91. On the other hand, BIGARELLA et al. (1969) believe that such strata became deformed as the result of oversteepening of the profile. Oversteepening (slopes greater than about 34°) can only occur on sand surfaces that are already damp. Under moist conditions, sand transport should be minimal, therefore oversteepening by sedimentation is unlikely to occur. Apart from the illustrations given by BIGARELLA et al. (1969), contorted bedding from the gypsum dunes of Whitesands National Monument, New Mexico, is figured by McKEE (1966, plates IVB and VE).

Slump structures have also been recognised in ancient dune sediments in Britain. Fig.93 shows slumped aeolian sandstone at the top of the Permian "Yellow Sands" of northeast England (looking down over the edge to the quarry floor some 25 m below). At this locality, there are two slumps, one above the other. Later, these slumped sands were covered by marls of the transgressing Permian "Zechstein Sea", suggesting that the formation of these Permian slumps was probably also due to dampness, either rain, or the effect of the transgression itself.

Similar slumps have been seen at Ledstone Quarry, near Leeds, Yorkshire, where again, the yellow dune sands are overlain by fossiliferous marine marls. About 20 cm of sand between the undoubted aeolian and marine horizons appears to have been reworked by water and contains some moulds of brachiopods.

At Hilton Beck, in the Vale of Eden, slumps also occur at the top of the Permian Lower Penrith Sandstone. The overlying sediments, in this case, are wadi conglomerates known locally as the Upper Brockram. These slumps were presumably caused by the flooding wadi or associated rain. Whether or not water scouring of dune sand was also involved is not certain. Bedding attitudes in the sands of the Lower Penrith Sandstone at this locality suggest that they were part of a seif dune formed by a wind that blew from the east. A little farther to the east, imbrication of the pebbles of the Upper Brockram indicates that here the wadi flowed roughly from south to north.

Wind, especially when associated with rain, can cause scouring followed by slumping of the sand. The result can be mistaken for contorted fluviatile or marine sands.

In North America, contorted bedding has been recorded from sandstones of aeolian origin from the Permian Coconino Sandstone (McKEE, 1944), the Triassic Moenkopi Formation (McKEE, 1954) and the Jurassic Navajo Sandstone of Utah (KIERSCH, 1950).

Contorted bedding occurs in the Lower Cretaceous Nubian Sandstone of the northern Fezzan, Libya, and has been discussed in some detail by McKEE (1962). He, probably rightly, ascribes their formation to "forward drag and overturning of the upper part of the beds... by a sudden rush of water and sand as demonstrated in laboratory experiments" (McKEE et al., 1962, pp.156–159). The same type of origin is assumed for the recumbent folds seen in Fig.94 and 95. These cores

Fig.91. Slump folds and fractures in dune sand. Zanzur, Libya.

Fig.92. A slump formed on the surface of a coastal dune following rain. West of Tripoli, Libya.

Fig.93. Slump folds in Permian dune sands. Crime Riggs, Durham, England.

were taken in the Recent sediments of a temporary delta built out into the Mediterranean Sea by a wadi in flood.[1] They might just as easily have been formed at the point where the sediment-laden water of a wadi in flood enters a temporary desert lake. They are included here for comparison with slump folds of undoubted aeolian origin.

In the Nubian Sandstone of the Fezzan, the recumbent folds sometimes form part of a graded bed. Associated quartz-pebble and curled clay-flake horizons are indicative of sedimentation under water. The curled clay flakes indicate that these beds have also been subjected to sub-aerial exposure. In such a sequence, especially where there are other features indicative of a desert environment[2], one may expect

[1] Some down-dragging of the laminae at the edge of these cores was probably caused by contact with the side of the core barrel as it was pushed into the soft sediment.

[2] Mud-cracks, shale pebbles and boulders, mud-flakes, ventifacts, cellular dolomite (BUSSON, 1967, p.143). Apart from these features, the widespread occurrence of silicified sands and the presence of silicified wood (DI CESARE et al., 1963; KLITZSCH, 1966) is believed by the writer to be related to diagenesis in a desert environment. Although the time and process of silicification is not known, petrified wood is sometimes found buried beneath what is believed to be cemented dune sand and its alteration may be connected with the depth of the water table below the desert surface. Similarly, silicified sandstones may also reflect diagenetic changes possibly involving an earlier history of cementation by calcite (calcretes) and the formation of silcretes.

to find aeolian sand. McKee (1962, p.551) states that no aeolian sands occur in the Cretaceous Nubian Sandstone.[1] On the other hand, when working in the same area, the present writer inferred the presence of aeolian sand on the basis of the criteria set out in chapter 2, p.11. Water-laid sediments undoubtedly exist in the Nubian Sandstone of this area, but then they are also a common feature in some parts of modern deserts and can still be associated with aeolian sands. Although the writer has not visited the other localities in North Africa and Arabia that are described by McKee in his paper, he could infer, from McKee's own descriptions, that many of these other areas possibly also possess aeolian Nubian Sandstone. McKee himself (1962, p.576) appeared to have difficulty in finding a suitable water-associated environment for cross-stratification that "in most respects... matches the structure of barchan dunes". Some of McKee's "recumbent folds" might well conform to slumps in dune sands. Perhaps further study of the Cretaceous Nubian Sandstone will permit its mode of deposition to be defined more precisely.

DIKAKA

Another type of structure that is fairly common on modern stabilised dunes and is occasionally seen in Cenozoic dune sands is that of plant-root moulds. The writer,

---

[1] The Cretaceous Nubian Sandstone of southern Egypt was named by RUSSEGGER (1837). Use of the term "Nubian Sandstone" has since spread greatly both geographically and stratigraphically. The name has been applied to clean and conspicuously cross-stratified sandstone bodies in most countries of northeast Africa and on the Arabian Peninsula, and has been used for rock of more varied lithology ranging in age from Cambrian to Cretaceous.

Although ideas concerning the genesis of the Nubian-type sandstone have been numerous, the theory of dune or aeolian origin, first presented by WALTHER (1888), was one of the most popular. Since then, the concept of a fluvial, estuarine or deltaic origin has been promoted by palaeontologists impressed by the mixture of marine and fresh-water fossils in certain beds (NEWTON, 1909; BUROLLET and MANDERSCHEID, 1963) and by geologists who noted the association of plant remains in many places (LYONS, 1894; BOWMAN, 1926). The theory of marine deposition has likewise had numerous supporters (SHUKRI and SAID, 1944; ATTIA, 1955). Others (KLITZSCH, 1966) describe the Nubian Sandstone (Messak Sandstone) as consisting of continental strata without further subdivision.

SANDFORD (1937, 1951) considered the Nubian sandstones of Libya primarily as a facies that kept recurring from the Devonian to the Late Cretaceous; he compared them to the Karroo of South Africa. It seems likely that the "Nubian Sandstone" (sensu lato) comprises rock sequences that were deposited in an arid continental environment over a time span from Cambrian to Late Cretaceous, but which are locally interbedded with strata resulting from intermittent marine transgressions.

Since the term "Nubian Sandstone" has lost its original meaning, POMEYROL (1968) suggests that it should be dropped. On the other hand, RIGASSI (1969) believes that "Nubian Sandstone" should be retained to designate a unit which ranges in age from Cambrian to Quaternary and comprises rocks that were deposited under arid continental conditions. Until further study permits more precise definition, perhaps the use of "Nubian-type sandstone" (McKEE, 1962) is more satisfactory when referring to these rocks of similar facies but of wide-ranging age; with this view, SHAWA (1969) concurs.

Fig.94   Fig.95

Fig.94. Recumbent folds in core taken in a temporary wadi delta. West of Tripoli, Libya. Half natural scale.

Fig.95. Recumbent folds in core taken in a temporary wadi delta. West of Tripoli, Libya. Half natural scale.

in conjunction with Evamy, has discussed the significance of the occurrence of these structures (GLENNIE and EVAMY, 1968). They use the word "dikaka" for them after an Arab word used on modern maps of Arabia to designate scrub-covered accumulations of dune sand (see also Bramkamp's dune classification in POWERS et al., 1966, p.D100).

   All plants require water in order to live, and none more so than in a desert. Desert plants have leaf adaptations to reduce evaporation to a minimum. Many also have root systems that penetrate deeply in order to reach a permanent supply of the moisture that is so necessary to life (see KASSAS, 1966, for a more general description of desert plants).

   On the surface of active sand dunes, plants have little chance to establish themselves because they are either smothered by drifting sand, or the sand is blown away from around their small young roots and they wither and die. Seeds that have been incorporated more deeply within a dune, however, can sprout after the dune has been dampened by rain. Provided its roots can reach a more permanent supply of water than is afforded by a surface wetting, the plant may survive and grow to maturity. Since these plants grow upwards, and extend their roots downwards through aeolian sand, they tend to disturb the previously formed aeolian bedding. When the plant dies, its tissue appears to be oxidised fairly rapidly to carbon dioxide in the arid environment of a desert, and sand from above fills the cavity so formed. Some of the dikaka found growing at the surface of stabilised dune systems possibly originally established itself from seed during the last pluvial phase of the Pleistocene. Once the dune is stabilised, it is relatively easy for the plants to spread. The large seif dunes of the central Rajasthan Desert, the northern Trucial States and the Wahiba Sands are all more or less stabilised and have a covering of dikaka. Over much of these areas there are no wadis to provide a shallow source of water. Apart from sporadic rainfall and dew, the life-giving moisture must be reached by long root systems.

Another way in which plants can become established on dunes is for pre-existing vegetation to become enveloped by drifting şand. Already in possession of a supply of ground water from a nearby wadi or coastline, the plant is often capable of maintaining upward growth as the sand drifts around it. Plants may also spread colonially by developing from near-surface lateral root systems. Since sand is trapped among the roots and branches of the plants, well-defined laminae are unlikely to form in the sand except in the lee of scrub bushes. Dikaka of this type is common on coastal dunes and sand drifts and where dunes migrate across old wadis.

Modern dikaka is most prevalent near to coastlines and wadis where a constant supply of water is available, and on stabilised dunes where their deep root systems possibly first became established during a late Pleistocene or early Holocene pluvial period.

Some plants had already adapted themselves to a desert environment by the Permian (e.g., *Walchia piniformis* and *Walchia filiciformis*; MÄGDEFRAU, 1956, pp.177–179), but appear to have grown in water-transported sediment. Their root systems, if any, seem not to have penetrated deeply into the underlying sediment. The earliest dune plants with sediment-penetrating roots *(Nathorstiana, Weichselia, Hausmannia)* are known from Lower Cretaceous dune sands of possible coastal origin from Germany (MÄGDEFRAU, 1956, pp.279–286). By Tertiary time, however, several root-forming plants had adapted themselves to living in the dune sands of arid deserts. Root penetration of Late Tertiary dikaka can be measured in lengths of at least tens of centimetres.

At Jebel Baraka, at the northeast corner of Sebkha Matti on the Trucial Coast (see Enclosure 1), the Late Tertiary[1] aeolian sands show a considerable

---

[1] Teeth, part of a jawbone and other bones assigned to *Mastodon* (*Tetralophodon*) sp. of Pontian age were found in a wadi conglomerate interbedded with the dikaka-rich aeolian sands. They were identified by Professor R. Dehm of the Institut für Paläontologie und Historische Geologie, Munich.

Fig.96. Preferentially cemented Pliocene plant-root moulds (dikåka) in dune sands in which the dune bedding is still clearly visible. Jebel Baraka, on the coast of the Trucial State of Abu Dhabi.

development of dikaka, but the original dune bedding of the sediment is still clearly visible (Fig.96). In other dune sands from the same locality (Fig.97) the dikaka root moulds are so numerous that the original dune bedding is only discerned with difficulty. Many of the moulds are oriented parallel to the sand laminations (almost horizontal in Fig.97), since this presumably was the direction of greatest permeability, and therefore the direction of flow of the intergranular water, so necessary for root-forming plants. Note the pebble horizon cutting across the top of the dikaka-riddled dune sand. These pebbles, deposited in a Pliocene wadi, are another indication of the relationship between dikaka and a nearby source of moisture.

The roots themselves are not preserved, apart from examples that were still living or had only recently died. The former distribution of roots in sediment deposited in an arid climate is, however, commonly exhibited by preferential cementation of the sand grains which had encased the roots. If, after such preferen-

Fig.97. Sub-horizontal Pliocene dune bedding almost destroyed by fossil dikaka. Jebel Baraka, on the coast of the Trucial State of Abu Dhabi.

tial cementation, wind deflation removes the more poorly cemented sand between the former roots, the root pattern becomes exhumed and stands out in relief.

Modern plants living along the Trucial Coast are generally halophytes which can live in soils having ground waters of high salinity. The fossil dikaka found in the same area is typically cemented by gypsum euhedra arranged in concentric patterns around former roots. The cement of the host rock, however, need not be gypsum. Along the Trucial Coast, for example, Quaternary dunes, away from localised gypsum-cemented dikaka, are cemented by calcite. Preferential cementation of fossilised mangrove roots has been reported from Florida by HOFFMEISTER and MULTER (1965). It is interesting to note that in Florida, where the climate is relatively humid, the cementing mineral is calcite, whereas along the arid Trucial Coast of the Persian Gulf, the cement is gypsum. Plants that grew on dune sands away from mineral-rich ground water are unlikely to be recorded in fossil sediments by the preferential cementation of their root moulds.

LOESS

Reference has already been made (p.24) to the fact that as particles decrease in size below about 80 μ, the wind velocity that is required to set them in motion becomes greater. Once airborne, however, these silt and clay-sized particles can readily be kept in suspension by strong turbulent winds by virtue of their small size and weight. They can be carried great distances over the earth's surface by persistent winds before being deposited as a layer of dust or loess.

Loess is an accumulation of such wind-blown dust ranging in size from fine sand to clay-sized particles. Most of the particles fall within the range 20 μ to 100 μ with the bulk varying between about 30 μ and 80 μ.

According to BRYAN (1945) and OBRUCHEV (1945), loess has two main areas of origin; one is associated with the outwash of glacial rivers and the other is in deserts: around desert highlands extensive deposits of water-laid sands and silts are exposed to deflation. Both areas of origin can have very dry climatic conditions. The dust picked up in periglacial regions is deposited in marginal areas by a combination of polar anticyclonic winds and the prevailing westerlies. Dust is normally carried out of desert areas as dust storms and it settles in adjacent steppe lands. Dust, blown from the Sahara is occasionally found covering snow on the southern slopes of the Alps.

Although not common in desert areas, BEYDOUN (1966) mentions the presence of loess in the tributaries to Wadi Hadramaut in southern Arabia. Dust particles blown across the southern Rub al Khali or derived from the highlands of the western Hadramaut are presumably trapped in these deep gorges. Pleistocene loess from the northern Negev (Israel) is occasionally reworked during storms associated with dry easterly winds (YAALON and GINZBOURG, 1966).

BARBOUR (1936) believes that the loess of China, although deposited predominantly during the Pleistocene, ranges in age from the Late Pliocene to the present. He considers that the loess was derived from the continental basins of the Gobi Desert. SMALLEY and VITA-FINZI (1968) suggest that the loess of China may have been derived, at least in part, from the glacial moraines of the Tienshan Range. They are not in favour of deserts as major source areas for the production of loess. They believe that very little silt will be formed by mechanical reduction of sand-sized particles during aeolian transport. With this, the writer concurs, but as has been described by HÖRNER (1936), there remain extensive areas of alluvial sediments in the deserts of Central Asia that are subjected to deflation during the long intervals in which the rivers do not flow with water; similar areas of alluvial sediments occur in most other deserts of the world.

Loess is typically soft and porous, and yellow or buff in colour. It usually has little or no bedding, but is often riddled with small tubules that are thought to have been occupied by rootlets. The tubules are often lined with calcite. The loess appears to be trapped between blades of grass that, like dikaka, prevent the formation of well-defined laminae.

Large accumulations of loess in the U.S.A. and Europe appear to have been deposited during the Pleistocene beyond the margins of ice sheets. Dust storms also occur over the Great Plains of the United States when dry soils, lacking sufficient protection of grass or other vegetation, are picked up by strong winds. SWINEFORD and FRYE (1945) collected dust from the roof of a Kansas hotel and found from its analysis that it compared well with the grain-size distribution of Pleistocene loess from Kansas State. They concluded that the wind is competent to sort material to the degree represented by loess deposits.

Chapter 7

DESERT COASTAL SEDIMENTS

Apart from isolated "desert islands", deserts are not usually surrounded by a coast line. Many deserts border coastlines along at least one edge, however (Fig.1). From the point of view of palaeogeographic reconstruction it is important to realise that continental (desert) shoreline and marine facies may all occur in close proximity.

DEVELOPMENT OF COASTAL SEBKHAS BEHIND LONGSHORE BARS

Fig.98 shows part of the Arabian coast near Ras al Khaimah, where the Oman Mountains approach close to the Persian Gulf (see Enclosure 2). Spreading out over the narrow coastal plain is a large alluvial fan built up by intermittently flowing braided wadi channels whose sediment is derived from the mountains (cf. Fig.16, 17). The dark line along the periphery of the fan is caused by the presence of palm groves situated in a zone of maximum supply of water of tolerable salinity (see also p.75). A coastal sebkha had developed between the conglomerate fan—which it partly also overlies—and the protection afforded by a long-shore sand bar. Much of the sand which went into the formation of the bar was probably obtained by erosion of coastal dune sands and longshore transport from areas of active carbonate-sediment production to the south. Wave action has built up this bar to above sea level and the wind has reworked the sediment into low dunes.

A coastal sebkha is an almost flat land area that occurs just above the level of normal high tides on the coasts of some low-lying hot, arid deserts. Its sediments consist of sand, silt and clay. Its surface is often covered by a salt crust that results from evaporation of water drawn to the surface by capilliary action and from occasional marine inundations. The sediments of a coastal sebkha are the same as those of adjacent lagoonal and intertidal areas (and therefore commonly carbonate in composition) with an admixture of wind-blown sand and silt from off-shore islands or more landward regions, and rare detritus from nearby hills carried in desert water courses (EVANS et al., 1964a, b). Because of its environment, the carbonate-rich sediments of a coastal sebkha are liable to early diagenetic altera-tion as the result of reaction with brines of high chlorinity; they are characterised by the presence of algal mats (KENDALL and SKIPWITH, 1968, 1969) and by the formation of evaporites (nodular anhydrite, gypsum and halite; SHEARMAN, 1963,

1966; BUTLER, 1969) and dolomite (WELLS, 1962; SHEARMAN, 1963; CURTIS et al., 1963).

The surface of a coastal sebkha is subject to deflation down to the level of the water table; the material so derived is often blown inland to be incorporated in nearby dunes. Large lenticular crystals of gypsum up to 20 cm across are exposed by deflation; they show a preferred orientation in that they grow with the plane of flattening in a vertical or near-vertical position. Many of these crystals enclose sand grains of the host sediment poikilitically (SHEARMAN, 1963, 1966).

PRESERVATION OF DUNES BEHIND PROTECTION OF SPIT/COASTAL-SEBKHA COMPLEXES

South of the Ras al Khaimah sebkha an extensive tract of dunes occupies the broader area of coastal plain between the peri-montane alluvial fans and the coast (Fig.99). The long, narrow coastal dune[1], which is here higher than any dune directly inland, is now being eroded by the sea except where protected by the recent northward extension of another spit/coastal-sebkha complex. This coastal dune probably owes its greater height to the combination of the strong onshore shamal winds and an almost unlimited supply of both quartz and carbonate grain from the beach and coastal sebkha.

The distribution and morphology of the coastal dunes found along the Pacific coast of U.S.A. has been described by COOPER (1958, 1967). He shows that there, coastal dunes form only where there is a good supply of beach sand that is replenished by longshore drift, and where the dominant wind is essentially onshore. Many coastal dunes form where coastal indentations are cut off by the formation of a marine sand bar that thus shortens the coastline. The predominant dune types appear to be transverse and parabolic, the latter being always associated with vegetation and partial stabilisation.

A feature that appears to be characteristic of some coastal dunes is the occurrence of bedding at the downwind side of the dunes that is convex upward. It has been reported by MACKENZIE (1964a,b) and BALL (1967) from Bermuda, and by BIGARELLA et al. (1969) from the coast of Brazil. According to these latter workers, it appears to form as the result of deposition on the windward side of the slip face because the wind is neither so intense nor dry enough to cause complete removal of previously deposited beds. BALL (1967) notes the occurrence of root

---

[1] It has been noticed in the field that the dunes which are nearest to a coastal beach tend to be oriented parallel to the coast line in contrast to those further inland whose orientation is commonly controlled by the prevailing wind. Similarly, MACKENZIE (1964a) and BALL (1967) have both noted that the cross-bedding of Pleistocene coastal carbonate dune sands in Bermuda and Florida is always directed inland. SNEAD and FRISHMAN (1968) have made a similar observation for Pleistocene and Recent dune sands on the coast of West Pakistan.

Fig.98. Oman Mountains (*M*), alluvial fan (*a*) with palm-tree oasis (*o*) along its outer rim and coastal sebkha (*cs*) protected by a sand spit (*s*). Ras al Khaimah, Trucial Coast.

Fig.99. Oman Mountains (*M*) flanked by alluvial fans (*a*), dune field (*d*) on broad coastal plain, and coastal dunes (*c*) partly protected from erosion by northward-extending sand spit/sebkha complex (*s*). South of Ras al Khaimah, Trucial Coast.

casts together with these structures and suggests that the dunes may have been partially stabilized. The presence of vegetation on the top of a dune and the resulting lowering of wind velocity near to the surface would certainly assist in the deposition of sand to windward of the slip face and the development of bedding that is convex upward. The coastal dunes described from Brazil are also at present stabilized by vegetation.

ABSENCE OF FLUVIAL DELTAS ALONG DESERT COAST LINES

Except in the case of large rivers, such as the Colorado, Nile, Indus and Tigris–Euphrates, that derive their water from beyond the desert, desert coasts do not have fluvial deltas. Wadi sediment which reaches the sea during flood may build a temporary delta, but redistribution of the delta sediments by wave action and longshore currents soon destroys it. An example of this observed by the writer was the delta of a Libyan wadi which was built some 500 m out into the Mediterranean Sea within a few days. Two months later, with no further flow of water or sediment from the wadi to maintain it, the delta had been so reduced that it protruded a mere 50 m beyond the original coastline. Fig.94 and 95 are cores from this temporary delta.

TIDAL DELTAS

Although fluvial deltas are generally absent along desert coastlines, tidal deltas may exist off the entrances to lagoons (EVANS et al., 1964b). In the tropical shallow-water environment of the coastal lagoons of Abu Dhabi, the sediment of the tidal deltas is largely carbonate (Foraminifera, ooliths and fragments of Bryozoa, coral and shells). Storm and tidal oscillations of sea level result in strong currents at the entrance to large lagoons. Sufficiently concentrated backward and forward flow of water results in the formation of both inward and outward facing deltas (although not necessarily in the same channel), which in some cases are built entirely of ooliths (BUTLER et al., 1965).

PROGRADING DESERT COASTS

Fig.100 shows the development of an outward-facing submarine delta south of Ra's Ghanadah, Abu Dhabi (Enclosure 2). On the north side of the main channel there is an extensive area of coastal sebkha where large quantities of calcium-carbonate grains are trapped behind the protection of a sand spit. The spit is surmounted by a low linear dune consisting mainly of carbonate sand. South of the

Fig.100. Tidal creek (t) with outward-facing submarine delta (sd), coastal sebkha (cs) behind protection of sand spit (s) north of the creek, and probable former coastal sebkha complex now covered by dune fields (d) south of the creek. South of Ras Ghanadah, Abu Dhabi, Trucial Coast.

main channel, a dune field covers sediments which probably represent an earlier coastal sebkha.

The manner in which this desert coastline has prograded may be imagined to a certain extent from a study of Enclosure 2. Off-shore bars have permitted the development of coastal lagoons and then coastal sebkhas behind their protection. Aeolian transport of carbonate sand has helped to raise the sebkha surface above storm-tide level and has resulted in the formation of carbonate dunes. The coast line will remain temporarily static until a further development of an offshore bar—perhaps a long-shore extension from a submarine delta—permits another phase of lagoonal sedimentation and coastal-sebkha development with its inevitable cover of aeolian sand.

When making a detailed study of the Quaternary, one must differentiate between Pleistocene sediments—aeolian sands and wadi gravels and sands that were deposited during a glacial lower stand in sea level—and the sediments that have been deposited since the post-Glacial rise in sea level. According to FAIRBRIDGE (1962, fig.9, 10), the Würm Glaciation resulted in a world-wide sea level that was something like 100 m lower than now. In the post-Glacial period, the sea level rose by a series of oscillations until about 6,000 years B.P. when it reached about the present level. In many parts of the world, the result of this post-Glacial rise in sea level is seen in widespread transgressions across what is now the continental shelf. In the warm, shallow, clear seas found along some river-free desert coasts, however, carbonate sediment can be rapidly "manufactured" by marine organisms living under optimum conditions.

The sediment sequence seen near Ras al Khaimah is complicated not only by the post-Glacial rise in sea level, but also by sub-Recent tectonic subsidence of the Musandam Peninsula. Further southwest, however, along the Abu Dhabi coast, Sebkha Matti, the Qatar coastal sebkhas, Bahrain Island and the eastern coast of Saudi Arabia, the coastline is prograding in areas where it can be assumed with reasonable certainty that there has been no marked change in sea level for the past two thousand years or more (Enclosure 1).

Although the Mediterranean is, in general, a region of coastal erosion, the coastline appears to be prograding south of Misurata, at the western end of the Gulf of Sirte, and on both sides of the Libyan/Tunisian border (Enclosure 4). This progradation is, no doubt, assisted by the rapid production of carbonate sediment associated with a river-free desert coast.

COASTAL CARBONATE DUNES

Coastal dunes which form in close proximity to a marine province of carbonate sediment production are themselves, in desert areas of prevailing onshore winds, often made up of the same carbonate grains. Early calcite (vadose?) cementation can result in the formation of a limestone which, when examined microscopically, is extremely difficult to differentiate from marine limestones since these are commonly composed of similar grains (Fig.127, 129). Foraminifera are well preserved[1], and a few of the more resistant of them (e.g., miliolids) may still be recognisable in dune sands after tens of kilometres of aeolian transport from the coast.

According to KUENEN (1960), aeolian abrasion of limestone proceeds 2 to 4 times as rapidly as that of quartz. With an increase in transport distance from a common quartz/limestone source area, the ratio of quartz to limestone will increase. If the carbonate fraction consists of diagenetically unaltered discrete skeletal fragments from the coast, then the rate of abrasion is probably even faster. Over the horizontal distance of 100 km, the quartz/carbonate ratio in the dune sands changed from 19:81 at locality *139* (see Enclosure 2) near the Abu Dhabi coast, to 76:24 at locality *131* near Buraimi. The situation here, however, is not that of a simple reduction in the carbonate content of the sand proportional to transport distance, because there are secondary sources of both quartz and carbonate sediment. Nearer to Abu Dhabi, the interdune areas undergoing deflation consist of the cemented carbonate sands of former coastal sebkhas, whilst near Buraimi, the interdune areas are rich in both quartz and limestone of older wadi deposits derived from the Oman Mountains.

Away from the coast, the bulk of the quartz sand in the dunes was possibly transported into the area during the Pleistocene, or even the Pliocene, to judge from dated aeolian sands from Sebkha Matti (GLENNIE and EVAMY, 1968). During these periods, the shores of the then Persian Gulf probably lay many tens of kilometres farther north than now, and there is a good chance that the westerly winds that moulded the major dunes during Pleistocene glaciations, blew parallel to the then coastline and transported only quartz sand derived from farther west in Arabia (Enclosure 1). With no knowledge of the earlier history of the area as a desert, a false impression might be gained of the resistance of carbonate grains to abrasion.

The Wahiba Sands, however, are rich in carbonate grains throughout their length. Much of this carbonate fraction is thought to have been blown from coastal sebkhas and marine terraces that existed between the mainland and Masira Island. These areas are assumed to have been exposed to the action of strong winds during a Glacial lower stand in sea level. The present strait is very shallow. Although further evidence is still lacking, it seems likely that the influence of a rich coastal supply of carbonate sand can still be detected at least 170 km from its source, even though Foraminifera can no longer be recognised.

---

[1] According to M. Hughes Clarke (personal communication, 1965), Foraminifera may be better preserved in a coastal carbonate dune than in a marine environment, since in the former they are not attacked by marine boring algae.

A cemented coastal carbonate dune can form a very effective barrier between the sea on one side and the desert on the other. It can prevent wadis from discharging their load of water and sediment into the sea and thus result in the creation of an inland sebkha on its landward side (Fig.60, 62); it can protect these desert sediments—whether of aeolian or fluviatile origin—from erosion by a (potentially) transgressing sea if it can maintain a rate of vertical growth equivalent to that of the relative rise in sea level (Fig.3). Under these circumstances, the coastal carbonate dune may tend to migrate landwards over penecontemporaneous non-coastal sediments, which are thus preserved from marine erosion. Early—perhaps almost contemporaneous—cementation of such carbonate dunes strengthens their resistance to erosion.

Fig.101 shows the present coastal carbonate-dune barrier on the coast of Libya west of Tripoli. The recent uncemented dune is overlying an older Late Quaternary cemented carbonate dune, part of which is now submerged beneath the sea. Behind the dune barrier are an inland sebkha and wadi (extreme right) which have no direct access to the sea.

Dunes that are rich in carbonate grains, border the low northern (Batinah) coast of Oman. They also form a barrier between the sea and the wadis that flow from the Oman Mountains. In many places the coastal dunes are cut by wadis, but occasionally wadis have failed to maintain a channel to the sea, and inland sebkhas have developed on the landward side of the dunes (see p.69). Carbonate sand is often carried inland from the beach by the daily onshore winds, and so the dunes are built up and maintained.

CEMENTED CARBONATE DUNES

Fig.102 shows a typical eroded outcrop of the cemented carbonate dunes west of Tripoli. The bedding is both dipping and horizontal; alternation of finer- and coarser-grained carbonate laminae is typical of aeolian sands; the foresets exhibit crumpling of some laminae, which is very suggestive of the slumping seen on the flanks of recent dunes from nearby (Fig.91, 92). A thin section of the limestone is given in Fig.127.

Occasional cemented plant-root moulds and borings by recent pholad molluscs (at present living in the splash zone of the sea), combined with Bryozoa, Foraminifera and shell fragments, make it likely that a marine environment of deposition will be interpreted for outcrops such as this unless the aeolian nature of the bedding is recognised. The chances of making an incorrect deduction of the depositional environment are high in some outcrops where distinctive dune bedding is poorly developed. These chances are greatly increased if the deduction has to be

Fig.101. Present coastal dune (P) overlying cemented pre-Roman coastal dune (R). Formation of present coastal dune has prevented the water in a wadi (w) from flowing into the sea and an inland sebkha (s) has developed. West of Tripoli, Libya.

Fig.101a. Simplified sketch of Fig. 101.

made from cores. With only drill cuttings available, these carbonate dunes are almost certain to be considered as representing a marine environment of deposition. Thus their true palaeogeographic significance will not be recognised.

A misinterpretation of the environment of deposition of carbonate dune sands may result in the geological necessity of invoking fictitious changes in sea level. The Pleistocene quartz–carbonate dune sand seen in Fig.128 was deposited on the hills of Kutch over 100 m above the present sea level (for location, see Fig.109). Both FEDDEN (1884, p.56) and AUDEN (1952, p.59) believed that these and other similar sands represent a rise in sea level because of the marine micro-faunas that they contain. On the other hand, EVANS (1900, p.566) and the writer

Fig.102. Dune bedding in pre-Roman cemented carbonate dune with slump structures in steeply dipping dune bedding at bottom right. Coast at Zanzur, West of Tripoli, Libya.

believe that these sands are of aeolian origin. Other similar Pleistocene carbonate dune sands have been found in western India at over 300 m above the present level of the sea (EVANS, 1900), but the only evidence to connect the sands with the marine environment of their origin is their rich faunal content of miliolids and other skeletal fragments. There is no necessity for invoking a 300 m Pleistocene rise in sea level to account for their presence; a slight lowering of sea level, to expose a broad area of the present continental shelf to the wind during a polar glacial period, seems a much more reasonable hypothesis to account for their presence. SEGERSTROM (1962) describes how a prevailing onshore wind in Chile carries sand inland from a deflated marine terrace for a distance of some 35 miles to a height of 2,800 ft. above sea level.

Coastal carbonate dunes are rich in particles consisting of complete or fragmented marine organisms that had first been washed onto the beaches and coastal sebkha and then transported to the dunes by the wind. These organisms had once lived in shallow sea water. Analyses by FRIEDMAN (1964) show that in the marine environment, their skeletons were generally composed of aragonite or high-magnesian calcite.

Many workers (GINSBURG, 1953; EMERY and COX, 1956; FRIEDMAN, 1964; STODDART, 1965) have shown that carbonate sands can lithify as "beach rock" in a tropical intertidal marine environment. The cementing material commonly consists of acicular crystals of aragonite.

FRIEDMAN (1964, has shown that if carbonate fragments of marine origin are brought into a sub-aerial environment, they may lithify and the aragonite and high-magnesian calcite alter to low-magnesian calcite. This is possibly brought about by solution of the aragonite and the precipitation of low-magnesian calcite as cement; high-magnesian calcite possibly alters to low-magnesian calcite by solution of magnesium or solution-deposition on a micro-scale that leaves the original texture intact.[1] FRIEDMAN (1964) has also shown that under sub-aerial conditions, aragonite grains have a metastability sequence in which the order of increasing stability is skeletal grains–ooids–pellets–cryptocrystalline grains. Aragonite grains are commonly leached to form moldic porosity and the molds are infilled by a drusy mosaic of low-magnesian calcite. MATTHEWS (1968) points out that ancient carbonates are composed of the stable minerals calcite and dolomite. He has demonstrated that subaerially exposed Pleistocene carbonates exhibit mineralogical stability, thus suggesting that the process of stabilization proceeds rather rapidly.

From studies of eolianites on the coastal plain of Israel, YAALON (1967) was able to infer that cementation must take place above the water table as the result of wetting by rainwater. From analyses of sands, he found that a minimum of about 8% $CaCO_3$ was probably necessary to initiate cementation under the environmental conditions prevailing locally. He, like FRIEDMAN (1964), believes that precipitation of the interparticle cement takes place close to where carbonate was dissolved. In general agreement with Yaalon's findings, the writer noticed that in the northern Trucial States (Enclosure 2), calcite-cemented dune sands were not exposed more than 30 or 40 km from the present coast. It is possible, of course, that cemented sands are present farther to the east but buried beneath a cover of uncemented sands.

As was mentioned on p.70, dune sands can also be cemented by gypsum. In that particular case, it seems likely that coastal dunes prevented the flow of water from a wadi and inland sebkha to the sea. The dune sands probably became cemented with gypsum as the result of slow evaporation of the ground water associated with the inland sebkha.

Gypsum cemented quartz dune sands of probable Pliocene age are also found in Sebkha Matti (Enclosure 1) close to the locality seen in Fig.61. The quartz grains are poikilitically enclosed within large gypsum crystals in a fashion that is reminiscent of the Fontainebleau Sandstone of the Paris Basin. In this latter case, however, the quartz grains are locally enclosed in calcite rhombohedra. ALIMEN (1936, p.236) believes that these Oligocene dune sands were cemented recently as the result of percolation of lime-rich water from the overlying Beauce Limestone. In support of this idea, she mentions the growth of small concretionary nodules on the surface of freshly exposed sandstone in quarries. Similar nodules

---

[1] Carbonate minerals can be identified by X-ray diffraction methods (FRIEDMAN, 1964) or by staining techniques (FRIEDMAN, 1959; EVAMY, 1963, 1969).

have been seen by the writer on freshly exposed surfaces of the Permian "Yellow Sands" at Houghton-le-Spring in Durham, but he does not believe that the cementation of the Fontainebleau Sandstone is of such recent origin. The Oligocene dunes of the Paris Basin were apparently partially flooded by lime-rich lake water prior to the deposition of the Beauce Limestone (see also p.58). The writer suggests that evaporation of this water within the dune sands could result in cementation by the growth of calcite rhombohedra. Had the area been more evaporitic, the dunes might instead have been cemented by gypsum.

TIME OF CEMENTATION OF CARBONATE DUNES

The conditions required to cement the Libyan carbonate dune sands are thought to be similar to those described by YAALON (1967) for Israel. They presumably involve rainfall and subaerial exposure. The cement is low-magnesian calcite. The dunes were already cemented in Roman times, for not only is the ancient Roman city of Sabratha built on the cemented dunes, but the already-formed limestone was quarried as a rough building stone which was then faced with ornamental limestone and marble imported from Italy. The time of deposition of similar cemented carbonate dunes on the coast of Cyrenaica can be correlated with the Early Würm Glacial of the Alps (McBURNEY, 1960, pp.163–165)—125,000 to 100,000 years B.P.[1] In Morocco, archaeological dating of two generations of carbonate dunes shows that the older ones were deposited after the onset of the Mindel Glacial (780,000 years B.P.) and were probably already cemented by the start of the Riss Glacial (360,000 years B.P.) (McBURNEY, 1960, pp.115–121). The younger dunes probably have an Early Würm age for the time of their deposition, like those of Cyrenaica.

There has been adequate time for slow cementation. A mechanism for the cementation of these carbonate dune sands could be solution of aragonite and high-magnesian calcite from skeletal particles and ooids by rainwater, followed by precipitation of low-magnesian calcite cement as the water evaporates. This explanation is supported by the archaeological dating of the artefacts from a cave which was carved out of the previously cemented dune sand (McBURNEY, 1960). The dune sand was cemented under subaerial conditions before an interglacial rise in sea level resulted in the cave formation.

An oyster bed on the coast of West Pakistan has yielded a radiocarbon age of about 23,000 years. The oyster bed is overlain by a dune sand that is lightly cemented by calcium carbonate and which, in turn, is covered by another dune system that is still not cemented (SNEAD and FRISHMAN, 1968).

---

[1] Dates taken from HOLMES (1965, pp.698–707). According to FAIRBRIDGE (1962, fig.10), however, the Mindel Glacial took place about 220,000 years B.P.; the Riss about 110,000 years B.P. and the Early and Late Würm glacials roughly 50,000 and 20,000 years B.P., respectively.

Fig.103. Suspected dune bedding in Permian sucrosic dolomite. Magnesian Limestone, Derby-shire, England.

DIFFICULTIES OF RECOGNISING ANCIENT CARBONATE DUNES

Unfortunately, undoubted limestone dunes have not been recognised in ancient sediments which have also been subjected to deep burial and diagenesis. In Britain, foreset bedding in a sucrosic dolomite of the Permian Magnesian Limestone from Scarcliffe, Derbyshire, suggests the possibility that this sediment was originally deposited as a carbonate dune on the desert shores of the Zechstein Sea, and was later dolomitised (Fig.103). Microscopic examination of a thin section cut from this dolomite, however, gives no indication as to either its original lithology or its mode of deposition (Fig.130).

THE SALTS OF COASTAL EVAPORITIC LAGOONS

Deposits of bedded evaporites (halite, gypsum, anhydrite[1]) are generally associated with seas and lagoons having a very restricted connection with the open ocean and are often bordered by deserts. Water is evaporated from the surface of these seas and is largely replenished by an intermittent or even steady influx of salt water through a narrow strait; such conditions exist at present in the Gulf of Kara Bogaz. Water of low salinity ($13^{\circ}/_{\circ\circ}$) flows continuously from the Caspian Sea into the gulf, which acts as a gigantic evaporating pan. Mostly gypsum was deposited in the past, but the salt concentration is now sufficiently high for a little halite to be precipitated in the hot season (GREEN, 1961; HOLMES, 1965, p.138; DICKEY, 1968).

[1] These evaporite minerals can be identified by their crystal form (SHEARMAN, 1966) and by X-ray diffraction methods.

According to DICKEY (1968), the rate of evaporation in the Gulf of Kara Bogaz is such that almost four times as much total salt is precipitated annually in the gulf as is carried into the Caspian Sea by rivers. The Caspian Sea is annually becoming less salty. On a smaller scale, gypsum and halite are also being deposited in the narrow estuary of Bocana de Virrila on the northern coast of Peru (MORRIS and DICKEY, 1957).

Salt deposition on the same scale as that of past geologic periods (Cambrian to Tertiary) is not seen today[1]. The writer suggests that this is, perhaps, due to Pleistocene climatic changes that brought about geologically rapid changes in sea level associated with repeated growth and reduction in size of the polar ice caps. The world is probably only slowly returning to a climatic and sea level situation conducive to evaporite formation in peri-desert seas.

The salinity of normal sea water is taken to be about $36^\circ/_{oo}$. Although the Red Sea has a narrow marine connection with the open ocean at its southern end, salinities of about $42^\circ/_{oo}$ have been recorded from the northern end (LOTZE, 1957). A slightly increased restriction of the already narrow strait at the southern end of the sea would, because of its hot, almost rain-free climate and lack of rivers, convert it once more into the basin of evaporite sedimentation that it was during parts of the Tertiary. A similar restriction of the Strait of Hormuz would soon turn the Persian Gulf into an evaporite basin similar to that which existed in northwest Europe during the Upper Permian.

On a much smaller scale, deposition of thin, bedded evaporites in continental basins of inland drainage, have already been referred to (Fig.49, 50, 59, 60). Any single bed of evaporite in these cases is usually the result of complete evaporation to dryness of lake water. Its thickness is limited by the volume of water evaporated and the original salinity of the water prior to evaporation.

On shores and in lagoons along desert coasts, intertidal and supratidal evaporation results in the precipitation of gypsum between grains of the existing sediment, and the formation of a thin crust of salt. The salt crust is usually either dissolved by the next high tide or is deflated by the wind and redeposited elsewhere.

RECENT ANHYDRITE AND CONTORTED BEDDING

Anhydrite has recently been described from the modern sediments of desert coasts (SHEARMAN, 1963; BUTLER et al., 1965; BUTLER, 1969). On the sebkhas of the Trucial Coast, gypsum is the stable calcium sulphate mineral in contact with brines of chlorinities less than $145^\circ/_{oo}$ and anhydrite at chlorinities greater than $145^\circ/_{oo}$. Anhydrite will be hydrated into gypsum where brine chlorinity falls to less than $145^\circ/_{oo}$ (BUTLER, 1969).

---

[1]See, for instance, KOZARY et al. (1968)

Fig.104. Contorted bedding in the evaporitic sediments of a coastal sebkha. Pisida, Libya.

Fig.104 shows a pit dug into the sediments of a coastal lagoon at Pisida, near the Libya/Tunisia border (Enclosure 4), that is cut off from the open sea during all but the highest storm tides. The sediment consists largely of quartz sand, halite and gypsum crystals and there is a thin crust of halite on the surface. The gypsum crystals are likely to be recognised in the subsurface as nodules of anhydrite in a sandy matrix (cf. Fig.113).

The contorted bedding seen near to the surface of a coastal sebkha in Fig.104 is not fully understood. There are several possible explanations for its presence. Two are given here; one, however, is particularly related to evaporites. Although the sediment was still wet from recent marine flooding at the time the pit was dug, there were traces of anhydrite in the sediment. This suggests the possibility that anhydrite had formed after gypsum above the water table (or from a brine with a chlorinity greater than $145^o/_{oo}$) during the hot dry summer season and that, because of local permeability barriers within the sediment (illite is also present), not all of it had been converted back into gypsum. There is a 38% volume reduction when gypsum alters to anhydrite. Volume changes connected with the alteration sequence gypsum–anhydrite–gypsum, may have caused lateral flow of wet sediment beneath a fairly hard and rigid surface crust. Another possible explanation is that sediment flow occurred because of changes in hydrostatic pressure due to various causes.

The dark colour of much of the sediment suggests that the environment was reducing. A core was taken from the sediment. Since exposure to the atmosphere, all the sediment has become white. Potash feldspars (microcline) and traces of dolomite are also present in the sediment.

GYPSUM DUNES

The flooding of another lagoon south of Misurata, Libya, was witnessed by the writer. Storm waves were breaking over the barrier beach and flooded the dried-up lagoon behind. The influx of water allowed stromatolite-forming algae to start growing along the edges of the polygonally cracked lagoon floor (Fig.105). Dunes along the landward side of the lagoon were composed almost entirely of gypsum grains derived, presumably, from the sediments of the lagoon during periods of deflation. The lagoon is dry for the greater part of the year. A small gypsum dune is seen in the background of Fig.105. Farther along the lagoon they attain a height of at least 10 m. Gypsum dunes occur along the edges of the evaporite-producing Ranns of Kutch in India, and dunes built almost entirely of gypsum grains are also described by McKee (1966a) from White Sands National Park, New Mexico. The source of the gypsum in this case, however, was an inland "playa" known as "Lake Lucero". Cross-laminated gypsum of possible aeolian origin occurs in the Triassic Moenkopi Formation of Arizona and is illustrated by McKee (1954). Here, the gypsum appears to have been deposited in a near-coastal environment and may well be analagous to the dunes described from Libya and India.

Cross-bedded gypsum also occurs in the Jurassic Todilto Formation in New Mexico. It is interpreted by Tanner (1965) as having been formed by the wind, the gypsum in this case possibly being derived from a desert lake.

THE RANNS OF KUTCH

An area of more widespread deposition of evaporitic minerals is formed by the Ranns of Kutch on the west coast of India (see Fig.109). Like the coastal sebkhas of the Persian Gulf, the surface of the Ranns of Kutch is at, or slightly above, sea level. During the three months of the Southwest Monsoon, storm tides, aided by the wind, force water from the Arabian Sea over the flat surface of the Ranns. Rainfall is fairly low, so that as the waters recede and evaporate, they leave behind a crust of halite, and gypsum crystals grow in the clays and sands. The few rivers (wadis) which flow into the eastern ends of the Ranns carry only limited fresh water and sediment for about one week during the monsoon. For the rest of the year they are dry. The result is that an area of about 30,000 km² (about the same size as The Netherlands) is subjected to annual flooding with the succeeding formation of evaporites.

Fig.106, from Great Rann of Kutch, shows a thin (2–3 cm) salt crust some

Fig.105. Preferential growth of algae around the edge of polygonal mud cracks. Gypsum dune sand behind. Coastal sebkha south of Misurata, Libya.

Fig.106. Salt crust of marine-flooded coastal sebkha 150 km from the open sea. Pachham Island, Great Rann of Kutch, India. (See Fig.109.)

Fig.107. Wavy lamination in gypsiferous argillaceous sands on the beach at Pachham Island. Great Rann of Kutch, India. (See Fig.109.)

Fig.108. Thin salt crust overlying horizontally bedded gypsiferous sands and clays. Tidal estuary of Kori Creek, Lakhpat, Kutch, India. (See Fig.109.)

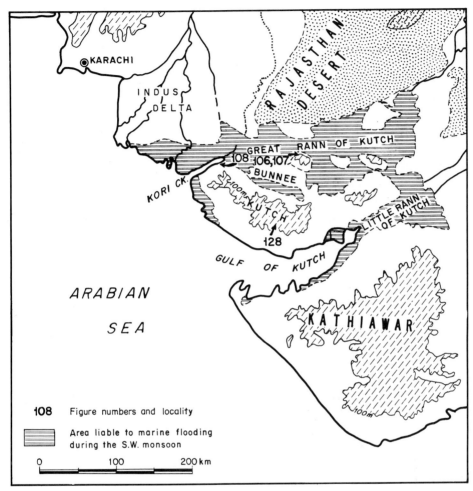

Fig.109. Sketch map of the Ranns of Kutch, India.

150 km from the open sea. The crust is buckled and thrust, probably by the forces of crystal growth of the salt.[1] In the left background are low, scrub-covered dunes of the north end of Pachham Island. Wind deflation during the dry season has resulted in the incorporation of halite[2], gypsum flakes and one species of Foraminifera into the dune sand.

Fig.107, from the shore of Pachham Island, shows wavy lamination which

[1] BOBECK (1959, p.22) ascribes the shape of salt polygons to horizontal expansion of the salt crust. "The polygons are not due to some process of shrinking in the course of drying out..." He also has noticed thrusting of the edges of some polygons over those of others, when studying the salt flats of the Great Kawir of Central Iran.

[2] WEDMAN (1964) has estimated that of the 30,000 tons of salt produced in Sebkra Sedjoumi, Tunisia, each year, 90% is removed by wind deflation.

is very reminiscent of the lamination seen in sediments of inland sebkhas (cf. Fig.55, 62). It is not certain whether this lamination is the result of current action, gypsum crystal growth, or the formation of adhesion ripples, although the last mentioned is thought the most likely.

In a tidal estuary much nearer to the open sea, the horizontally bedded clays and sands are rich in gypsum crystals (Fig.108). The surface of the sediment is covered by a thin halite crust as the water recedes and evaporates after high diurnal or spring tides.

In contrast to the coastal sebkhas of the Persian Gulf, the sediments of the Ranns of Kutch are poor in carbonate minerals. This is thought to reflect an influx of sediment from the Arabian Sea which, in the vicinity of the Indus Delta, is rich in fluvial sand and clays.

The evaporitic clays and sands found in the Ranns of Kutch have many similarities with the Triassic Keuper sediments of northwest Europe. Perhaps some of the Keuper evaporitic sediments were deposited under similar conditions of storm tide over broad flat areas at, or slightly above, normal high tide in an area of hot, arid climate.

Chapter 8

SUBSURFACE RECOGNITION OF DESERT SEDIMENTS

GENERAL

In the foregoing chapters, an attempt has been made to relate different desert sediments to their specific environments of deposition and to show some of the relationships that exist between these environments. The examples of ancient desert sediments that have been given so far all occur in outcrop, where recognition of the environment of deposition is sometimes relatively easy. The broader picture as seen in Enclosures 1–4 may help in envisaging possible palaeogeographic relationships of rocks in which their desert origins have already been recognised. Now, however, we must consider in more detail those features of desert sediments that may be recognised from cores, drill cuttings and the individual grains of sand of which they are composed. The criteria for the recognition of subsurface desert sediments are still essentially the same as in chapter 2. The scale on which these criteria must be recognised, however, is very small. Diagenetic changes may make the recognition of some criteria more difficult, and if they lead to the obliteration of primary depositional features, even impossible. Some criteria by which desert sediments may be recognised from cores, and more doubtfully from drill cuttings, are given in Table I.

Before the recognition of a desert environment of deposition can be inferred from a particular sequence of rocks, all the available petrographic, structural and stratigraphic data must, of course, be considered. For a well sequence, some of this evidence may come from lateral differences or correlations seen in other wells, or from inferences made from a regional study of the area.

SUN-DRIED SEDIMENT

Four pieces of core of roughly the same age and from the same area have been chosen by E. Oomkens[1] to illustrate one aspect of sedimentation in a desert environment (Fig.110–113). The slightly curled and cracked clay flakes in Fig.110 indicate sub-aerial exposure and drying of water-transported sediment. This, with perhaps a conglomerate below, might suggest a wadi environment, but would not

---

[1] Unpublished K.S.E.P.L. report.

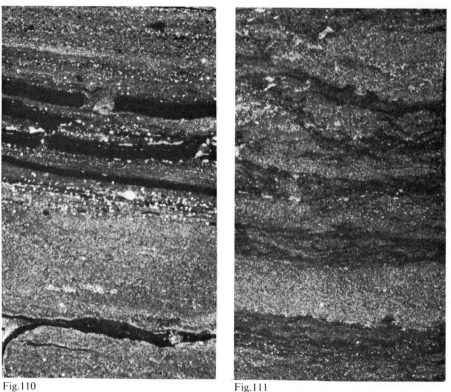

Fig.110   Fig.111

Fig.110. Subaerial exposure and drying of sediment is indicated by cracked and slightly curled clay flakes. Natural scale.

Fig.111. Sub-parallel to wavy lamination of adhesion ripples. White specks of anhydrite suggest that the environment is also evaporitic. Natural scale.

prove it. It could also have been deposited by a river with a high annual variation in water level (cf. Fig.40).

EVAPORITE ENVIRONMENT

The wavy silt and sand laminae in Fig.111 suggest adhesion ripples formed by wind-blown sediment adhering to a damp surface. They could represent a temperate climate, and were, in fact, first described from the recent sediments of the north German coast (REINECK, 1955). The presence of small white specks of anhydrite, however, makes one think of the possibilities of an associated evaporitic environment—either coastal or inland. The interpretation of a desert environment of deposition is possible.

    A similar analysis was made by Oomkens with Fig.112 and 113. The cracks in the clay flakes (Fig.112) have been filled in from above by (windblown?) sands

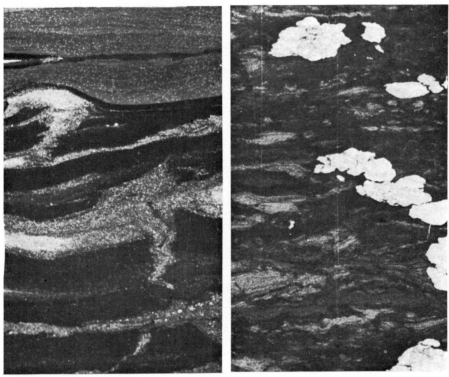

Fig.112   Fig.113

Fig.112. Sand dykes and sandy infill of mud cracks from above indicate an environment that alternates between wet and aeolian. Natural scale.

Fig.113. Anhydrite nodules in sand-laminated silt indicate an evaporitic environment. Natural scale.

and also injected from below by (wet?) sand in the form of a sand dyke that locally forced a layer of clay to arch upwards. Sand dykes have been recognised in inland sebkha environments (cf. Fig.56–58). The well-developed anhydrite nodules in the sand-laminated silt of Fig.113 confirm a slightly evaporitic environment. Evidence leading to a fuller environmental interpretation might be provided by cores from higher or lower in the sequence. These evaporitic sediments are likely to be overlain by dune sands, wadi conglomerates or a marine sequence.

The above example shows that a desert environment can be inferred from an association of sediments that does not include typically foresetted dune sands. It also emphasises that not all desert sediments are dune sands.

RECOGNITION OF DUNE SANDS IN CORES

Dune sands are sometimes easily recognised in a core (see Table I). The characteristic sharp differences in grain size between different laminae, and the clean, often uniformly dipping sand beds with dips of up to 34°, are highly suggestive. Some dune sands, however, have an almost uniform grain size, and may be very difficult to distinguish from a well-sorted beach sand. SHEPARD and YOUNG (1961)

TABLE I

SUBSURFACE RECOGNITION OF DESERT SEDIMENTARY ROCKS IN CORES

A. *Wind-deposited sands*

1. Sequences of sands that may vary in thickness from a few centimetres to several hundred metres and whose laminae dip at angles from horizontal to 34° (after allowing for hole deviation or structural tilt). Dips may be of constant or multiple orientation (Fig.114–117, 120–122).
2. Laminae commonly planar, but ripples occasionally seen on steeply-dipping foresets (Fig.120).
3. Individual laminae well sorted, especially in finer grain sizes; sharp differences in maxi-   +
   mum grain size between laminae common (Fig.124–126).   +
4. Larger sand grains tend to be well rounded (Fig.126).   +
5. Percentage of silt and clay generally well below 5% or even absent (authigenic clay may   +
   modify this criterion, but if present, should be recognisable by X-ray diffraction analysis
   or in thin section).
6. Clay drapes very rare, and when present should be accompanied by evidence that it was water-laid (Fig.114, 115, 117).
7. Quartz sands at shallow depths commonly friable or lightly cemented with haematite. Local discolouration of red haematite-coated grains to green or white is not uncommon (see also chapter 9).
8. Presence of adhesion ripples with associated increase in clay content and common presence of gypsum or anhydrite cement.   +

B. *Water-laid sands*

1. Most sedimentary features similar to those of water-laid sediments from non-desert continental environments but modified by the presence of one or more of the following:
2. Commonly calcite-cemented, or locally cemented by gypsum or anhydrite.   +
3. Many grains coated with haematite.   +
4. Conglomerates may be common, and sometimes with several cycles of deposition that lack a sand-sized fraction at the top of the cycle (deflation of the sand and silt).
5. Presence of mud-flow conglomerates (Fig.118).
6. Sharp upward decrease in grain size (especially from sand to clay) indicating a rapid fall in water velocity.
7. Common presence of clay pebbles and curled clay flakes (Fig.110).
8. Presence of mud cracks with sandy infill (Fig.112).
9. Presence of sandstone dykes (perhaps implying interbedded aeolian sands) (Fig.112).
10. Calcite cement stained with a solution of Alizarin red S and potassium ferricyanide in   +
    hydrochloric acid commonly stains red (had the cement formed in a reducing environ-
    ment, the rock might have contained ferrous iron and would stain violet; EVAMY, 1963).

Criteria marked + in right-hand column can also sometimes be recognised in drill cuttings (see remarks in text on p.156).

and SCHOCK (1965) have presented evidence to show that there are only slight statistical differences between beach sands and sands of nearby dunes. In this case it may be possible to differentiate between them on the assumption that the grain size of beach sands tends to increase upwards, whereas the opposite is true of dune sands (see Fig.66, 134–136). Ancient aeolian sands are also often more poorly cemented than other sands from the same sequence which were deposited in water.

Continuous coring through a thick sequence of sediments naturally gives the geologist the best chance of determining the environment of deposition of that sequence correctly. If the cores consist mainly of dune sand, the investigator will not only recognise the characteristics of individual laminae, but will be able to build up a picture of the changes in bedding attitude with changes in depth. He may even measure the dips and deduce palaeo-transport directions.

If cores have been taken at only rare intervals, these must be used for determining the characteristics of the sand—uniform bedding generally with no ripple structures or evidence of scouring or slumping; the bedding is either horizontal or dipping at angles of up to 34°; the orientation of the bedding is either uniform in direction or shows changes in direction; each set of laminae tends to show a slight upwards reduction in grain size.

The cores seen in Fig.114 and 115 show both sub-horizontal and foresetted Permian aeolian sandstone. The aeolian sandstone in Fig.114 overlies a fine sandy conglomerate (not shown) some 2 m below, that is interpreted as having been deposited by water. The dip of the bedding in the sandstone slowly increases from sub-horizontal, at its contact with the conglomerate, to about 17° when it is truncated by a second set of aeolian sandstone laminae dipping gently in an opposing direction (wind at right angles to the plane of the photo, or winds from two different directions?). This latter sandstone has a few larger granules incorporated in the lowermost laminae. Another sequence of fluvial sandstones and clays starts 1 m above the laminae seen at the top of the photo. By analogy with Recent desert areas, one assumes that here we have a wadi in which at least one of the local channels has been filled with wind-blown sand. When thin sequences of aeolian sands are associated with wadi sediments, care must be taken in assuming any regional palaeo-wind direction from the aeolian foresets. In the vicinity of hills or mountain ranges, irrespective of the regional prevailing wind direction, there is often a strong wind that blows "upstream" towards the hills during the day, and a milder wind that blows "downstream" at night.[1] Fluvial transport directions are often opposite to apparent wind-transport directions, and accretion slopes along the

---

[1] This general principle is well known to helicopter pilots who fly in mountainous areas. The writer once made the mistake of camping opposite the mouth of a gorge cut through the Siwalik Hills on the northern edge of the Ganges Plain. In the late afternoon, very strong "upstream" winds prevented the cooking of the evening meal. At dawn, almost equally strong "downstream" winds upset the timing of a hot breakfast. In this area, the periods of calm air were around midday and midnight. In deserts, where the lack of vegetation permits much more rapid temperature changes, the times of calm air are shortly after sunrise and sunset.

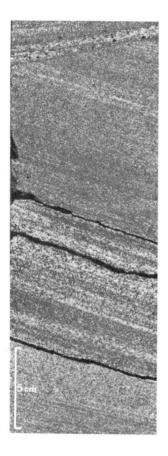   

Fig.114   Fig.115

Fig.114. Core from Permian aeolian sands associated with wadi sediments (not shown).
Fig.115. Core from Permian dune sands.

protected banks of the wadi may dip at almost 90° to the local wind direction (i.e.,
towards the centre of the wadi). See the arguments applied to the formation of a
seif dune, p.90 and Fig.73.

Fig.115, on the other hand, shows the central portion of a sequence of aeolian sandstone 6 m thick that started with sub-horizontal laminae at the base and
ends with laminae dipping at over 20° at the top (not shown). It represents a very
small portion of a more or less continuous aeolian sequence well over 100 m thick
and is interpreted as representing dune sands of a sand sea. Each dune sequence
usually starts at the base with horizontal or low-angle dips that increase in angle
upwards. Often, the dip may be constant in both angle and orientation through
several metres of vertical sequence; it may be at about 34°, thus implying slip-face
conditions of deposition, or at any lesser slope. It is in major dune-sand sequences

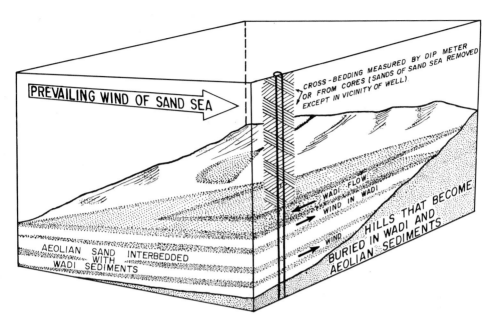

Fig.116. Schematic block diagram to illustrate the relation between opposed wind and water transport of sediment in wadis and its possible lack of connection with the prevailing wind as deduced from the dune sands of a later sand sea. All these deductions can be made from cores.

such as this that, from an analysis of the bedding styles and orientations, an interpretation of dune type can be made. Once this is decided, then the palaeo-wind direction can be worked out with reasonable accuracy.

A reconstruction of the history of sedimentation, as seen from the cores taken from a single well, may follow the following lines. The lowest cores show opposed fluviatile and aeolian transport directions. The fluviatile sediments can be assumed to have been transported away from a range of hills and the aeolian sands towards them. If, higher in the sequence, the attitudes of the more continuous dune bedding seen in the cores suggests that the wind came from another direction—perhaps at right angles to the earlier wind and water-transport directions—then this later direction probably coincides with the prevailing wind. If the cores have all been oriented with respect to the north, then directions become available for reconstructing the palaeogeography as suggested in Fig.116.

This situation of differing wind and water-transport directions is, perhaps, easier to follow if the southwest corner of Enclosure 1 is studied.

When the wadis are in flood, sediment is transported from the highlands of the Hadramaut towards the north. The Pleistocene to Early Recent gravels, now exposed in the feidjes (interdune corridors) of the southern edge of the Rub al Khali, probably show the same transport direction. The linear dunes of this part of the Rub al Khali are oriented east-northeast–west-southwest in response to the dominant east-northeast sand-transporting winter wind of this area. According to BEYDOUN (1966), however, many of these dunes have slip-faces directed to the south. These slip-faces are probably formed by local winds that blow "upstream" towards the hills in response to convection currents that build up over the Hadramaut (see also Fig.75).

An example of contrasting wadi and aeolian transport directions has been described from the Permian desert sediments of Devon, England, by LAMING (1966). See also Fig.27 and 29.

Fig.117 and 118 are of Triassic cores from Algeria. In Fig.117, uniformly oriented steeply dipping foresets suggest an origin on a dune. A grain-size analysis, however, might be rather confusing, for 19% of the sediment would appear to have a grain size of less than 32 μ (Fig.119). Dune sands should be almost free from silt and clay. The explanation is given by a microscope examination of the sandstone. The silt and clay is in the form of sand-sized particles composed of silty clay which were deposited on the dune as such. They are probably the deflation products of a nearby interdune (feidj or inland sebkha?) lightly cemented soil. Laboratory techniques involving water in a sedimentation balance[1] resulted in the disintegration of these grains into their constituent particles (cf. Fig.45, 132).

The mud-flow conglomerate seen in Fig.118 is overlain by sharply contrasting foresets of a slightly pebbly sandstone. This sandstone is gradually replaced upwards by sandstone that possesses more typical aeolian characters. The presence of pebbles in the sandstone and an obviously water-laid conglomerate beneath, could lead to an interpretation in which a stream-flow origin is assumed for the sandstone; and yet, we have seen with Fig.26 and 36, that the presence of pebbles in an aeolian sand can be explained. The sharp line of contact between the conglomerate and the overlying sandstone is possibly more easily explained if the sandstone is considered to be of aeolian origin and deposited at the foot of the avalanche slope of a dune. When undoubted aeolian characters develop upwards with no obvious lithological break, then an aeolian origin for the pebbly portion of the sandstone is also likely. Other evidence, including the nature of the laminae and the degree of sorting, could also affect the final interpretation.

---

[1] See also PLANKEEL (1962) and SENGUPTA and VEENSTRA (1968).

Fig.117. Foresets in Triassic dune sand. Micro-fracturing is associated with a fault zone. 19% of the sediment consists of silt and sand-sized grains of silty clay. Toual No. 3 Well, Algeria.
Fig.118. Contact between a Triassic mudflow-conglomerate and overlying foresets of a slightly pebbly sand. Toual No. 3 Well, Algeria.
Fig.119. Grain-size distribution curve and sorting coefficient of sand taken from core seen in Fig.117.

Fig.117

Fig.118

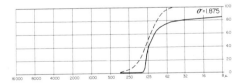

Fig.119

DIFFICULTIES OF DEDUCING PALAEO-WIND DIRECTIONS FROM CORES

In order to stress the limitations imposed by the dimensions of a core, oriented "cores" have been cut from the lacquer peels of dune sands shown in Fig.120–122. The bedding seen on Fig.120 has almost unidirectional dips. The corresponding core has been given a hypothetical tectonic tilt which has almost removed the appearance of foresetted sands. The assumed original transport direction of the sediment is now much less certain. Without great care, the set of foresets, now apparently dipping to the right nearly half way up the core, could be mistaken for "climbing ripples" in a clean river sand (cf. Fig.43). Since the dips are uniformly oriented, it is impossible to deduce an accurate palaeo-wind direction (Fig.123A and B), because it cannot be known whether the dips were formed on a barchan or a seif-like dune. The error in the deduced palaeo-wind direction could ecxeed 90°. The lacquer peel was actually made in the centre of a barchan dune. The horizontal surface accretion dips are not shown. The same uncertainty in interpretation will be found with a non-oriented core from a hole that had deviated from the vertical. With a hole deviation of 15°, apparent horizontal bedding could, in reality, dip in any direction. If the visible dip in the core from this deviated hole is 15°, the true dip of the bedding could vary from 0° to 30° with vastly different interpretations of environment of deposition within the desert and of possible palaeo-wind directions.

A THREE-DIMENSIONAL MODEL OF BARCHAN BEDDING

Fig.121 is of lacquer peels made at right angles to each other in the same pit dug into a barchan dune. A three-dimensional model of the bedding can be imagined by folding the two photos at right angles to each other. Note that for directional orientation, these photos should face outwards since they represent sections peeled off the inside walls of the pit.

Changes in the dip of the bedding are self-explanatory. The thin laminae that appear to stand out, do so because they are made up of the finer sand. When lacquer peels are made, the greater capillarity of the finer sand permits greater penetration of the lacquer. This should not be confused with the better permeability which exists in the coarser sand laminae. The few small burrows must not be confused with similar phenomena occurring in, say, estuarine sands and formed by burrowing animals. The burrow-like structures seen here were made by plant roots. The peel represents an area of limited dikaka.

Fig. 120. Lacquer peel and "core" of barchan dune sand. The "core" has been given a 15° tectonic tilt. Bandah, Rajasthan Desert, India.

not to be confused
with water-formed
climbing ripples
cf. fig. 43

Fig.121. Two lacquer peels and "cores" from a barchan dune. A three-dimensional model of the bedding may be made by folding the two photographs at right angles to each other, facing outwards. Buraimi, eastern Arabia.

PALAEO-WIND DIRECTION DEDUCED FROM CORE OF BARCHAN DUNE

The palaeo-wind direction can be deduced from the dip attitudes measured on the oriented cores. The distribution of dip attitudes (Fig.123C) roughly fits the pattern to be expected for a barchan dune. High-angle dips oriented in the direction of the palaeo-wind are absent, and there is a tendency for lobate asymmetry. This is because the "core" was taken from the broad right-hand horn of the barchan where a tendency to develop a seif-like pattern is present (Fig.82). The higher dips are directed towards the slip face on the inner edge of the crescentic dune.

Fig.121 (continued).

CORES FROM SEIF DUNES

The lacquer peel and "core" seen in Fig.122 are taken from a seif dune. Normally, a core taken on the flank of a seif will show almost unidirectional dips. As may be gathered from the opposed directions of dip (gently to the right, above; steeply to the left, below) a location near the crest of the seif may be assumed. This is partly confirmed by the rare 34° dip near the base of the core. It suggests the presence of an occasional slip-face which is sub-parallel to the predominant wind direction. The asymmetry in the distribution of the dip attitudes (Fig.123D) also reflects a location to one side of the crest line.

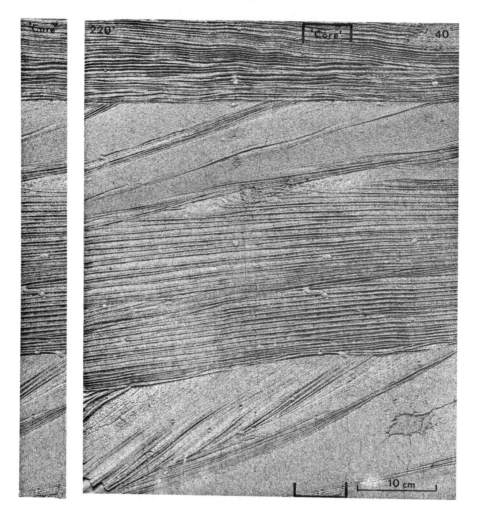

Fig.122. Lacquer peel and "core" from a seif dune. Dubai, Trucial Coast.

It should be realised, however, that for instance, 10 small seif dunes with an inter-crest spacing of 100 m could be replaced upwards, in time, by 5 larger seifs with an inter-crest spacing of 200 m, the larger seifs probably representing a long period of stronger winds. The presence of these two stages in the development of dune systems may not be readily recognised in a vertical sequence. Dip measurements taken on an oriented core or series of cores, from well down the flank of the larger dune may include dips belonging to the opposite flank of an older and smaller dune.

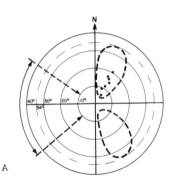

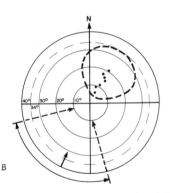

Possible range in deduced palaeo-wind directions taken from the almost unidirectional dip attitudes measured on the oriented core Fig. 120 (after correction for tectonic tilt).

A. Assuming the dips to be representative of a seif dune. Wind from N 265°E ± 37°.

B. Assuming the dips to be representative of a barchan dune. Wind from N 210°E ± 45°.

Note: The lacquer peel was actually made on a barchan dune formed by a wind which blew from about SSW (N 205°E).

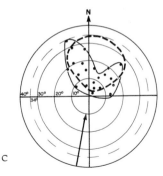

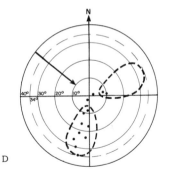

Palaeo-wind direction deduced from dip attitudes measured on the oriented cores figure 121 (reconstructed 3-dimensionally). The distribution of dip attitudes fits a pattern comparable to that found in barchan dunes. Deduced palaeo-wind from ca. N 190°E.

Note: These lacquer peels were made on the broad horn of a barchan where dip attitudes are not unidirectional.

Palaeo-wind direction deduced from dip attitudes measured on the oriented core figure 122 (reconstructed 3-dimensionally). The distribution of dip attitudes fits a pattern comparable to that found in seif dunes. Deduced palaeo-wind from ca. N 310°E.

Note: The lacquer peel was made on the flank of a seif dune not far from the crest line. The dune was formed by the Shamal which blows from the NW.

Fig.123. Palaeo-wind directions deduced from cores of dune sands.

Fossil dune bedding is rarely as simple as the examples given here. With the present state of our knowledge, it should be sufficient to recognise that the sediment is aeolian sand, that the dune is, perhaps, of barchan or seif type, and if oriented cores have been taken, that the palaeo-wind probably blew in a certain approximate direction.

PERMEABILITY IN DUNE SANDS

In order to make lacquer peels of dune sands in the arid climate of a desert, it was found necessary to first wet the sand with water so that the sub-vertical walls of a pit dug into the dune would remain standing during the process of peel making. It was noticed that owing to increased capillarity, the water travelled further along the fine grained laminae than along those of coarser grain. It was also noticed that vertical penetration of water through horizontal sand laminae was very poor. In fossil dune sands, the finer grained laminae tend to be better cemented than coarser-grained laminae. It is suggested, therefore, that in an oil-bearing fossil dune sand, these finer sands will, because of their greater cementation and capillary action, act as semi-permeable barriers to oil flow; the better permeability will be found parallel to these lamellae in the coarser grained sands. It follows, therefore, that an oil field producing from what is essentially a barchan-type dune complex, may have different production characteristics from one producing from a seif-like reservoir because of differences in permeability distribution related to the bedding styles found in the two dune types.

DRILL CUTTINGS

If only drill cuttings are available for examination, the problem of recognising desert lithologies is naturally increased. Comparison of different cuttings may give some indication of the degree of sorting within sand lamellae. The round-ness of larger sand grains and the presence or otherwise of frosting on the surfaces of the grains (provided that the cuttings have not been cemented with calcite—see p.166) may give some indication as to whether or not the sediments could have been deposited in a desert, and if so, whether they could include dune sands. The presence of Foraminifera or other calcareous skeletal fragments need not preclude the possibility that the environment of final deposition was that of a desert. As pointed out on p.127, Foraminifera have been recognised in dune sands many tens of kilometres from the coast, and have also been found in the fluvial sands of wadis. They are typically abraded and normally free of signs of boring by algae.

A clean sandstone that is cemented with anhydrite may lead to an inter-pretation that the sands were deposited in an area where the ground water was rich in Ca^{2+} and SO_4^{2-} ions. Here also, a desert environment of deposition might be suspected. If the sandstone chips contain no clay particles, then the presence of dune sands is also a possibility.

With such a series of "suspicions" concerning the possible environment of deposition, one would naturally wish to core the interval if another well is to be drilled nearby. Support may also be found in the interpretation of well logs. This book is not the place for discussing their possible uses for interpretation of lithology, but it is perhaps pertinent to refer to the dip meter and the possibility it offers for distinguishing between sands deposited on dunes and sands deposited in other environments (see GILREATH and MARICELLI, 1964, and CAMPBELL, 1968).

BEDDING AND SORTING IN DUNE SANDS

It has been previously stated that individual laminae are well sorted in a dune sand. This is illustrated in Fig.124 by a sandstone of Permian age. It is typical of what can be seen through a microscope of the surface of an unpolished piece of sandstone. Each lamina is really the thickness of one grain. A group of laminae may all contain grains of roughly the same size (well sorted). Alternating laminae (or groups of laminae) can differ in grain size from say $100\,\mu$ to $1,000\,\mu$ thus giving a high (poor) sorting coefficient for a bulk sample. Grain-size differences are not usually so great, however. The coarse white patches (in Fig.124) consist of kaolinite, altered post-depositionally from what are presumed to have been sand-sized grains of alkali feldspar.

Alternation of groups of laminae of markedly different grain sizes is characteristic of some dune sands. This is illustrated in Fig.124–126 where groups of laminae rich in coarse grains alternate with those that are much finer. By contrast, some dune sands are of remarkably uniform grain size. This presumably occurs where either the source area provides grains of uniform size or, more likely, where the source area is far distant from the site of deposition and original variations in grain size have been selectively reduced during transport.

Fine sand and silt and even clay particles can become trapped in the interstices between larger grains. By contrast, large individual grains are not normally found in the middle of fine grains unless they are relics of temporary deflation. It follows, therefore, that sorting is usually better in bulk samples of fine-grained dune sands than in coarse-grained dune sands. This can be seen more clearly in the photomicrographs made from thin sections of Permian aeolian sandstone (Fig. 125, 126) and in the grain-size distribution graphs of modern dune sand (Fig.66). The sandstones illustrated in Fig.124 and 125 came from the locality shown in Fig.81. The sandstone seen in Fig.126 is from the locality shown in Fig.79.

Fig.124. GL.343. Bedding and sorting in a Permian dune sand (k = grain of kaolinite). South-west Scotland (location seen in Fig. 81). Reflected light.

THIN SECTIONS OF CARBONATE DUNE SANDS

The difficulties of recognising carbonate dune sands in outcrop and core has already been mentioned. It is even more difficult to recognise the aeolian origin of a carbonate dune sand from cuttings. The individual grains can consist of well-preserved Foraminifera, Bryozoa and other skeletal fragments (Fig.127), which give little indication of their aeolian mode of deposition. If cementation, leaching and other diagenetic changes have not gone too far, it may be possible for a palaeontologist to recognise a surface polish on the Foraminifera. This could be diagnostic if a marine limestone of similar age and depth of burial were available for comparison, but the chances are that the sediment would be interpreted as wholly marine. The thin section (Fig.127) was made from a sample taken from the outcrop shown in Fig.102. It contains about 5% scattered quartz grains.

The grains seen in Fig.128 consist of a mixture of quartz and Foraminifera. The range in grain size is much greater than that seen in Fig.127. This Pleistocene example of a quartz–carbonate dune sand from Kutch, India (for location, see Fig.109) was found about 50 km from the present coast. The carbonate grains are thought to have been transported inland by the wind when a broad expanse of the present continental shelf in the Gulf of Kutch became exposed during a glacial period of lower sea level; the quartz could have been derived more locally. It is assumed to be a correlative of the purely calcareous Porbander Limestone (Miliolite[1]) found on the southwest coast of Kathiawar, India (WADIA 1957, p.409).

Fig.129 shows typical carbonate grains taken from a dune 3 km inland from the coast at Dubai (see Enclosure 2). The grains, which are well rounded and polished, include occasional recognisable Foraminifera such as the specimen near the right-hand edge of the figure.

DOLOMITISED CARBONATE DUNE SANDS

Recognition of carbonate dune sands which have been diagenetically altered may well be impossible. Ordinary cementation with associated leaching of some grains can make it difficult to recognise an aeolian origin in a purely carbonate rock (Fig.127). After dolomitisation, however, there may be no characters left which indicate aeolian deposition. Fig.130 is a photomicrograph of a thin section made

---

[1] The term "miliolite" was first used by CARTER (1849) when describing granular calcareous rocks from the coast of southeast Arabia, Sind, Kutch and Kathiawar that contain ooliths and miliolids. EVANS (1900) and CHAPMAN (1900) produced arguments to support an aeolian origin for many of these miliolite occurrences, including some on the islands of the Persian Gulf. PILGRIM (1908) also assumed an aeolian origin for the miliolite of the Persian Gulf and that of Kathiawar. The term is still used in India and the Persian Gulf, but its aeolian character is not always recognised (see, for instance, HOLM, 1960, p.1377). The Persian Gulf "miliolite" is often rich in ooliths, Foraminifera and other skeletal debris.

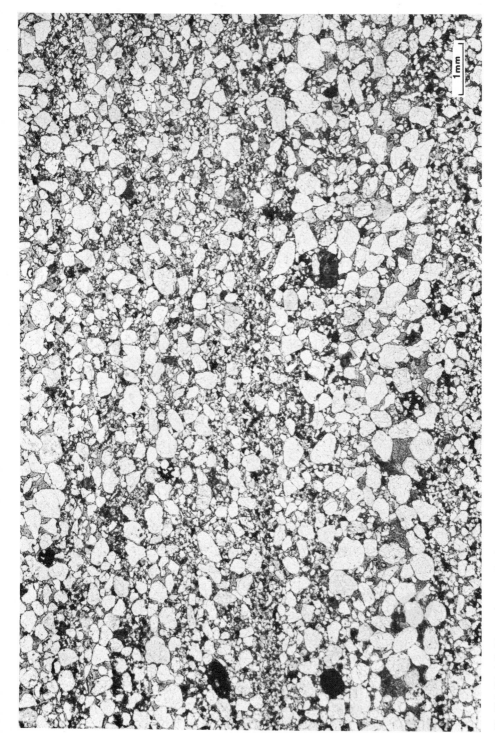

Fig.125. GL.343. Photomicrograph of Permian dune sand illustrating bedding and sorting. Southwest Scotland (location seen in Fig.81). Plane polarised light.

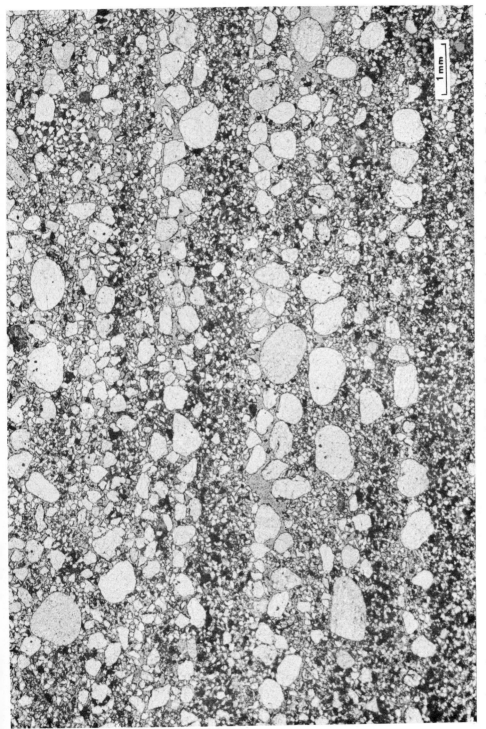

Fig. 126. GL.241. Photomicrograph of Permian Yellow Sands illustrating bedding and sorting in dune sand. Durham, England (location seen in Fig. 79). Plane polarised light.

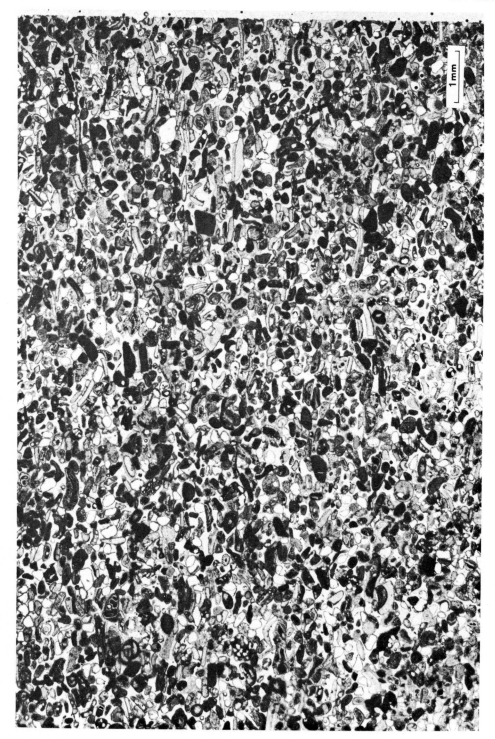

Fig.127. GL.69. Photomicrograph of Pleistocene (pre-Roman) cemented carbonate dune sand. Zanzur, West of Tripoli, Libya (location seen in Fig.102). Plane polarised light.

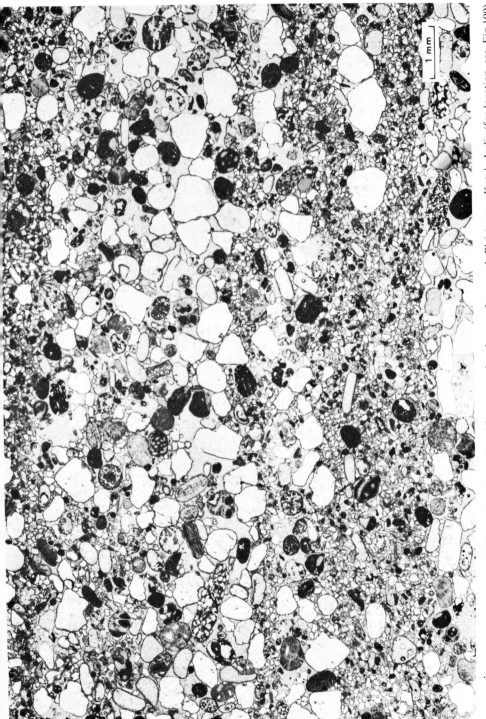

Fig.128. 'GL.360. Photomicrograph illustrating alternations of quartz and carbonate dune sand. Pleistocene. Kutch. India (for location see Fig.109). Plane polarised light.

Fig.129. GL.615. Carbonate dune sand. Locality 152, Dubai, Trucial Coast. Reflected light.

Fig.130. GL.127. Photomicrograph of sucrosic dolomite suspected of having been originally deposited as a carbonate dune sand. Permian Magnesian Limestone, Derbyshire, England (location seen in Fig.103). Crossed polarised light.

from the dolomite seen in Fig.103. Its aeolian origin is suspected only on the basis of its dune-like bedding. It is unlikely that this would be recognised in a core, and would be impossible, with present techniques, to determine from drill cuttings. In the subsurface, the horizon would be described as a dolomite and interpreted as of marine origin.

DUNE SAND AND ROUNDNESS OF QUARTZ GRAINS

The well-rounded sand grains that are considered by many authors as typical of dune sands acquire their shape after long-distance aeolian transport and abrasion (see Fig.131)[1]. Well-rounded grains are, however, usually those of larger diameter. With decreasing grain diameter, a point is reached – TANNER (1956) places this point at about $100\,\mu$ – where there is a change in degree of angularity. Either the saltating grain is so light that it is incapable of self-abrasion on impact with other grains, or it is so small that it falls between larger grains and is thus protected from the abrasive action of other saltating grains. For any particular grain size above a certain minimum limit, the degree of roundness will depend essentially upon the distance of travel; that is, upon the number of impacts with other grains. Because of its greater mass (and therefore, potentially, greater kinetic energy) a larger grain should achieve a certain degree of roundness in a shorter travel distance (fewer saltations) than is required by a smaller grain. KUENEN (1960) has carried out some experiments on aeolian abrasion, but it is still not possible to estimate the distance which any particular grain has travelled, since its history prior to its aeolian existence will not be known in sufficient detail. The roundness of larger quartz grains may be indicative of an aeolian environment, but large quartz grains also become rounded in other environments (see, for example, INMAN et al., 1966, p.800). Dune sands, however, also possess many angular grains that are derived from larger particles as the result of insolation (see Fig.132–136).

FROSTING OF QUARTZ GRAINS IN A DESERT

The large grains seen in Fig.131 are frosted as well as rounded. They have possibly been reworked from older Tertiary dune sands. The frosted appearance, typical of many aeolian sands, appears under the normal optical microscope to result from light diffraction associated with small pits on the surface of the grain. KUENEN and PERDOK (1962) claim that the frosting is not the result of pits made by the impact

---

[1] It is assumed here that the grains under discussion became rounded solely as the result of aeolian transport and abrasion. Many grains that occur in dune sands, however, have probably also had an earlier history involving transport and rounding in entirely different environments (e.g., fluvial or marine).

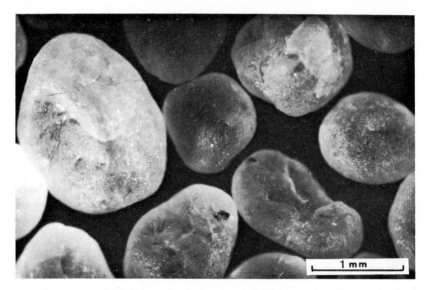

Fig.131. GL.664. Well-rounded, frosted grains of quartz between 1 and 2 mm in diameter. Southern end of Sebkha Matti, Trucial Coast. Reflected light.

on one grain against another. They suggest that it is caused by micro-chemical attack of the quartz surface associated, perhaps, with desert dews. Similar frosting is, however, also associated with peri-glacial and coastal dune sands where other climatic conditions prevail. No illustrations are given here as the writer has so far failed to obtain satisfactory photographs of the surface of a grain under high optical magnification.

FROSTING AND CALCITE CORROSION OF QUARTZ GRAINS

Frosted quartz grains are typical of many modern dune sands. If, however, the quartz grains have been cemented by calcite in a fossil sediment, the surface of the grains are corroded by the calcite to give the grain a frosted appearance (ALIMEN, 1944; WALKER, 1957, 1960). Under the optical microscope these corrosion pits appear as light diffraction rings similar to, but often bigger than, those associated with the frosting of Recent dune sands. In the early stages of corrosion, however, the pits will be about the same size as those associated with desert frosting. It may be possible to recognise the differences between desert frosting and calcite corrosion by use of an electron microscope. Without such means of differentiation, it is at present very dangerous to use the frosting of a carbonate-cemented quartz sand as evidence for a desert environment of sedimentation. Electron-microscope investigations may help to resolve this problem. Excellent electron-microscope photographs have been published of the surfaces of quartz grains that are thought to have acquired characteristic markings in different geologic environments: glacial and fluvio-glacial, rivers and beaches; aeolian sands from both hot deserts and non-desert areas; sands whose surfaces are chemically etched or altered by authigenic overgrowths (BRAMER, 1965; KRINSLEY and FUNNEL, 1965; WAUGH, 1965; SOUTENDAM, 1967; WOLFE, 1967; KRINSLEY and DONAHUE, 1968a, b).

This type of study is still in its infancy; the reasons for the development of certain markings on the surface of grains is still under active discussion (see, for instance, SOUTENDAM, 1967, and discussion by KRINSLEY and DONAHUE, 1968b). Further detailed studies of this type may eventually reveal patterns of surface markings on quartz grains that conform to particular climatic and depositional environments. This, in turn, may lead to a better understanding of the diagenetic changes (quartz overgrowths as well as corrosion) that can alter the surfaces of grains after burial.

FROST-FREE CONCHOIDAL FRACTURES ON DESERT QUARTZ SAND AND RELICT DESERT SOILS

One grain in Fig.131 (top, right of centre) is about to calve a flat flake of quartz along a fracture formed by the effects of insolation. The conchoidally fractured surface which results will not be frosted. The elongate grain below it has earlier lost a similar flake. Its fracture surface has already undergone further abrasion and frosting.

Most of the sand grains seen in Fig.132 have probably not suffered extensive aeolian transport. A few quartz and carbonate grains are very well rounded and almost spherical, but some are angular. Brown, irregularly shaped grains form almost 50% of this size fraction. They consist of silt, or fine sand-sized particles cemented together by an earthy looking brown oxide of iron. They are thought to have been deflated from nearby interdune desert-soil crusts (cf. Figs.117, 119).

A finer fraction, from the same locality, is formed from almost equal amounts of carbonate grains and quartz together with grains of heavy minerals. The grains tend to be more angular than those in the coarser fraction. The "shiny" surfaces on many of the quartz grains are unfrosted conchoidal-fracture surfaces. This lack of frosting on the surfaces of grains of fine angular aeolian sand has also been noted by SNEAD and FRISHMAN (1968, p.1673). The angularity of aeolian sand grains increases with a decrease in grain size. The sand grains illustrated in Fig.132 and 133 are from the same locality as the lacquer peel and core, Fig.120.

DUNE SAND FROM DEFLATION PLAIN TO TOP OF DUNE

It has already been remarked that the grain size of dune sand tends to diminish

Fig.132. GL.426. Rounded to angular grains of quartz and carbonate with irregular iron-cemented aggregates representing former interdune desert soil. 480–500 μ. Bandah, Rajasthan Desert, India. Reflected light.

Fig.133. GL.426. Sub-rounded to angular quartz, carbonate and heavy-mineral grains. Many grains are partly frosted, with unfrosted conchoidal-fracture surfaces. 250–297μ. Bandah, Rajasthan Desert, India. Reflected light.

Fig.134. Sample taken from a dune at 27.5 m above the deflation plain (cf. Fig.66). Locality 92, near Barik, Oman. GL.559. 53–220 μ. $\sigma = 0.22$. Reflected light.

Fig.135. Sample taken from a dune at 1.5 m above the deflation plain (cf. Fig.66). Locality 92, near Barik, Oman. GL.555, 53–260 μ. $\sigma = 0.36$. Reflected light.

Fig.136. Sample taken at the foot of a dune. The grains are mostly limestone, products of deflation of the interdune outcrop. Locality 92, near Barik, Oman (cf. Fig.66). GL.553. 53–10,000 μ. $\sigma =$ 2.38. Reflected light.

from bottom to top of the dune. The three examples of sand shown on Fig.134–136 are comparable to three of the grain-size distribution curves given in Fig.66. It will be noted that there are several angular grains in the example taken from the top of the dune (Fig.134). As with the examples from India (Fig.132, 133), many of the sand grains have only partial frosting of their surfaces. At the foot of the dune (Fig.136), locally derived deflation products of the limestone interdune area make up the bulk of the sand. They resemble in form the similarly derived sand seen in Fig.6. The presence of large angular grains at the base of an undoubted aeolian sequence could therefore suggest that they represent the products of a nearby deflation surface.

POSSIBLE PRESERVATION OF ENVIRONMENTAL HISTORY ON A QUARTZ GRAIN

Fluviatile transport is slow to polish the surface of an already frosted grain. Grains of wadi sand are usually just as frosted as grains of aeolian sand. This is not surprising since much of the wadi sand has probably been airborne at some stage in its history. As KUENEN and PERDOCK (1962) have already pointed out, however, it may be that sub-aerial corrosion in a desert climate is a more important

Fig.137. LP 273. Rounded to angular grains of quartz river sand. Niger River Delta, Nigeria. 250–297 μ. Reflected light.

Fig.138. GL.30. Typical frosted, rounded to sub-rounded modern dune sand. Northern edge of the Ubari Sand Sea, Libya. Reflected light.

Fig.139. GL.241. Typical frosted, rounded, Permian dune sand. Durham, England. Reflected light.

cause of frosting than aeolian transport. Fig.137 is of a river sand from the Niger Delta. Although the surfaces of the grains are fairly well polished, microscope examination shows that they have relict markings reminiscent of desert frosting. This might imply an earlier history of aeolian transport in the Sahara Desert, all traces of which have not been removed by its subsequent fluviatile transport, or the markings may reflect an earlier period of calcite cementation. The environment of final deposition was fluvial, in a hot, humid climate. For the present, one can only speculate as to the reasons for the markings. The possibility of recognition of relict environmental features has recently been presented by KRINSLEY and FUNNEL (1965) and KRINSLEY and DONAHUE (1968a) in papers describing electron-microscope photomicrographs of the surfaces of some quartz grains. CAILLIEUX (1937) believes that relict peri-glacial aeolian features can be recognised in the present North Sea sands.

There are few criteria that can be used as direct evidence of a fossil desert environment when only drill cuttings are used. In the absence of bedding features, well-rounded, frosted sand grains are perhaps the best indicator of the environment (Fig.138, 139), but the possibility that these grains have been reworked into a non-desert (marine?) environment must not be overlooked. At present, frosting on calcite-cemented quartz grains cannot be accepted as evidence of a desert environment.

THE SIGNIFICANCE OF RED-STAINED QUARTZ GRAINS

The red iron oxide coating found on quartz grains is often accepted as evidence of deposition in a continental environment. Recognition of this iron oxide on the grains can be taken as additional evidence in support of a hot arid or seasonally wet climate. Here again, however, later reworking into a marine environment need not result in the removal of all the red coating. Grains that are covered with patches of iron pyrites altered from haematite indicate a colour change caused by an alteration from an oxidising to a more reducing environment. This could be caused by reworking into a marine environment, a change in the ground-water chemistry, or even, perhaps in some instances, the migration through the sands of undersaturated hydrocarbons. The whole question of the significance of red beds in desert sediments is dealt with in some detail in the following chapter.

Chapter 9

THE RELATION BETWEEN RED BEDS AND DESERTS

INTRODUCTION

No account of the various aspects of desert sedimentation would be complete without considering the significance of red beds.

Since the beginning of the century there has been much controversy concerning the interpretation of red beds. The only subjects on which all geologists agree are that the cause of the colour in red beds is the presence of red-stained clays and a coating of the red oxide of iron (haematite) on grains of sand and silt, and that most red bed sequences are terrestrial in origin.

The conditions under which the red pigment formed and then coloured grains of sand or particles of clay red are assumed by various authors to be related to different environments ranging from hot, humid tropics to hot, arid deserts. Some geologists believe that the red pigment is detrital; others believe that it forms penecontemporaneously in situ. Still others point out that some beds appear to have been reddened long after deposition. The history of this controversy over the origin of red beds, which appears to have been gathering in momentum since the late 1940's, is outlined in chronological order in Table II.

In the following pages, it is hoped to establish the probable conditions under which sediments—especially desert sediments—can acquire a red colour, and also to consider other factors related to the formation or loss of colour in sediments that, apparently, were deposited in similar environments.

HOT, WET TROPICAL ORIGIN FOR RED SEDIMENTS

WALTHER (1900) thought that desert sediments inherited the colour of the rocks from which they were derived. If desert sediments were red, then they were derived from a source that became reddened in a hot, humid climate associated with the formation of lateritic soils. He, like DORSEY (1926) and RAYMOND (1927), was impressed by the common yellow and dun colours of the desert. These latter geologists concluded that red colour is not produced in Recent deserts.

GÈZE (1947) and WAHLSTROM (1948) state correctly that red laterite soils form in hot, humid climates. Pigment derived from such areas should stain red a sediment that is otherwise non-stained. This is the argument followed by KRYNINE

TABLE II

HISTORY OF THE CONTROVERSY OVER THE ORIGIN OF RED BEDS

Year	Author	Nature of hypothesis
1900	WALTHER	Red beds formed in a hot, humid climate and preserved in an arid desert climate.
1908 1916	BARRELL	Red beds formed in a hot climate with alternate wet and dry seasons. Applied to fluviatile Old Red Sandstone of Scotland.
1926	BAILEY	Secondary reddening of previously deposited beds by penetration of oxidising conditions resulting from overlying arid desert. Applied to reddened Carboniferous strata in Scotland.
1926 1927	DORSEY RAYMOND	Red colour is not produced in (dune sands of) Recent deserts.
1937 1937 1938	DE LAPPARENT BOURCART	Red colour of ancient sedimentary rocks is the result of intermittent humidity in a desert environment.
1947 1948	GÈZE WAHLSTROM	Red colour is produced during laterite formation in hot, humid areas.
1949	ROBB	Intra-stratal alteration of iron-bearing minerals as a source of iron for haematite pigment in red beds.
1949	KRYNINE	(a) Red beds produced from red soils or primary red beds. (b) Red beds produced from non-red detritus by oxidation within the sediment itself. (c) Red beds produced through the reworking of older red beds. (d) Red beds produced chemically by precipitation from a solution within the basin of sedimentation.
1953	CHOUBERT	Suggested that even in deserts, some humidity is necessary to produce the red stain.
1953	DUNHAM	Carboniferous red beds of Britain resulted from period of sub-tropical humid soil formation between end of Carboniferous and transgression of Zechstein Sea. Permian dune sands reddened in similar manner from an area of not too remote subtropical humid climate.
1953 1954	TROTTER	Red Carboniferous strata of north England secondarily reddened by oxidising conditions of overlying Permian desert.
1955	MILLER and FOLK	Intra-stratal alteration of iron-bearing minerals as source of red colour. Pigment lacking at contact point between grains, therefore in situ readening.
1957	DUNBAR and ROGERS	Source area will determine whether or not a sediment will be initially red. Environmental conditions in basin of deposition determine whether or not it remains red.

TABLE II (*continued*)

Year	Author	Nature of hypothesis
1960	BLUNDELL and MOORE	Red Carboniferous strata of South Wales secondarily reddened by oxidising conditions of overlying Permian desert.
1960	MYKURA	Similar secondary reddening of Carboniferous strata in southwest Scotland.
1961	VAN HOUTEN	(*a*) Ferric oxides originated in red lateritic upland soils in a tropical or subtropical climate. (*b*) Oxidising conditions necessary in place of deposition -- a drier climate, possibly local desert conditions, but not in great desert like those of today. (*c*) Possibility of ageing of hydrohaematite to haematite after deposition.
1963	WALKER	In situ formation of red beds in an arid to semi-arid climate.
1964	VAN HOUTEN	(*a*) Most of ferric oxide pigment found in red beds brought from source area in colloidal suspension or in solution and precipitated as cement. (*b*) Some pigment supplied by alteration of iron-bearing minerals. (*c*) Diagenesis has played a significant role in modifying components inherited from source area.
1964	MILLOT	Red beds deposited in hot, seasonally wet climate. Inferred from Permo-Triassic rocks of the Vosges, France.
1965	DOWNING and SQUIRREL	Red colour in Upper Carboniferous strata of South Wales contemporaneous or penecontemporaneous and either: (*a*) derived from source areas where red soils or red rocks existed; or (*b*) resulted from subaerial processes that produced red soils from grey sediment in situ by weathering of iron-bearing minerals.
1965	ARCHER	Formation of red beds and other associated phenomena in South Wales resulted from penecontemporaneous lowering of water table.
1966	FRIEND	(*a*) Redness develops in situ and does not result directly from presence of red soils in source areas. (*b*) Alteration of red to non-red occurs post-depositionally as result of differences in oxidation/reduction potential, which is determined by position of water table—applied to water-laid Devonian sediments.
1967	WALKER	Red colouration in desert sediments is due to presence of haematite that forms in sediments after deposition. Critical factors that control formation of haematite are: (*a*) Presence of iron-bearing grains in original sediment. (*b*) Post-depositional conditions favouring intra-stratal alteration of iron-bearing grains. (*c*) Eh-pH interstitial environment that favours formation of ferric oxide (probably as limonite in initial stages of formation). (*d*) Absence of subsequent reduction of ferric iron. (*e*) Enough time for alteration of iron-bearing minerals and formation of haematite from limonite. (*f*) Possibly an elevated temperature.

(1949; (*a*) in Table II), DUNHAM (1953), DUNBAR and ROGERS (1957) and VAN HOUTEN (1961, 1964). Deposition of organic-rich sediment that has been stained red by lateritic muds can, however, result in reduction of the sediment to a greenish-grey or even a grey colour (see, for example, core description by NOTA, 1958, p.23 etc., of the sediments off the mouth of the Orinoco River).

That red continental sediments can be reduced when transported into a marine environment is supported by BORCHERT (1965). In a discussion on marine sedimentary iron ores[1], BORCHERT (1965, p.180) assumed from earlier arguments "that most of the source material for marine iron ores originated from the continents, and that the separation of iron from this detrital sial material took place principally not on the continents, but rather in sea basins by the leaching of ferrous iron from clay minerals". Later, he says: "In both the continental and the marine environments, iron can be dissolved from the sialic detritus only under conditions in which ferrous solutions are stable (i.e., the low pH and Eh values of the CO_2-zone)." "A CO_2-zone can develop in certain confined sea basins in which ... stratified water masses can develop." This condition of stratified water masses is found off the mouth of the Orinoco River where the river water flows over the more dense sea water. "In the main CO_2-zone there exists a moderately strong reducing environment (Eh = $+0.05$–0.2 V and pH 6–7.5) and iron may be dissolved from the bottom sediments" (Borchert, 1965, p.183 and fig.9). Ferric minerals carried in suspension in the river water will become reduced to the ferrous state as the clay particles flocculate on contact with the sea water and settle down in the underlying CO_2-zone.

Further evidence is provided by HINZE and MEISCHNER (1968) who show that although red detritus from the Istrian Peninsula is carried into the Adriatic Sea, red marine sediments do not result. The water at a depth of 30 m has a seasonal fluctuation in temperature of between $10°$ and $19°$ C, in salinity of between $37°/_{oo}$ and $38°/_{oo}$ and in oxygen saturation of between 70% and 100%. Cores show a transition with depth of penetration into the sediment from red-brown (at the surface near the source area), through brown-grey to grey (at a depth of a few centimetres below the surface of the open-sea floor). Hinze and Meischner believe that the haematite is partly destroyed during fluviatile transportation. Because of burrowing, those ferric hydroxides that reach the sea bottom are gradually carried down into the zone of negative Eh and low pH, where they are reduced and partly fixed as siderite and pyrite.

---

[1] Throughout this discussion, the writer assumes that the colour of red beds is very close to 5R or 10R on the Geological Society of America Rock Color Chart (GODDARD, 1951), although sediments that have other colours (yellow, brown, green etc.) may be related to red beds in some aspects of the process of reddening. The iron ores that form in the marine environment discussed by BORCHERT (1965) are mainly yellow-brown limonite and brown siderite; they cannot be considered as representing a marine equivalent of the continental red beds discussed in the remainder of this chapter.

The proponents of the detrital pigments hypothesis state that once a red pigment has formed, the environmental conditions in the area of deposition will determine whether or not the sediment will remain red. An oxidising environment is necessary, otherwise the red ferric oxides will be reduced to a non-red ferrous state. VAN HOUTEN (1961; (b) in Table II) provides this oxidising environment by transporting the sediment and the red pigment into a region having a drier climate. The pigment is brought from the source area either as a colloidal suspension, or in solution to be later precipitated as red cement (VAN HOUTEN, 1964, p.653; (a) in table II). He considers that the area of deposition could, possibly, be locally a desert, but not "in vast deserts like the great high pressure or trade wind deserts (of) today" (VAN HOUTEN, 1961, p.122).

DUNHAM (1953, p.27) states that "red oxides require hot humid, or rapidly alternating hot dry and humid conditions for their generation". He applies this idea to the reddened Carboniferous sediments of Britain by assuming that the red oxide that coloured these sediments was formed during a period of subtropical humid soil formation between the Carboniferous and Zechstein. This is not supported by the work of LAMING (1965), MYKURA (1965) and WAGNER (1966). They date the onset of desert conditions with accompanying dune sands as Upper Carboniferous (Stephanian), thus permitting no time for an Early Permian period of soil formation.

In addition, WALKER (1967b) shows that although red soils occur in hot humid areas of tropical Mexico, the Recent alluvium is grayish brown because the red detritus is masked by more abundant non-red material.

RED SEDIMENTS IN TROPICAL CLIMATE HAVING SEASONAL RAINFALL

An alternative hypothesis for the formation of red beds was proposed by BARRELL (1908). He suggested that they occur in sediments deposited in a tropical area subjected to a seasonal rainfall. This provides conditions both for transport of the pigment in solution and its later oxidation to haematite. BARRELL (1916) later applied this idea, with apparent success, to the predominantly fluviatile Old Red Sandstone sediments of Scotland.

This hypothesis finds favour with MILLOT et al. (1961) and MILLOT (1964) who studied water-transported sediments of the Permo-Triassic New Red Sandstone in the Vosges. MILLOT (1964, pp.184–192) presents criteria found in the fossil red beds of the Vosges and compares them with palaeoclimatic characters recognised in the sediments of a hot, humid climate (Table III). From this comparison, he concludes that these Permo-Triassic sediments cannot have been deposited in a hot, humid climate.

Probably influenced by the water-transported nature of the sediments which he and his co-workers studied, Millot was in favour of a hot climate with alternate

TABLE III

CRITERIA FOR DEDUCING PALAEOCLIMATES
(From MILLOT, 1964)

Climatic characters recognised in Permo-Triassic sediments of the Vosges	Climatic characters recognised in sediments of a hot, humid climate
Presence of polycrystalline grains	No polycrystalline grains
Alkali feldspars preserved	All feldspars destroyed
Quartz grains not corroded	Quartz grains corroded
Quartz grains not micro-fractured	Quartz grains micro-fractured
Quartz grains ferruginous	Quartz grains with ferruginous corrosion cavities
Clay fraction essentially illite	Clay fraction essentially kaolinite
Accidental presence of arid-type soils	Lateritised soils with haematite concretions

wet and dry seasons to account for the red colouration of these sediments of the New Red Sandstone. He points out that humidity is necessary for the hydrolysis of the ferromagnesian silicates that must precede the liberation of iron, which, during the dry season, can be converted into the sesquioxides of iron.

The origin of red and non-red Devonian fluviatile sediments is discussed by FRIEND (1966). He considers that the reason for the differences between red and non-red rock sequences is the presence of fine-grained haematite, often of hexagonal crystal form, in the red sediments. He says (on p.285): "The redness developed in situ, and did not result directly from the presence of red soils in the source areas." Although the haematite is often intimately connected with clay minerals, the clays are not themselves a cause of the red colour, for the same type of clay minerals occur in non-red sediments.

Friend considers that the localised presence of organic material causes reducing conditions below the water table, which result in ferrous solutions. The ferrous–organic complexes so formed can be carried away in solution, thus causing a drop in the total iron content of the rock. Under strongly reducing conditions associated with the presence of organic material (and sulphur), pyrite may form. Localised green patches within the red beds are often associated with dark plant fragments. The formation of the green colour is also post-depositional, and follows the formation of red colour.

IN-SITU FORMATION OF RED BEDS

The association of some red beds with evaporites, and locally with dunes, influenced many earlier workers to consider red beds as the product of an arid or semi-arid environment. DUNBAR and ROGERS (1957), like WALTHER (1900), were more impressed by the presence of dun and buff colours and the apparent lack of red sediments in Recent deserts. There is, however, mounting evidence to support a hypothesis that supposes postdepositional in situ reddening of sediment under suitable conditions. As we have just seen, FRIEND (1966) proposes in situ reddening for the Devonian fluviatile sediments of the Catskill Mountains. Both DE LAPPARENT (1937) and BOURCART (1937, 1938) considered the colour of red fossil sediments to be the result of intermittent humidity in a desert environment. They were supported by CHOUBERT (1953) who pointed out that, even in deserts, some humidity is necessary to produce the red stain. Moreover, the lack of pigment at the contact points between grains suggests reddening of the sediment after deposition (MILLER and FOLK, 1955).

The clearest reasons for an in-situ, postdepositional origin for the red colour of ancient desert sediments so far published are given by WALKER (1967a). They are based on a study of Pliocene to Recent sediments in the Sonoran Desert of Baja California, Mexico, and their Late Palaeozoic analogues from Colorado. He provides convincing evidence that the haematite pigment formed after deposition, in a hot arid or semi-arid environment, by tracing stages in the in-situ colour change from Recent non-red desert sediments to red Pliocene desert sediments.

Walker's interpretation is based essentially on the widespread presence of unstable iron-bearing minerals such as hornblende and biotite in the non-red Recent alluvium, and the presence of corroded iron-bearing minerals (e.g., hornblende extensively altered-to montmorillonite clay; see Walker et al., 1967) with halos of haematite in red Pliocene desert sediments. The varying degrees of alteration of these iron-bearing minerals appear to be related to an increase in the presence of haematite and the increasing degree of redness of the sediments from the Recent, through the Pleistocene to the Pliocene. Time is needed for desert sediments to become red. Time is apparently also required for the haematite to become sufficiently ordered structurally to allow X-ray identification. The red pigment found in the Pleistocene alluvium seems to be some form of ferric oxide that is either amorphous to X-rays or is too poorly crystallised to give a diagnostic X-ray diffraction pattern.

In the Palaeozoic red beds of Colorado, Walker finds that biotite, with a red halo of haematite, is particularly abundant in the red mudstones and shaly sandstones. Hornblende, however, is almost completely lacking, in spite of the fact that the rocks from which the biotite and haematite are derived—again exposed to erosion—are rich in the mineral. Alteration of iron-bearing minerals as a source of iron for the haematite pigment found in red beds has also been advocated to various extents by ROBB (1949), MILLER and FOLK (1955), SHOTTON (1956), WALKER (1963) and VAN HOUTEN (1964, 1968). In addition, WALKER and HONEA (1969) point out that the clay fraction of desert soils contains an average of about 4.5% total iron, most of which is held in the clay-mineral lattices. Under favourable interstitial chemical conditions, the iron-bearing clay should undergo post-depositional alteration and yield additional iron which will ultimately also form haematite pigment.

WALKER (1967a) lists six critical factors that he believes control the formation of red pigment in the Baja California beds. They are given in Table II. He includes his last factor, "possibly an elevated temperature", because the formation of the red pigments studied by him took place in a hot climate where the ground-water temperature is approximately 72 °F (22 °C). He is not certain, however, whether elevated temperatures are necessary for haematite formation in situations where long periods of ageing are involved. Other authors (by implication) also appear to favour a hot climate as an additional factor in the formation of red beds. VAN HOUTEN (1961) has suggested the possibility of "ageing" brown hydrohaematite to red haematite after deposition—the time factor required by WALKER'S (1967a) hypothesis for the conversion of limonite into haematite. This is supported by BERNER (1969), who shows that goethite is unstable relative to haematite, and given sufficient time, the yellow-brown goethite could dehydrate to red haematite. Obviously following similar lines of thought, NORRIS and NORRIS (1961), PRICE (1962) and NORRIS (1969) suggest that the colour of dune sands is, in part, a measure of their age.

From studies undertaken both in desert and non-desert areas, WALKER and HONEA (1969, p.542) conclude that "special types of climate in the source areas are not essential for the formation of red beds". "Essentially all sediments, regardless of type of parent material or type of source-area weathering conditions (moist or arid), contain enough iron to produce bright red sedimentary rocks if the interstitial environment, either during or subsequent to the time of deposition, favours the formation and preservation of iron oxide." "The vital factor for the formation and preservation of red beds is the occurrence within the depositional basin of special interstitial conditions (for example, favourable Eh and pH) that favour the formation and preservation of hematite."

ARE RED BEDS RED THROUGHOUT?

The above remarks by WALKER and HONEA (1969) and WALKER'S (1967a, p.363) statement that the red colour will probably form after deposition in any climate where his six conditions are satisfied, are worthy of further study. Both the Old Red Sandstone of Scotland and the Tertiary Siwaliks of the Himalayan foothills are fluviatile and lacustrine sequences that contain red beds. Neither of these sequences, however, is so consistently red as many fossil dune sands. In the writer's experience, probably less than 20% of the Old Red Sandstone and Siwaliks can be described as red.[1] The remainder of these sequences—for which a hot climate and seasonal rainfall have been invoked to account for the conglomeratic and graded nature of the fluviatile sediments—consist of brown, yellow, green, grey or even white sediments. By contrast, the aeolian desert sediments of the Permo-Triassic New Red Sandstone of southwest Scotland, the Vale of Eden and the Midlands of England are virtually red throughout. It would appear that in the case of the dune sediments a more efficient process of reddening—or of preservation of the red colour—has been active than that affecting the fluviatile Old Red Sandstone and Siwaliks. WALKER'S (1967a) criteria would appear to have been met fully in the one case, but not in the other. It is, perhaps, worthwhile considering the environments of deposition and preservation of other sediments that are, or might once have been red, in order to see whether there are other factors that help in the formation of red beds or cause their later alteration to other colours.

THE "BARREN RED MEASURES"

There are areas of Britain (southwest Scotland, north and central England, South Wales) where Carboniferous strata are red. Some of these sequences can be traced from normal productive Coal Measures into areas that are barren of coal seams. BAILEY (1926) suggested that the Carboniferous sediments of Arran were reddened by the penetration of oxidising conditions resulting from an overlying arid desert during the Permo-Triassic. This hypothesis is extended to the mainland of southwest Scotland by MYKURA (1960) who considers that there, overlying desert conditions caused the reddening of Upper Carboniferous strata to a maximum depth of 1,950 ft. He has also suggested (Fig.140) that, at the same time, the deeper Westphalian coal seams in the Mauchline Basin of Scotland were replaced by dolomitic limestone[2] and the shallower ones by ironstone. The oxidation (and replacement)

---

[1] JONES (1965) describes the three sequences of red beds from the Cretaceous Bima Sandstone of northern Nigeria. This sandstone is assumed to be of fluviatile and lacustrine origin and deposited in a climate which was seasonally wet. In one section, 9% of the beds were red, in another, 4% and in a third, only 3%. On the other hand, ARNDT et al. (1962, Fig.72.2) show two sequences of the Catskill Formation of Pennsylvania, one of which has 68% "red beds" and the other 40% "red beds". Included in the red beds, however, are rocks that are "grayish-red, pale brown, brownish-gray and yellowish-brown" (ARNDT et all., 1962, p.C35). In the Catskill sediments studied by FRIEND (1966, p.281), 73% of the thickness of coarse beds in a local section of 5 cyclothems are non-red and 98% of the fine beds are red. His non-red group includes grey, greenish-grey, olive-grey and brownish-grey. The reds fall in the range 5R, 10R, on the Geological Society of America Rock-Color Chart (GODDARD, 1951). See also GILL (1951, pp.382–384) for description and colours of Siwalik sedimentary rocks.

[2] Desert erosion of early New Red Sandstone volcanic lavas is thought to have given rise to a concentration of Ca^{2+} and Mg^{2+} ions in the ground water of the area. This is assumed to have been the reason why the coals were replaced by dolomitic limestone.

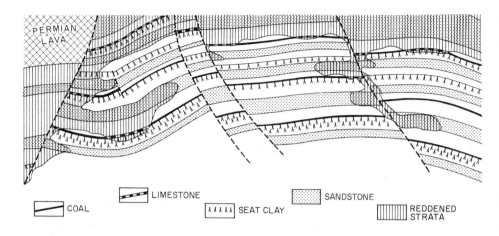

LIMESTONE   SANDSTONE

COAL   SEAT CLAY   REDDENED STRATA

Fig.140. Relation between red beds and post-depositional conditions of reddening. Possible relationship between faulting and the lower limit of reddening on the Coal Measures of Ayrshire. From MYKURA (1960, Fig.4). Crown Copyright Geological Survey diagram. Reproduced by permission of the Controller of H.M. Stationery Office.

of the coal seams—which were originally formed in a tropical humid climate—is also believed to be associated with overlying arid desert conditions which resulted in a great lowering of the water table.[1]

Sediments associated with the Carboniferous coals were probably not red when deposited, and even though red lateritic clays may originally have been deposited, the presence of so much organic matter in the environment of deposition must soon have caused the reduction of the oxides to non-red colours. For the reddening of these organically rich sediments, there must have been very strong post-depositional oxidising conditions. These are unlikely to have been met by the presence of oxygenated ground water at great depths below the water table (see WALKER, 1967a, p.363, reference to GERMANOV et al., 1959). Something stronger was needed, but once oxidised, there was no more organic matter with which to bring about a return to reducing conditions.

Reddening of Carboniferous strata in Permo-Triassic time is also proposed for the north of England by TROTTER (1953, 1954). The same hypothesis was applied to South Wales by BLUNDELL and MOORE (1960) but is opposed by DOWNING and

---

[1] In some deserts, the water table is at a considerable depth below the surface. This depth may be as much as 700 m in mountainous areas such as the Hoggar Mountains in the Sahara (A.A.E.A. Coffinier, personal communication, 1966). In depositional basins, however, the water table is usually somewhere between 10 and 100 m below the surface of wadis or interdune areas. The water is at, or very close to, the surface in inland sebkhas. The level of the water table may fluctuate several metres annually, or even, in some cases, daily (A.A.E.A. Coffinier, personal communication, 1966). Tidally controlled fluctuation of the water level occurs in water wells in Dubai, Trucial Coast.

SQUIRREL (1965) and ARCHER (1965) who present convincing evidence to support contemporaneous or pene-contemporaneous reddening of these sediments.[1] They point out that the red beds are both overlain and underlain by typical grey sediments of the Coal Measures. Downing and Squirrel assume that the red colour found in the Upper Coal Measures of the eastern part of the South Wales Coalfield were either derived from source areas where red soils or red rocks existed, or it resulted from subaerial processes that produced red soils from grey sediments in situ by the weathering of iron-bearing minerals. Archer, who worked in the western part of the South Wales Coalfield, concluded that the red beds and other associated phenomena were related to pene-contemporaneous lowering of the water table.

In the Midlands of England, there is similar conflicting evidence. Analysed, it might well be suggested that some of the rock sequences that are classed as "Barren Red Measures" may have been reddened in post-Carboniferous time, but the majority of the red beds are probably part of a sequence of terrestrial rocks that reflect increasing aridity laterally, away from low-lying coal-forming areas, and upwards into passage beds that herald the approaching Late Carboniferous (Stephanian) and Permian desert conditions (EDMUNDS and OAKLEY, 1958, pp.40–42, 48–50).[2]

RECENT DESERT SANDS

Some modern desert sands are red, but most are buff coloured, yellow or even white. The darkest colours in a desert are usually associated with areas of outcrop where the yellow, dark brown or even almost black "desert varnish" (p.19) is thought to be associated with the frequent presence of dew (ENGEL and SHARP, 1958) or moisture brought to the surface by capillary action (OPDYKE, 1961). The most strongly coloured sediments are normally those of wadis, where the older wadi sands and gravels exhibit darkish-brown to pink shades, whilst the youngest wadi sediments are usually light brown or yellow. Pebbles on the deflated surfaces of wadi gravels that have not been covered by flood waters for many years—perhaps many decades—also show the dark brown or almost black colouration of desert varnish (Fig.19). Water may only be present in these wadis seasonally or at longer intervals, but the intermittant soaking of the wadi sediments with long

[1] The origin of the red colour in Carboniferous sediments of this part of Wales has also, for many years, been the subject of controversy following the lines of argument given earlier in this chapter. MOORE (1948) suggested that the red colour may have been derived from nearby outcropping Old Red Sandstone rocks. COX (in discussion of BLUNDELL, 1952) said that the beds may represent red muds brought by rivers from areas of lateritic weathering.

[2] The Permian aeolian sands of the Midlands of England have long been shown on Geological Survey maps as Triassic. According to these maps, Permian strata are virtually absent, an age classification that is not accepted by the writer, SHOTTON (1956) and many others.

dry periods between, permits the sporadic solution of ferrous oxides and their later oxidation to the ferric state.

In southeastern Arabia, an interesting comparison can be made between two areas in which older dune sands are being currently remoulded. To the north and west of the Buraimi oasis (Enclosure 2), reddened dunes occur that are now being reshaped. The reworked sands are lighter in colour than the underlying sands from which they are being eroded. In the Wahiba Sands, although the recently reworked sands are lighter in colour than the underlying cemented dunes, these latter are not red.

As was suggested on pp.90 and 98, the large seif dunes of both the Wahiba and Buraimi areas were probably moulded into their present broad outlines during the Pleistocene. Why then, is there a difference in degree of reddening between two dune systems that were, apparently, formed more or less contemporaneously? Also, according to WALKER'S (1967a) findings in the Sonoran Desert, dunes that were formed in the Pleistocene (and perhaps very late Pleistocene at that) should not have had sufficient time to properly redden post-depositionally.

In the vicinity of Sebkha Matti, in western Abu Dhabi (Enclosure 1), are Pliocene dune sands. They have been dated by means of mastodon teeth and bones found in an interbedded wadi conglomerate (see p.115 and GLENNIE and EVAMY, 1968). These sands are red and had probably already acquired much of their red colour by the end of the Pliocene.[1] Sands of similar age were probably remoulded by strong winds during the Pleistocene to give rise to the present dune distribution in the Buraimi area. Loss of pigment due to aeolian abrasion would be kept to a minimum because during the process of reshaping, the bulk of the sands were probably not moved, and for the rest, transport distances were possibly small. On the other hand, NORRIS (1969) suggests that in spite of minor losses by abrasion, sand grains can add to their coating of iron oxide even during aeolian transport. By analogy with the present, some lightening in the colour of the surface sands probably occurred during the Pleistocene. It is thought that this local loss of colour is now either masked by the stronger colour of the mass of sand that was not reworked, or, it is possible that a slight addition of red oxide to partly coloured sand grains is sufficient to bring back the full colour in a shorter time interval.

The winds that formed the large dunes of the Wahiba crossed no known source of red sediment; all the iron-oxide now found in these sediments is assumed to have been forming and ageing since sometime in the Pleistocene and they are still not red.[2] The wind that formed similar-looking large dunes in the Buraimi

---

[1] From regional evidence, it seems possible that desert conditions existed over much of southeast Arabia from the Miocene onwards.

[2] THESIGER (1959, p.307) noted that locally in the Wahiba Sands, the sand of the interdune areas was "rusty red whereas the dunes on either side were honey-coloured, both colours becoming paler as we travelled farther north". The same conditions seem also to apply to the large seif dunes of the Rajasthan Desert in India. They also are thought to have formed during the Pleistocene, are slightly reddened, and yet have no known source of red sediment.

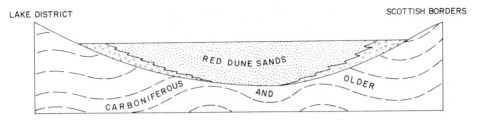

Fig.141. Relation between red beds and post-depositional conditions of reddening. Schematic cross-section through the Vale of Eden, England, to illustrate the relation between the New Red Sandstone dune accumulations, lateral wadi deposits and areas of outcrop.

area, however, did cross a known source of probably already-red dune sands that, away from the coast, were unlikely to have been cemented. Pleistocene reworking of older red sands seems a very plausible explanation for the occurrence of modern red dunes.

PERMIAN RED BEDS OF BRITAIN

In the Vale of Eden, the centre of the elongate Permo-Triassic basin is occupied by nearly 400 m of Permian aeolian sandstones that are red throughout. Wadi conglomerates are found on the flanks of the basin (Fig.141). All the quartz grains of aeolian sand have a coating of red haematite and yellowish-brown goethite. At the contact points between grains, no haematite exists (Fig.142) although haematite can be traced around the points of contact.[1] The surfaces of individual grains have circles free from pigment at the contact points. This suggests that the formation of the haematite coating is post-depositional.

Grain-like patches of white kaolinite are also coated with haematite and goethite. The kaolinite is thought to be a post-depositional product of alteration from feldspar. The feldspars were probably derived by erosion from Late Carboniferous (Stephanian) to Early Permian volcanics which, in southwest Scotland, are interbedded with dune sands (MYKURA, 1965), or from older igneous outcrops. They may be found in other beds as feldspar, in which case kaolinite need not be present, although feldspar, partly altered to kaolinite, is common (Fig.142, 143, 145). A similar situation of no pigment at the contact points between grains, and partial alteration of feldspar to kaolinite is found in the Permian dune sands of Devon (Fig.143) and the Midlands of England.

One of MILLOT's (1964) criteria for deducing palaeoclimates (Table III), implies that feldspars are destroyed in climates that are hot and humid. Kaolinite

---

[1] This was found to be the case in all thin sections examined. The evidence, as seen in thin section, does not, of course, permit one to say that none of the grains had any haematite coating prior to deposition, but it certainly implies that much, if not most, of the haematite is post-depositional.

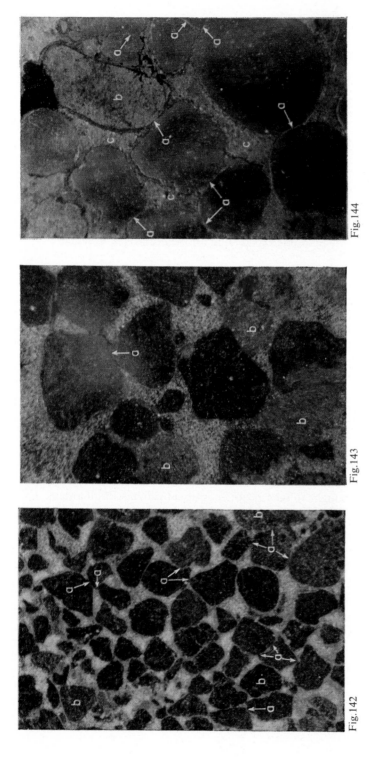

Fig.142

Fig.143

Fig.144

Fig.142. Haematite-coated grains of Permian dune sand with haematite-free contact area between the grains (*a*). Occasional partly altered feldspar (*b*). Pore space impregnated with plastic. GL.313. Hilton Beck, Vale of Eden. England. Magnification ×45; reflected light.

Fig.143. Haematite-coated grains of Permian dune sand with haematite-free contact area between the grains (*a*). Occasional partly altered feldspar (*b*). Pore space impregnated with plastic. GL.97. Mamhead House, south Devon, England. Magnification ×70; reflected light.

Fig.144. Carbonate-cemented Permian dune sand. Except for the contact area between grains (*a*) the grains are coated with haematite which in turn is encrusted with dolomite crystals. The dolomite crystals also, appear to have a thin coat of haematite. A feldspar grain (*b*) has been altered to kaolinite, but it also has a crust of iron-oxide coated dolomite. The remaining pore space (*c*) has been filled with calcite. GL.229. Downhill Quarry, Durham, England. Magnification ×45; reflected light.

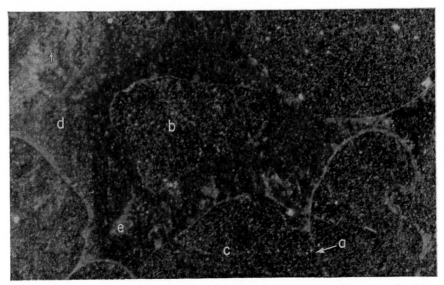

Fig.145. Calcite-cemented Permian dune sand. Haematite is absent at the point of contact *a* between grains, around quartz grain *b* and the upper half of grain *c*. The calcite has been stained with a solution of alizarin red S and potassium ferricyanide in hydrochloric acid. The calcite that is free of ferrous iron stains red (*d*) and is in contact with haematite-coated grains. The calcite that contains ferrous iron stains violet (*e*) and is in contact with haematite-free quartz surfaces (*b* and *c*). A grain of feldspar (*f*) is partly altered to kaolinite. GL.243. Crime Riggs Sand Pit, Durham, England. Magnification ×50; reflected light.

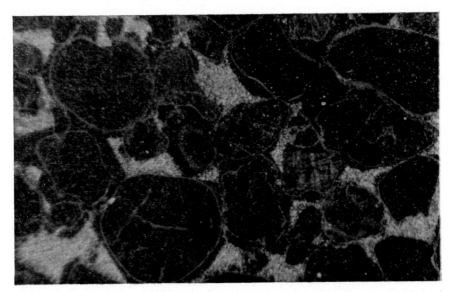

Fig.146. Grains of Permian quartz and feldspar dune sand with quartz overgrowths. The grains were coated with haematite prior to the formation of the overgrowths. Pore space impregnated with plastic. GL.338. Corncockle Quarry, Dumfriesshire, Scotland. Magnification ×50; reflected light.

apparently forms from feldspar under these conditions. It seems probable that below the arid surface of a desert, the humid and relatively hot conditions directly associated with the ground-water/air-filled pore-space interface reproduces a "physico-chemical climate" suitable for the alteration of feldspar to kaolinite, and for the oxidation and precipitation of ferrous solutions to haematite. That some feldspar-bearing horizons remain unaltered is the result, perhaps, of the chance circumstances of a locally more rapid rise in the permanent level of the ground water, or of local differences in the permeability of the sands.

On the flanks of a continental basin where wadi sedimentation predominates, post-depositional reddening will occur, but since there is likely to be more organic matter associated with wadi sediments than with dune sands, it is possible that in the former, patches may occur locally which have been permanently reduced to a green or even a white colour. Such discoloured patches are common in the wadi conglomerates of south Devon and the Vale of Eden. Sporadic patches of iron pyrites on the surfaces of some fossil desert sand grains may also indicate post-depositional organic reduction of a previous red coating.

THE APPARENT ANOMALY OF YELLOW ANCIENT DUNE SANDS

An area which does not appear to fit the pattern of reddening of dune sands is that of the Permian "Yellow Sands" of northeast England, which are shown in Fig.79. They directly overlie Carboniferous strata of Namurian and Westphalian age. The sands are themselves overlain by marine shales and dolomites of the Magnesian Limestone (Zechstein equivalent). The "Yellow Sands" are dune sands which, as their name implies, are yellow and not red, and yet they represent part of the same desert that filled other Permian continental basins with sands that are now red from Devon to the Highlands of Scotland (Elgin), and from Britain to Germany.

Many of the quartz grains from the "Yellow Sands" have little or no coloured oxides on their surfaces. X-ray analysis shows that part of the yellow colour comes from a thin coating of goethite and a trace of haematite on the surface of grain-like patches of white kaolinite. The sands are lightly cemented by calcite and dolomite. Occasionally, a yellow iron mineral (siderite or limonite?) is found disseminated through the calcite cement. If this yellow mineral is limonite, this might suggest early calcite cementation of the sands that arrested its alteration to haematite. Small patches and aggregates of haematite also occur in the intergranular spaces.

How is it that grains of kaolinite sometimes have a thick coat of iron oxide whilst many quartz grains have only a thin coat or no coat at all? One possible explanation involves the ground water chemistry that gave rise to a carbonate cement. In Fig.144 the lack of iron oxide at the contact points of the grains a implies that the deposition of a film of oxide on the sand grains was post-depositional.

A feldspar grain b has been altered to kaolinite. HALL (1967) has shown that plagioclase feldspars can contain 15 to 30 times as much iron in their molecules as alkali feldspars. Plagioclase feldspars are generally more readily destroyed by weathering than alkali feldspars, but they have been found preserved in desert sediments. K^+, Ca^+ and Na^+ ions are removed from feldspar during kaolinisation. It seems reasonable to assume that ferrous iron, resulting from post-burial alteration of plagioclase feldspar, could be trapped in the intercrystallite spaces on the surface of the kaolinite grains and later oxidised. Similar alteration of alkali feldspars would give rise to a much thinner zone of iron oxide. Quartz has no such intercrystallite spaces, so ferrous iron cannot be trapped. If a change to a reducing environment follows the original deposition of iron oxide, much of the oxide, if not all of it, will be lost from the surfaces of the quartz grains. This explanation would appear to fit the observed relationship between grains of much of the Permian "Yellow Sands".

In Fig.145, iron oxide is again absent at the contact point a between two grains. It also appears that the calcite cement has locally removed the iron oxide from around the central grain b and the upper surface of grain c.

When the calcite cement of Fig.145 is treated with acidified alizarin red S and potassium ferricyanide (EVAMY, 1963), calcite free of ferrous iron stains red (Fig. 145, d) and calcite containing ferrous iron stains violet (Fig.145, e). After staining, it can be seen that the iron-oxide films around the quartz grains are absent next to former pore space only where the cement contains ferrous iron.

It requires reducing conditions to incorporate ferrous iron in carbonates (EVAMY, 1969). B. D. Evamy (personal communication, 1965) suggests that the reducing environment concerned might first locally have taken the iron-oxide films into solution and that the ferrous iron so produced might then have been incorporated in the calcite cement e of Fig.145.

In Fig.144, a rather similar situation occurs, but is not so clear. The iron-oxide coated quartz grains are encrusted with a thin layer of dolomite crystals. Some solution of the iron oxide may have occurred, but is not so obvious. Some of the dolomite crystals also appear to have a very thin crust of iron oxide. The final stage of cementation was the deposition of pore-filling calcite c.

The pore-destroying calcite cementation seen in Fig.144 and 145 has resulted in a partial loss of colour subsequent to the diagenetic reddening. In Fig.146, the development of quartz overgrowths has had no effect on the iron-oxide films around the grains, suggesting that the diagenetic environment for their precipitation remained constantly oxidising. Fig.144 and 145 are of dune sands deposited on the continental margin of the transgressive Zechstein Sea. The ground water which gave rise to the calcite and dolomite cementation and subsequent loss in colour of the "Yellow Sands" is almost certainly associated with the Zechstein Sea. Fig.146, on the other hand, is, like Fig.142 and 143, of dune sands deposited in a continental basin where oxidising conditions prevailed continuously after deposition.

Further study may show that there is a more widespread palaeogeographical significance attached to some yellow and white fossil dune sands, in that they may imply deposition on a continental margin whose ground waters became saturated with respect to calcium carbonate derived from a transgressing sea. Had a former continental basin of desert deposition been transgressed by the sea, the red colour of the topmost sands might have been reduced as the result of carbonate cementation, but those beneath, whose ground waters remained oxidising, would still retain their red colour.

Non-red dune sands are also known that are overlain and underlain by red desert sediments. The diagenetic processes that brought about these local colour differences are still not fully understood. Much has yet to be learned about the authigenic formation of clay films and quartz and feldspar overgrowths on grains of fossil desert sand, and their relation to colour and diagenetic environment.

THE NECESSITY FOR WATER IN THE FORMATION OF RED DESERT SEDIMENTS

WALKER'S (1967a) criteria for the in-situ reddening of desert sediments appear to be sound. Although he implies the necessity for the presence of water to bring about the diagenetic changes that result in the reddening of desert sediments, he says little about it. Whilst concurring with Walker, the present writer also believes that much of the oxidation of iron in solution takes place at the interface between the ground-water saturated sediment below the water table and the air-filled pore space above. In support of the idea, oxidation of ferrous iron has been noticed in the laboratory by BLOOMFIELD (1964) at the interface between air and water in a water-saturated soil (see also the discussion SCHMALZ, 1968; WALKER, 1968). This principle also applies to the seasonally flooded wadi and river sediments and locally, to dune sands that may acquire a perched water table following rain.

Rain water is known to remain in the pore spaces of mobile dune sands for many years. THESIGER (1948, p.4) refers to vegetation deriving moisture from sand dunes in the Rub al Khali which had received no rainfall for at least four years. The writer has also encountered moist sand when digging deeply into the base of desert sand dunes. Such moisture, in the form of perched water tables or adhering around the contact points between grains even without free ground water, could well account for some minor reddening (such as is seen in the darker colours of the older dunes of the Rajasthan Desert or the Wahiba Sands), but is thought unlikely to cause strong reddening of the total dune sediment as seen in the Permian dune sands of southwest Scotland or the Vale of Eden. A similar argument may be applied in connection with the frequent and often heavy dews encountered in desert regions. The surface grains which are dampened are those which are most likely to suffer further transport and abrasion. There is, moreover, less chance of the grains, coming into contact with a solution containing ferrous iron.

For dune sands to become strongly reddened throughout their total thickness, they must first be buried to the level of the water table in order to come into contact with ferrous solutions. Then, repeated daily and annual fluctuations in the level of the water table will permit the formation of the red oxides of iron over a zone of sediment a metre or more in thickness. As the desert basin slowly fills with sediment, this fluctuating water table will also slowly rise and will soak buried dune sands that have not previously been wet, thereby assisting in the alteration of iron-bearing minerals and permitting ferrous solutions to come into contact with the sand grains. Annual fall in the level of the water table will permit drying of the sand grains and oxidation of ferrous iron to ferric iron. In time, all the sediment through which the interface between the ground water and air-filled pore-space passes will be reddened.

The same principle should apply to annually flooded wadi sediments, or sediments that are affected by the annual rise and fall of the water level in tropical rivers which are controlled by seasonal rainfall.

In contrast to the above ideas, BERNER (1969) supports WALKER (1967a, 1968) in thinking that yellow limonite can be converted into red haematite within water-saturated sediments.

The solution which provides the ferrous iron is reducing. It must have, however, a very low reducing capacity, so that contact of this solution with any previously deposited iron oxide will not lead to re-solution of the oxide. This is thought to be the case for the following reasons:

The most common reducing agents encountered in sediment are dissolved sulphide (S^{2-}) and organic matter. If dissolved sulphide is present, this would react with ferric oxide to form pyrite. Since this, in general, is not found, the presence of sulphide in quantities large enough to redissolve the ferric oxide may be excluded. Plants are generally absent from desert sediments except on stabilised dunes and wadi sediments, where they are usually oxidised soon after they die. This lack of organic matter, together with the absence of sulphide, leads one to assume that there are insufficient reducing agents in desert basins to reduce ferric oxide to ferrous oxide. The sediment will, therefore, normally retain its red colour after it has passed permanently beneath the water table.

CRITERIA FOR THE RECOGNITION OF A DESERT PALAEOCLIMATE

The palaeoclimatological significance of desert sandstones has been discussed in some detail by OPDYKE (1961), and some of the problems connected with the recognition of arid and hot climates of the past have been discussed by McKEE (1964). Following Millot's climatic criteria given in Table III, additional criteria indicative of desert conditions of deposition in ancient sediments are given in Table IV. They are mostly additional to the criteria already given in chapter 2 for the recognition of ancient desert sediments and are closely allied to the problem of why some ancient desert sediments are red.

TABLE IV

MILLOT'S (1964) CLIMATIC CRITERIA APPLIED TO DESERTS

A. Modern desert sediments	B. Ancient desert sediments
Polycrystalline grains occur	Polycrystalline grains occur
Feldspars are preserved	"Grains" of kaolinite are thought to represent diagenetic alteration from grains which were deposited as feldspar, especially plagioclase feldspar; alkali feldspars often partly or wholly preserved
Quartz grains are not micro-fracture	Quartz grains are not post-depositionally micro-fracture
Quartz grains are not corroded; they are usually "frosted" at the time of deposition	Quartz grains are only corroded if they are cemented by calcite or dolomite; otherwise the original "frosting" is still apparent
Grains not normally covered with a strong coating of red iron oxide unless they were derived from nearby red outcrop or already red wadi or dune sediments	Grains often strongly red in colour; evidence of former red colour sometimes visible in sediments that are now yellow, or almost grey or white
Larger detrital aeolian grains are often rounded; no overgrowths present on grains of quartz or feldspar	Larger detrital aeolian grains are often rounded but may develop overgrowths on grains of quartz and feldspar both before and after reddening
The clays are usually detrital, in which case their composition appears to depend entirely on provenance; some desert salt lakes contain authigenic Mg-rich clay minerals (D.H. Porrenga, personal communication, 1966)	The clays are detrital and their composition appears to depend on provenance and post-depositional alteration.

CONCLUSIONS

From a study of both ancient and modern desert sediments, it seems probable, as has been suggested by many recent authors, that most of the red pigment found in ancient desert sediments formed in situ.

Post-depositional reddening can take place if WALKER's (1967a) six critical factors for the breakdown of iron-bearing detrital grains and the formation of haematite are met. For this to happen, the desert sediments must become alternately wet and dry. These conditions are related to sporadic flooding of wadis or the seasonal change in the water level of rivers, and to the slow rise of a daily and annually fluctuating water table in a continental basin. A post-depositional origin for the reddening appears to be confirmed by the lack of an iron-oxide coating on the sand grains at their points of contact. This process often gives rise to the reddening of a complete desert sequence because there is a general lack of organic matter in deserts to cause later reduction of the pigment, and what little is originally present is rapidly removed by oxidation.

Walker's statement that red sediments probably form after deposition in any climate (environment) where these conditions are satisfied appears to be valid for some of the reddening of the Carboniferous "Barren Red Measures" of Britain. The conditions, in this case, resulted from the presence of an overlying desert in Permian time and a possible drastic initial lowering of the water table.

Some red desert sediments are the result of erosion and transport over short distances of sediments that are already red. Their occurrence is not thought to be widespread.

Calcite cement, precipitated from ground waters associated with a transgressing sea, may result in the partial or even complete removal of iron oxide which was earlier deposited on the surfaces of grains of quartz desert sand.

GLOSSARY[1]

Adhesion ripples: Adhesion ripples and adhesion warts form when dry sand is blown onto humid surfaces and is fixed there by the surface tension of the water that ascends through the sediment. It follows that a dry area of deflation (as the source of wind-blown sand) and a damp area of sedimentation are both necessary for their formation. Adhesion ripples are oriented transverse to the wind direction. The smooth windward slope is steeper than the wart-covered lee slope. Surfaces that are covered exclusively with adhesion warts form preferentially under conditions of strongly varying wind direction. Adhesion ripples and adhesion warts are different from other ripples in that the laminae within the ripples are concave upwards (REINECK, 1955).

Adhesion warts: Small sedimentary adhesion structures that commonly form part of the larger adhesion ripples (*see also* Adhesion ripples).

Arroyo: American synonym for wadi.

Avalanche slope: That slope which forms on the lee side of a dune at the maximum angle of repose for dry sand, 34°. Any tendency to overload this slope results in an avalanche of sand down the slope. Synonym for "slip-face".

Bahr: Interdune area in the region of Lake Chad, flooded during seasonal rise of the water of the lake.

Bir: Water well (Arabic). Similar to tawi.

Braided streams: A braided river is an interlacing network of distributaries with shoals and islands of gravel and sand between. The river channel as a whole is characteristically wide and shallow (HOLMES, 1965, p.538). This definition for braided rivers may be extended to the braided channels of wadis. The sediments of a braided system of wadi channels consist of inter-tonguing lenses of fluvial gravels and sands that have been subjected to deflation, and upon which aeolian sands may also have been deposited.

Calcrete: Horizon of hard, dense calcium carbonate or sediment cemented by calcium carbonate, found in soils of hot, arid and semi-arid regions.

Caliche: Surface sediments in arid or semi-arid areas that become cemented by evaporation of lime-rich ground water.

Deflation: The blowing away of dry incoherent rock material, sand and dust by the wind; a form of transport (denudation) chiefly at work in deserts. (CHALLINOR, 1962, *Dictionary of Geology*).

Desert: An almost barren tract of land in which precipitation is so scanty and spasmodic that it will not adequately support vegetation, and where the potential rate of evaporation far exceeds precipitation.

---

[1] A compilation of terms used in describing deserts and their land forms can be found in "A desert glossary" by STONE (1967, pp.211–268). His terms are listed according to country with a marked emphasis on North America—a reflection of the relatively much greater volume of literature associated with one of the world's less extensive areas of desert.

Dikaka: Accumulations of dune sand covered by scrub or grass vegetation, ex-
                            tended to include plant-root burrows in ancient dune sediments.

Eolianite: All consolidated sedimentary rocks deposited by the wind (STONE, 1967).
                            More commonly used in connection with calcite-cemented dune sands of
                            coastal regions.

Erg (pl. uruq):   Arabic word for vein. Applied to linear dunes or belts of dunes (HOLM,
                            1960, p.1329).

Falaj (foggara):   A long underground aquaduct used for irrigation in Arab countries
                            Synonym for the Persian qanat, or the Morrocan foggara.

Feidj: Sand-free interdune corridor in area of linear dunes.

Frosted sand grains: Sand grains, typical of desert and aeolian sediments, whose roughened
                            surface causes a scattering of the light; the opposite of glassy or polished
                            sand grains.

Gibber plain: Australian synonym for "serir". A gibber is an aborigine word for pebble.

Hammada: Rocky desert. A tableland or plateau of rock denuded by wind erosion.

Insolation: Exposure to radiation from the sun. More particularly, the term implies
                            the wide diurnal temperature range found in desert areas, and the tem-
                            perature differences encountered between the hot surface of rock exposed
                            to the sun's rays and the cooler interior of the rock, which are liable to
                            cause splitting.

Jebel (jabal, djebel):   Hill or mountain.

Kavir (kawir):   Desert (Persian).

Loess: Soft, porous, yellow or buff coloured accumulation of wind-laid particles
                            predominantly of silt size.

Mamlahah: Inland sebkhas that have been excavated for salt. (POWERS et al., 1966,
                            p.D100).

Monsoon: A monsoon is the type of wind system in which there is a complete or
                            almost complete reversal of prevailing direction from season to season. It
                            is especially prominent within the tropics on the eastern sides of great
                            landmasses (MOORE, 1949). The Southeast Trade Winds in the southern
                            Indian Ocean are warm and saturated with moisture. Because of intense
                            heating of the land in summer, a low-pressure area develops over north-
                            western India and West Pakistan which deflects the Southeast Trades
                            northwards across the equator. Part of these deflected trade winds travel
                            parallel to the east coast of Africa and then swing parallel to the South
                            Arabian coast (as the *Southwest Monsoon*) where the hill slopes facing the
                            sea receive some rain. These moist winds bring torrential rainfall to much
                            of central and northern India. This summer monsoon lasts between April
                            and September, although its duration at any one place depends upon its
                            geographical location. The winter monsoon of reversed direction usually
                            produces only light winds in northern India and Arabia because of the
                            protection afforded by the mountain masses to the north. Where the
                            Southwest Monsoon blows (north) across the Wahiba Sands, the elevation
                            of the sands above sea level is too low to induce rainfall over this hot area.
                            The winds are, however, strong. Similarly over the Rajasthan Desert, the
                            Southwest Monsoon brings little rainfall because of the desert's relatively
                            low elevation.

Qanat:	A long underground aquaduct used for irrigation in Iran. Persian synonym for falaj.
Ra's:	Arabic word for cape or headland.
Reg:	Algerian synonym for "serir".
Saltation:	The repeated forward movement of wind- (or water-) driven sand grains along low parabolic trajectories.
Sand drift:	Aeolian sand that is deposited as the result of a fall in the wind velocity. Commonly found on the leeward side of wind-breaks such as vegetation, boulders, outcrops or a sharp change in surface relief such as the bank of a wadi, or to the lee of a gap between two obstructions. It can also form on the windward side of obstructions where the wind passes over or around the obstruction but cannot maintain its velocity at the foot of it. The size of a sand drift is limited by the size and shape of the obstruction in whose protection it forms. Its surface can be covered with ripples. Where sand drifts around or envelops plant stems and branches, clearly defined lamellae are usually absent, but lamellae may be more clearly defined on the edges of the drift where the action of the wind is more constant.
Sand dune:	Wind-formed accumulation of sand in which the finest grains tend to be found at the top. Although sand dunes differ widely in morphology and in their relation to dune-forming winds, there are two simple types that appear to be basic: barchan (crescent-shaped dune, the bulk of whose foresets are directed down-wind), and seif (linear dune whose axis is sub-parallel to the predominant sand-transporting wind direction). The bulk of the dune bedding is directed almost at right angles to the axis of the dune.
Sand ripples:	Those surface forms whose wavelength depends on the wind strength and remains constant as time goes on. The coarsest grains collect at the crest.
Sand sea:	Area of sand dunes in which the interdune areas are covered by aeolian sand.
Sebkha, sabkha(t), sebkra (pl. sibakh):	Flat area of clay, silt or sand often with saline encrustations. Subdivided into:

(1) coastal sebkha: a coastal flat that occurs just above the level of the normal high tide in a hot, arid, desert climate. Its sediments consist of sand, silt or clay and its surface is often covered with a salt crust that results from evaporation of water drawn to the surface by capillary action and from occasional marine inundations. Its sediments are mostly derived from adjacent marine environments (commonly carbonate in composition) with an admixture of material of continental origin; they are liable to diagenetic alteration as the result of its environment. These sediments of the coastal sebkha are characterised by the presence of algal mats and the formation of evaporites (nodular anhydrite, gypsum and halite) and dolomite. During much of the year, the surface of the coastal sebkha is subject to deflation down to the level of the water table.

(2) Inland sebkha: flat areas of clay, silt or sand, often with saline encrustations. Their salts may be derived from intermittently flowing wadis that have no access to the sea, from fluctuating saline ground water, from relict salts left behind by an advancing coastline or from salt crystals blown from another locality, often the coast. The sediment may consist of clays and sands carried in wadis, wind-blown silt and sand trapped on the moist surface as adhesion ripples, or of small sand dunes and sporadically drifting sand that has migrated over the dry salt crust. (Often referred to in North America as a playa or salina.) Algae are known but algal mats have not been recognised.

Serir: Deflation lag of pebbles, often of alluvial origin, on the desert surface. Libyan synonym of "reg".

Shamal: Arabic word for north; applied to north or northwest wind that blows down the Persian Gulf.

Silcrete: Horizon of siliceous material found in hot, arid and semi-arid regions; possibly formed by silicification of a sediment.

Slip-face: The slope which forms when wind-blown sand from the windward side of a dune passes into relatively calm air of the leeward side. The maximum angle of repose for dry sand is 34°. Also referred to as "avalanche slope".

Tawi: Water well (Arabic). Similar to bir.

Wadi (pl. widyan): Desert watercourse, dry except after rain. The American equivalent is "arroyo". In mountainous areas, little sediment is deposited. Beyond the mountains, or in broad intermontane valleys, alluvial fans are formed by rapid deposition of sediment resulting from sporadic flow of water over a lessening slope; here, this flow of water may be in the form of a spreading sheet-flood, or may be confined to an interlacing network of distributaries. Beyond the limits of the fan, the wadis spread out over the desert plain unless confined by the presence of outcropping strata or sand dunes. The water in a wadi may flow into the sea, a desert (temporary?) lake or sebkha (inland or coastal); often there may be insufficient rain for the water to flow the full length of its channel. The unconsolidated fluvial sediments of a system of wadis may be deflated and so form an important source for aeolian sand. Conversely, aeolian sand may be deposited on the bed of a wadi and so form a part of the sedimentary sequence.

REFERENCES

ALIMEN, H., 1936. Étude sur le Stampien du bassin de Paris. *Mém. Soc. Géol. France*, 14: 309pp.

ALIMEN, H., 1944. Roches gréseuses à ciment calcaire du Stampien—Étude pétrographique. *Bull. Soc. Géol. France*, 14 (7-8-9): 307-329.

ALIMEN, H. et FENET, D., 1954. Granulométrie des sables d'erg aux environs de la Saoura Ougaita (Sahara occidental). *Compt. Rend.*, 239: 1231-1233.

ALLEN, J. R. L., 1963. Asymmetrical ripple marks and the origin of water-laid cosets of crossstrata. *Liverpool Manchester Geol. J.*, 3 (2): 187-236.

ALLEN, J. R. L., 1968a. On the character and classification of bed forms. *Geol. Mijnbouw*, 47 (3): 173-185.

ALLEN, J. R. L., 1968b. The nature and origin of bed-form hierarchies. *Sedimentology*, 10: 161-182.

ALMEIDA, F. F. M., 1953. Botucatú, a Triassic Desert of South America. In: *Déserts Actuels et Anciens—Congr. Géol. Intern., Compt. Rend., 19e, Algiers*, 1952, 7:9-24.

ANDERSON, R. V., 1947. Origin of the Libyan oasis basins. *Bull. Geol. Soc. Am.*, 58 (12):1163.

ARCHER, A. A., 1965. Red beds in the Upper Coal Measures of the western part of the South Wales coal field. *Bull. Geol. Surv. Gt. Brit.*, 23: 57-64.

ARNDT, H. H., WOOD, G. H. and TREXLER, J. P., 1962. Subdivision of the Catskill Formation in the western part of the Anthracite Region of Pennsylvania. *U.S. Geol. Surv., Profess. Papers*, 450-C: 32-36.

ATTIA, M. I., 1955. *Topography, Geology and Iron-ore Deposits of the District east of Aswan.* Geol. Surv., Mineral Resources Dept., Cairo, 262 pp.

AUDEN, J. B., 1952. Some geological and chemical aspects of the Rajasthan salt problem. *Proc. Symp. Rajasthan Desert-Bull. Natl. Inst. Sci. India*, 1:53-67.

BAGNOLD, R. A., 1941. *Physics of Blown Sand and Desert Dunes.* Methuen, Londen, 265 pp.

BAGNOLD, R. A., 1954. Experiments on a gravity dispersion of large solid spheres in a Newtonian fluid under stress. *Proc. Roy. Soc. London*, 225: 49-63.

BAGNOLD, R. A., 1956. The flow of cohesionless grains in fluids. *Phil. Trans. Roy. Soc. London, Ser. A*, 249: 235-297.

BAILEY, E. B., 1926. Subterranean penetration by a desert climate. *Geol. Mag.*, 53: 276-280.

BALL, J., 1927. Problems of the Libyan Desert. *Geograph. J.*, 70: 209-244.

BALL, J., 1933. The Qattara Depression of the Libyan Desert and the possibility of its utilisation for power production. *Geograph. J.*, 82: 289-314.

BALL, M. M., 1967, Carbonate sand bodies of Florida and the Bahamas. *J. Sediment. Petrol.*, 37 (2): 556-591.

BARBOUR, G. B., 1936. The loess of China. *Intern. Geol. Congr., 16th*, New York, N.Y., (2):777-778.

BARRELL, J., 1908. Relations between climate and terrestrial deposits. *J. Geol.*, 16: 159-190; 255- 295; 363-384.

BARRELL, J., 1916. The dominantly fluviatile origin under seasonal rainfall of the Old Red Sandstone. *Bull. Geol. Soc. Am.*, 27: 345-386.

BEAUMONT, P., 1968. Salt weathering on the margin of the Great Kavir, Iran. *Geol. Soc. Am. Bull.*, 79: 1683-1684.

BERNER, R. A., 1969. Goethite stability and the origin of red beds. *Geochim. Cosmochim. Acta*, 33: 267–273.

BEYDOUN, Z. R., 1966. Geology of the Arabian Peninsula. Eastern Aden Protectorate and part of Dhufar. *U.S. Geol. Surv., Profess. Papers*, 560-H: 1–49.

BIGARELLA, J. J. and SALAMUNI, R., 1961. Early Mesozoic wind patterns as suggested by dune bedding in the Botucatú Sandstone of Brazil and Uruguay. *Bull. Geol. Soc. Am.*, 72: 1089–1106.

BIGARELLA, J. J. and SALAMUNI, R., 1964. Palaeowind patterns in the Botucatú Sandstone (Triassic–Jurassic) of Brazil and Uruguay. In: A. E. M. NAIRN (Editor), *Problems in Palaeoclimatology*. Interscience, New York, N.Y., pp. 406–409.

BIGARELLA, J. J., BECKER, R. D. and DUARTE, G. M., 1969. Coastal dune structures from Parana (Brazil). *Marine Geol.*, 7: 5–55.

BLACKWELDER, E., 1928. Mudflow as a geologic agent in semi-arid mountains. *Bull. Geol. Soc. Am.*, 39: 465–484.

BLACKWELDER, E., 1933. The insolation hypothesis of rock weathering. *Am. J. Sci., 5th Ser.*, 26 (152): 97–113.

BLACKWELDER, E., 1936. The insolation hypothesis of rock weathering (Abstract). *Intern. Geol. Congr., 16th*, New York, N.Y., (2):780–781.

BLISSENBACH, E., 1954. Geology of alluvial fans in semi-arid regions. *Bull. Geol. Soc. Am.*, 65 175–190.

BLOOMFIELD, C., 1964. Mobilization and immobilization phenomena in soils. In: A. E. M. NAIRN (Editor), *Problems in Palaeoclimatology*. Interscience, New York, N.Y., pp.661–665.

BLUCK, B. J., 1965. The sedimentary history of some Triassic conglomerates in the Vale of Glamorgan, South Wales. *Sedimentology*, 4 (3): 225–246.

BLUCK, B. J., 1967. Deposition of some Upper Old Red Sandstone conglomerates in the Clyde area: a study in the significance of bedding. *Scot. J. Geol.*, 3 (2): 139–167.

BLUNDELL, C. R. K., 1952. The succession and structure of the northeastern area of the South Wales Coal Field. *Quart. J. Geol. Soc. London*, 107: 307–333.

BLUNDELL, C. R. K. and MOORE, L. R., 1960. Mid-Coal Measures "Red Beds" in the South Wales Coal Field. *Congr. Avan. Études Stratigraph. Géol. Carbonifère, Compt. Rend., 4°*, 1:41–48.

BOBECK, H., 1959. Features and formation of the Great Kawir and Masilek. *Arid Zone Res. Centre, Univ. Tehran, Publ.*, 2: 63 pp.

BORCHERT, H., 1965. Formation of marine sedimentary iron ores. In: J. P. RILEY and G. SKIRROW (Editors), *Chemical Oceanography*. Academic Press, London, 2nd ed., pp.159–204.

BOURCART, J., 1937. Les pénéplains du Maroc et du Sahara. In: *Melanges de Géographie et d'Orientalisme offert à E. F. Gauthier*. Arrault, Tours, 464 pp.

BOURCART, J., 1938. La marge continentale. Essai sur les regressions et transgressions marines. *Bull. Soc. Géol. France, 5° Ser.*, 8: 393–474.

BOWMAN, T. S., 1926. *Report on Boring for Oil in Egypt*. Mines and Quarries Dept., Cairo, Sect. 2, 91 pp.

BRAMER, H., 1965. Bestimmung der Oberflächenbeschaffenheit von Quarzkörnern mit dem Elektronenmikroskop. *Geologie*, 14 (9): 1114–1116.

BREDEHOEFT, I. D., BLYTH, C. R., WHITE, W. A. and MAXEY, G. B., 1963. Possible mechanism for concentration of brines in subsurface formations. *Bull. Am. Assoc. Petrol. Geologists*, 47: 257–269.

BRUCK, P. M., DEDMAN, R. E. and WILSON, R. C. L., 1967. The New Red Sandstone of Raasay and Scalpay, Inner Hebrides. *Scot. J. Geol.* 3 (2): 168–180.

BRÜCKNER, W. D., 1966. Salt weathering and Inselbergs. *Nature*, 210 (5038): 832.

BRYAN, K., 1945. Glacial versus desert origin of loess. *Am. J. Sci.*, 143: 245–248.

BUHSE, F. A., 1892. Die grosse Persische Salzwüste und ihre Umgebung. *Deut. Rundschau Geograph. Statistik*, 15: 49–59.

BUROLLET, P. F. et MANDERSCHEID, G., 1965. Le Crétacé inférieur en Tunisie et en Libye. *Mém. Bur. Rech. Géol. Minières*, 34:785–794.

BUSSON, G., 1967. Mesozoic of southern Libya. In: L. MARTIN (Editor), *Guidebook to the Geology and History of Tunisia—Petrol. Exploration Soc. Libya, Ann. Field Conf.*, 9 th, pp.131–151.

BUTLER, G. P., 1969. Modern evaporite deposition and geochemistry of coexisting brines, the sabkha, Trucial Coast, Arabian Gulf. *J. Sediment. Petrol.*, 39 (1): 70–89.

BUTLER, G. P., KENDALL, C. G. S. C., KINSMANN, D. J. J., SHEARMAN, D. J. and SKIPWITH, P. A.,
    1965. Recent evaporite deposits along the Trucial Coast of the Arabian Gulf. *Proc. Geol.
    Soc. London*, 1623: 246–252.
BUTZER, K. W., 1961. Climatic change in arid regions since the Pliocene. In: L. D. STAMP (Editor),
    A History of Land Use in Arid Regions—UNESCO Arid Zone Res., 17:31–56.
BUTZER, K. W., 1963. The last "pluvial" phase of the Eurafrican sub-tropics. In: *Changes in
    Climate—UNESCO Arid Zone Res.*, 20:211–221.
CAILLEUX, A., 1937. Traces d'action du vent dans les dépôts du fond de la mer du Nord. *Compt.
    Rend. Soc. Géol. France*, 5:63–65.
CAMPBELL, R. L., 1968. Stratigraphic applications of dipmeter data in Mid-Continent. *Bull.
    Am. Assoc. Petrol. Geologists*, 52 (9): 1700–1719.
CAPOT-REY, R., 1949. La morphologie de l'Erg occidental. *Trav. Inst. Rech. Sci. Algiers*, 2: 69–103.
CARTER H. J., 1849. On Foraminifera, their organisation and their existence in a fossilized state
    in Arabia, Sindh, Kutch and Khattyawar. *J. Bombay Branch Roy. Asiatic Soc.*, 3: 158–173.
CHAPMAN, F., 1900. Notes on the consolidated aeolian sands of Kathiawar. *Quart. J. Geol. Soc.
    London*, 56: 584–589.
CHOUBERT, G., 1953. Les rapports entre les formations marines et continentales quaternaires.
    Actes IV. Congr. INQUA, pp.576–591.
COOKE, R. U. and SMALLEY, I. J., 1968. Salt weathering in deserts. *Nature*, 220: 1226–1227.
COOPER, W. S., 1958. Coastal sand dunes of Oregon and Washington. *Mem. Geol. Soc. Am.*,
    72:169 pp.
COOPER, W. S., 1967. Coastal dunes of California. *Mem. Geol. Soc. Am.*, 104: 131 pp.
COQUE, R. and JAUZEIN, R., 1967. The geomorphology and quaternary geology of Tunisia (transl.
    by: G. L. de Coster). In: L. MARTIN (Editor), *Guidebook to the Geology and History of
    Tunisia—Petrol Exploration Soc. Libya Ann. Field Conf., 9th, Tripoli* pp.227–257.
CURRAY, J. R., 1956. The analysis of two-dimensional orientation data. *J. Geol.*, 64: 117–131.
CURTIS, L., EVANS, G., KINSMAN, D. J. J. and SHEARMAN, D. J., 1963. Association of dolomite and
    anhydrite in the Recent sediments of the Persian Gulf. *Nature*, 197 (4868): 679–680.
DAVIS, W. M., 1936. Geomorphology of mountainous deserts. *Intern. Geol. Congress, 16th*, New
    York, N.Y., 2:703–714.
DE LAPPARENT, J., 1937. Les phénomènes anciens de rubéfaction dans le Sahara central. *Compt.
    Rend.*, 205: 196–198.
DE SITTER, L. U., 1947. Diagenesis of oil field brines. *Bull. Am. Assoc. Petrol. Geologists*, 31:
    2030–2040.
DE TERRA, H., 1933. Blackwelder's challenge of the insolation hypothesis of rock weathering.
    Am. J. Sci., 26 (152): 523–524.
DI CESARE, F., FRANCHINO, A. and SOMMARUGA, C., 1963. The Pliocene-Quaternary of Giarabub
    Erg region. *Rev. Inst. Franc. Pétrole, Ann. Combust. Liquides*, 18 (10): 1344–1362.
DICKEY, P. A., 1968. Contemporary nonmarine sedimentation in Soviet Central Asia. *Bull.
    Am. Assoc. Petrol. Geologists*, 52 (12): 2396–2421.
DOEGLAS, D. J., 1962. The structure of sedimentary deposits of braided rivers. *Sedimentology*,
    1: 167–190
DORSEY, G. E., 1926. The origin of the colour of red beds. *J. Geol.*, 34: 131–143.
DOWNING, R. A. and SQUIRREL, H. C., 1965. On the red and green beds in the Upper Coal Meas-
    ures of the eastern part of the South Wales Coal Field. *Bull. Geol. Surv. Gt. Brit.*, 23:
    45–56.
DUBIEF, J., 1952. Le vent et le déplacement du sable au Sahara. *Trav. Inst. Rech. Sahariennes*, 8:
    123–162.
DUNBAR, C. O. and ROGERS, J., 1957. *Principles of Stratigraphy*. Wiley, New York, N.Y., 356 pp.
DUNHAM, K. C., 1953. Red colouration in desert formations of Permian and Triassic age in
    Britain. *Congr. Géol. Intern., 19°, Algiers*, 7: 25–32.
EDMUNDS, F. H. and OAKLEY, K. P., 1958. *British Regional Geology, The Central England District*
    (2nd ed. revised). H. M. Stationary Office, London, 90 pp.
EMERY, K. O. and COX, D. C., 1956. Beach rock in the Hawaiian Islands. *Pacific Sci.*, 382–402.
ENGEL, C. G. and SHARP, R. P., 1958. Chemical data on desert varnish. *Bull. Geol. Soc. Am.*, 69:
    487–518.

EVAMY, B. D., 1963. The application of a chemical staining technique to a study of dedolomitisation. *Sedimentology*, 2: 164–170.

EVAMY, B. D., 1969. The precipitational environment and correlation of some calcite cements deduced from artificial staining. *J. Sediment. Petrol.*, 39 (2): 787–793.

EVANS, G., KENDALL, C. G. ST. C. and SKIPWITH, P., 1964a. Origin of the coastal flats, the sabkha, of the Trucial Coast, Persian Gulf. *Nature*, 202 (4934): 759–761.

EVANS, G., KINSMAN, D. J. J. and SHEARMAN, D. J., 1964b. A reconnaissance survey of the environment of Recent carbonate sedimentation along the Trucial Coast, Persian Gulf. In: L. M. J. U. VAN STRAATEN (Editor), *Deltaic and Shallow Marine Deposits*. Elsevier, Amsterdam, pp.129–135.

EVANS, J. W., 1900. Mechanically-formed limestones from Junagarh (Kathiawar) and other localities. *Quart. J. Geol. Soc. London*, 56: 559–583.

FAIRBRIDGE, R. W., 1962. World sea-level and climatic changes. *Quaternaria*, 6: 111–134.

FAIRBRIDGE, R. W., 1964. African Ice-Age aridity. In: A. E. M. NAIRN (Editor), *Problems in Palaeoclimatology*. Interscience, New York, N.Y., pp.356–360.

FEDDEN, F., 1884. The geology of the Kathiawar Peninsula in Guzerat. *Mem. Geol. Surv. India*, 21 (2): 1–64.

FINKEL, H. J., 1959. The barchans of southern Peru. *J. Geol.*, 67: 614–647.

FLINT, R. F., 1959. Pleistocene climates in eastern and southern Africa. *Bull. Geol. Soc. Am.*, 70: 343–374.

FLINT, R. F. and BOND, G., 1968. Pleistocene sand ridges and pans in western Rhodesia. *Geol. Soc. Am. Bull.*, 79 (3): 299–314.

FRIEDMAN, G. M., 1959. Identification of carbonate minerals by staining methods. *J. Sediment. Petrol.*, 29: 87–97.

FRIEDMAN, G. M., 1964. Early diagenesis and lithification in carbonate sediments. *J. Sediment. Petrol.*, 34 (4): 777–813.

FRIEND, P. F., 1966. Clay fractions and colours of some Devonian red beds in the Catskill Mountains, U.S.A. *Quart. J. Geol. Soc. London*, 122: 273–292.

GAUTHIER, E. F., 1935. *Sahara (The Great Desert)*. Columbia Univ. Press., New York, N.Y., 264 pp.

GERMANOV, A. I., VOLKOV, G. A., LISTIN, A. K. and SEREBRENNIKOV, V. S., 1959. Investigation of the oxidation-reduction potential of ground waters. *Geochemistry*, 3: 322–329.

GERSTER, G., 1960. *Sahara*. Barrie and Rockliff, London, 302 pp.

GÈZE, B., 1947. Paléosols et sols dûs à l'évolution actuelle. Importance relative en pédologie théorique et appliquée. *Ann. École Natl. Agr. Montpellier*, 27: 263–288.

GIBBONS, S. G., 1967. Shell content in quartzose beach and dune sands, Dee Why, New South Wales. *J. Sediment. Petrol.*, 37 (3): 869–878.

GILL, W. D., 1951. The stratigraphy of the Siwalik Series in the northern Potwar, Punjab, Pakistan. *Quart. J. Geol. Soc. London*, 107 (4): 375–394.

GILREATH, J. A. and MARICELLI, J. J., 1964. Detailed stratigraphic control through dip computations. *Bull. Am. Assoc. Petrol. Geologists*, 48 (12): 1902–1910.

GINSBURG, R. N., 1953. Beach rock in South Florida. *J. Sediment. Petrol.*, 23 (2): 85–92.

GLENNIE, K. W. and EVAMY, B. D., 1968. Dikaka: Plants and plant-root structures associated with aeolian sand. *Palaeogeography. Palaeoclimatol., Palaeoecol.*, 4: 77–87.

GLENNIE, K. W. and ZIEGLER, M. A., 1964. The Siwalik Formation in Nepal. *Intern. Geol. Cong.*, 22nd, New Delhi, Sect. 15, pp. 82–95.

GODDARD, E. N., 1951. *Rock-Colour Chart*. Geol. Soc. Am., New York, N.Y.

GREEN, R., 1961. Palaeoclimatic significance of evaporites. In: A. E. M. NAIRN (Editor), *Descriptive Palaeoclimatology*. Interscience, New York, N.Y., pp.61–88.

HALL, A., 1967. The distribution of some major and trace elements in feldspars from the Rosses and Ardara granite complexes, Donegal, Ireland. *Geochim. Cosmochim. Acta*, 31 (5): 835–847.

HAMILTON, N., OWENS, W. H. and REES, A. I., 1968. Laboratory experiments on the production of grain orientation in shearing sand. *J. Geol.*, 76: 465–472.

HARE, F. K., 1961. The causation of the arid zone. In: L. D. STAMP (Editor), *A History of Land Use in Arid Regions—UNESCO Arid Zone Res.*, 17:25–30.

HARMS, J. C., 1965. Sandstone dikes in relation to Laramide faults and stress distribution in the southern Front Range, Colorado. *Geol. Soc. Am. Bull.*, 76: 981–1002.

HARSHBARGER, J. W., REPENNING, C. A. and IRWIN, J. H., 1957. Stratigraphy of the uppermost Triassic and Jurassic rocks of the Navajo country. *U.S. Geol. Surv., Profess. Papers*, 291: 74 pp.

HASTENRATH, S. L., 1967. The barchans of the Arequipa region, southern Peru. *Ann. Geomorphol.*, N. S., 2 (3): 300–331.

HIGGINS, C. G., 1956. Formation of small ventifacts. *J. Geol.*, 64: 506–516.

HILLS, E. S., OLLIER, C. D. and TWIDALE, C. R., 1966. Geomorphology. In: E. S. HILLS (Editor), *Arid Lands*. Methuen, London, pp.53–75.

HINZE, C. und MEISCHNER, D., 1968. Gibt es Rezente Rot-Sedimente in der Adria? *Marine Geol.*, 6: 53–71.

HOBBS, W. H., 1907. *Earthquakes*. Appleton, London, 336 pp.

HOFFMEISTER, J. E. and MULTER, H. G., 1965. Fossil mangrove reef of Key Biscayne, Florida. *Geol. Soc. Am. Bull.*, 76: 845–852.

HOLM, D. A., 1953. Dome-shaped dunes of Central Nejd, Saudi Arabia. In: *Déserts Actuals et Anciens—Congr. Géol. Intern., Compt. Rend., 19e, Algiers*, 7.

HOLM, D. A., 1960. Desert geomorphology in the Arabian Peninsula. *Science*, 132 (3427): 1369–1379.

HOLMES, A., 1965. *Principles of Physical Geology* (revised ed.). Nelson, London and Edinburgh, 1288 pp.

HÖRNER, N. G., 1936. Geomorphic processes in continental basins of Central Asia. *Intern. Geol. Congr., 16th*, New York, N.Y., 2:721–735.

HOUBOLT, J. J. H. C., 1968. Recent sediments in the southern bight of the North Sea. *Geol. Mijnbouw*, 47 (4): 245–273.

INMAN, D. L., EWING, G. C. and CORLISS, J. B., 1966. Coastal sand dunes of Guerrero Negro, Baja California, Mexico. *Geol. Soc. Am. Bull.*, 77: 787–802.

JONES, G. P., 1965. Red beds in northeastern Nigeria. *Sedimentology*, 5 (3): 235–247.

JOPLING, A. V., 1963. Hydraulic studies on the origin of bedding. *Sedimentology*, 2: 115–121.

KAISER, E., 1925. *Die Diamantenwüste Südwest-Afrikas*. Reimer, Berlin, 535 pp.

KASSAS, M., 1966. Plant life in deserts. In: E. S. HILLS (Editor), *Arid Lands*. Methuen, London, pp. 145–180.

KENDALL, C. G. ST. C. and SKIPWITH, P. A. D'E., 1968. Recent algal mats of a Persian Gulf lagoon. *J. Sediment. Petrol.*, 38 (4): 1040–1058.

KENDALL, C. G. ST., and SKIPWITH, P. A. D'E., 1969. Geomorphology of a Recent shallow-water carbonate province: Khor al Bazam, Trucial Coast, southwest Persian Gulf. *Geol. Soc. Am. Bull.*, 80: 865–892.

KIERSCH, G. A., 1950. Small-scale structures and other features of Navajo Sandstone, northern part of San Rafael Swell, Utah. *Bull. Am. Assoc. Petrol. Geologists*, 34: 923–942.

KLITZSCH, E., 1966. Geology of the northeast flank of the Murzuk Basin. In: J. J. WILLIAMS (Editor), *South-central Libya and Northern Chad. A Guidebook to the Geology and Prehistory—Petrol. Exploration Soc. Libya, Ann. Field Conf., 8th, Tripoli*, pp.19–32.

KOZARY, M. T., DUNLAP, J. C. and HUMPHREY, W. E., 1968. Incidence of saline deposits in geologic time. In: R. B. MATTOX (Editor), *Saline Deposits—Geol. Soc. Am., Spec. Papers*, 88:43–57.

KRYNINE, P. D., 1949. The origin of red beds. *Trans. N.Y. Acad. Sci.*, 2: 60–68.

KRINSLEY, D. H. and FUNNEL, B. M. 1965. Environmental history of quartz sand grains from the Lower and Middle Pleistocene of Norfolk, England. *Quart. J. Geol. Soc. London*, 121: 435–461.

KRINSLEY, D. H. and DONAHUE, J., 1968a. Environmental interpretation of sand grain surface textures by electron microscopy. *Geol. Soc. Am. Bull.*, 79: 743–748.

KRINSLEY, D. H. and DONAHUE, J., 1968b. Methods to study surface textures of sand grains; a discussion. *Sedimentology*, 10: 217–221.

KUENEN, Ph. H., 1960. Experimental abrasion, 4. Eolian action. *J. Geol.*, 68: 435–449.

KUENEN, Ph. H. and PERDOK, W. G., 1962. Experimental abrasion, 5. Frosting and defrosting of quartz grains. *J. Geol.*, 70: 648–658.

LAMB, H. H., 1961. Fundamentals of climate. In: A. E. M. NAIRN (Editor), *Descriptive Palaeoclimatology*. Interscience, New York, N.Y., pp.8–44.

LAMING, D. J. C., 1965. Age of the New Red Sandstone in S. Devonshire. *Nature*, 207 (4997): 624–625.

LAMING, D. J. C., 1966. Imbrication, palaeocurrents and other sedimentary features in the Lower New Red Sandstone, Devonshire, England. *J. Sediment. Petrol.*, 36 (4): 940–959.

LAWRENCE, T. E., 1935. *Seven Pillars of Wisdom*. Jonathan Cape, London, 700 pp.

LOGAN, R. F., 1960. *The Central Namib Desert, South West Africa*. National Research Council, Washington, D.C., Publ. nr. 758, 162 pp.

LOTZE, F., 1957. *Steinsalz und Kalisalze*. Borntraeger, Berlin, 455 pp.

LYONS, H. G., 1894, On the stratigraphy and physiography of the Lybian Desert of Egypt. *Quart. J. Geol. Soc. London*, 50: 531–547.

MACKENZIE, F. T., 1964a. Bermuda Pleistocene eolianites and palaeowinds. *Sedimentology*, 3 (1): 52–64.

MACKENZIE, F. T., 1964b. Geometry of Bermuda calcareous dune cross-bedding. *Science*, 144: 1449–1450.

MADIGAN, C. T., 1946. The Simpson Desert Expedition, 1939, 6. Geology—The sand formations. *Trans. Roy. Soc. S. Australia*, 70 (1): 45–63.

MÄGDEFRAU, K., 1956. *Paläobiologie der Pflanzen*, 3. Aufl. Fischer, Jena, 443 pp.

MATTHEWS, R. K., 1968. Carbonate diagenesis: equilibration of sedimentary mineralogy to the subaerial environment; Coral Cap of Barbados, West Indies. *J. Sediment. Petrol.*, 38 (4): 1110–1119.

MAXSON, J. H., 1940. Fluting and facetting of rock fragments. *J. Geol.*, 48: 717–751.

McBURNEY, C. B. M., 1960. *The Stone Age of Northern Africa*. Penguin Books, Harmondsworth, 288 pp.

McCoy, F. W., NOKLEBERG, W. J. and NORRIS, R. M., 1967. Speculations on the origin of the Algodones Dunes, California. *Geol. Soc. Am. Bull.*, 78: 1039–1044.

McGEE, W. J., 1897. Sheet-flood erosion. *Bull. Geol. Soc. Am.*, 8: 87–112.

McKEE, E. D., 1934. The Coconino Sandstone-its history and origin. *Carnegie Inst. Wash. Publ.*, 440: 77–115.

McKEE, E. D., 1940. Three types of cross-lamination in Palaeozoic rocks of northern Arizona. *Am. J. Sci.*, 238: 811–824.

McKEE, E. D., 1945. Small-scale structures in the Coconino Sandstone of northern Arizona. *J. Geol.*, 53: 316–320.

McKEE, E. D., 1954. Stratigraphy and history of the Moenkopi Formation of Triassic age. *Geol. Soc. Am. Mem.*, 61: 133 pp.

McKEE, E. D., 1962. Origin of the Nubian and similar sandstones. *Geol. Rundschau*, 52 (2): 551–582.

McKEE, E. D., 1964. Problems on the recognition of arid and of hot climates of the past. In: A. E. M. NAIRN (Editor), *Problems in Palaeoclimatology*. Interscience, New York, N.Y., pp.367–377.

McKEE, E. D., 1966a. Structures of dunes at White Sands National Monument, New Mexico (and a comparison with structures of dunes from other selected areas). *Sedimentology*, 7 (1): 1–69.

McKEE, E. D., 1966b. Significance of climbing-ripple structure. *U.S. Geol. Surv., Profess. Papers*, 550-D: 94–103.

McKEE, E. D. and TIBBITTS, G. C., 1964. Primary structures of a seif dune and associated deposits in Libya. *J. Sediment. Petrol.*, 34 (1): 5–17.

McKEE, E. D., REYNOLDS, M. A. and BAKER, C. H., 1962. Experiments on intraformational recumbent folds in cross-bedded sand. *U.S. Geol. Surv., Profess. Papers*, 450-D; 155–160.

McKEE, E. D., CROSBY, E. J. and BERRYHILL, H. L., 1967. Flood deposits, Bijou Creek, Colorado, June 1965. *J. Sediment. Petrol.*, 37 (3): 829–851.

MEIGS, P., 1953. World distribution of arid and semi-arid homoclimates. In: *Reviews of Research on Arid Zone Hydrology—UNESCO Arid Zone Res.*, 1:203–210.

MERRIAM, R., 1969. Source of sand dunes of southeastern California and nortwestern Sonora, Mexico. *Geol. Soc. Am. Bull.*, 80: 531–534.

MIDDLETON, G. V., 1965. Antidune cross-bedding in a large flume. *J. Sediment. Petrol.*, 35: 922–927.

MILLER, D. N. and FOLK, R. L., 1955. Occurrence of detrital magnetite and ilmenite in red sediments: new approach to significance of red beds. *Bull. Am. Assoc. Petrol. Geologists*, 39: 338–345.

MILLOT, G., 1964. *Géologie des Argiles*. Masson, Paris, 500 pp.

MILLOT, G., PERRIAUX, J. and LUCAS, J., 1961. Signification climatique de la couleur rouge des grès Permo-Triassiques et des grandes séries détritiques rouges. *Bull. Serve Carte Géol. Alsace Lorraine*, 14 (4): 91–100.

MOORE, L. R., 1948. The sequence and structure of the southern portion of the east crop of the South Wales Coalfield. *Quart. J. Geol. Soc. London*, 103: 261–294.

MOORE, W. G., 1949. *A Dictionary of Geography*. Penguin Books, Harmondsworth, 182 pp.

MORRIS, R. C. and DICKEY, P. A., 1957. Modern evaporite deposition in Peru. *Bull. Am. Assoc. Petrol. Geologists*, 41 (11): 2467–2474.

MYKURA, W., 1960. The replacement of coal by limestone and the reddening of coal measures in the Ayrshire Coal Field. *Bull. Geol. Surv. Gt. Brit.*, 16: 69–109

MYKURA, W., 1965. Age of the New Red Sandstone in southwest Scotland. *Scot. J. Geol.*, 1: 9–18.

NAGTEGAAL, P. J. C., 1969 Sedimentology, palaeoclimatology, and diagenesis of post-Hercynian continental deposits in the south-central Pyrenees, Spain. *Leidse Geol.Mededel.*, 42: 143–238.

NEAL, J. T., LANGER, A. M. and KERR, P. F., 1968. Giant dessication polygons of Great Basin playas. *Geol. Soc. Am. Bull.*, 79: 69–90.

NEWTON, R. B., 1909. Fossils from the Nubian Sandstone of Egypt. *Geol. Mag.*, 6: 352–397.

NORRIS, R. M., 1969. Dune reddening and time. *J. Sediment. Petrol.*, 39 (1): 7–11.

NORRIS, R. M. and NORRIS, K. S., 1961. Algodones dunes of southeastern California. *Geol. Soc. Am. Bull.*, 72: 605–630.

NOTA. D. J. G., 1958. Sediments of the Western Guiana shelf. *Mededel. Landbouwhogeschool, Wageningen*, 58 (2): 98 pp.

OBRUCHEV, V. A., 1945. Loess types and their origin. *Am. J. Sci.*, 243: 256–262.

OOMKENS, E., 1966. Environmental significance of sand dikes. *Sedimentology*, 7: 145–148.

OPDYKE, N. D., 1961. The Palaeoclimatological significance of desert sandstone. In: A. E. M. NAIRN (Editor), *Descriptive Palaeoclimatology*. Interscience, New York, N.Y., pp.45–60.

OPDYKE, N. D. and RUNCORN, S. K., 1960. Wind direction in the western United States in the Late Palaeozoic. *Bull. Geol. Soc. Am.*, 71: 959–972.

PETERSON, G. L., 1966. Structural interpretation of sandstone dikes, Northwest Sacramento Valley, California. *Geol. Soc. Am. Bull.*, 77: 833–842.

PILGRIM, G. E., 1908. Geology of the Persian Gulf and adjoining portions of Persia and Arabia. *Mem. Geol. Surv. India*, 34 (4): 1–179.

PLANKEEL, F. H., 1962. An improved sedimentation balance. *Sedimentology*, 1: 158–163.

POMEYROL, R., 1968. Nubian Sandstone. *Bull. Am. Assoc. Petrol. Geologists*, 52 (4): 589–600.

POOLE, F. G., 1964. Palaeowinds in the western United States. In: A. E. M. NAIRN (Editor), *Problems in Palaeoclimatology*. Interscience, New York, N.Y., pp.394–405.

POWERS, R. W., RAMIREZ, L. F., REDMOND, C. D. and ELBERG, E. L., 1966. Geology of the Arabian Peninsula. In: *Sedimentary Geology of Saudi Arabia—U.S. Geol. Surv, Profess. Papers*, 560-D:1–147.

PRAMANIK, S. K., 1952. Hydrology of the Rajasthan Desert: rainfall, humidity and evaporation. *Proc. Symp. Rajasthan Desert—Bull. Natl. Inst. Sci. India*, 1:183–197.

PRICE, W. A., 1962. Stages of oxidation coloration in dune and barrier sands with age. *Geol. Soc. Am. Bull.*, 73: 1281–1284.

RAMANATHAN, K. R., 1952. Atmospheric conditions over the Rajasthan Desert. *Proc. Symp. Rajasthan Desert—Bull. Natl. Inst. Sci. India*, 1:179–182.

RAYMOND, P. E., 1927. The significance of red colour in sediments. *Am. J. Sci.*, 13: 234–251.

REES, A. I., 1968. The production of preferred orientation in a concentrated dispersion of elongated and flattened grains. *J. Geol.*, 76: 457–465.

REICHE, P., 1938. An analysis of cross-lamination, the Coconino Sandstone. *J. Geol.*, 46: 905–932.

REINECK, H. E., 1955. Haftrippeln und Haftwarzen, Ablagerungs Formen von Flugsand. *Sencken-bergiana Lethaea*, 36: 347–357.

RIGASSI, D. A., 1969. "Nubian Sandstone": Discussion. Should the term "Nubian Sandstone" be dropped? *Bull. Am. Assoc. Petrol. Geologists*, 53 (1): 183–184.

ROBB, G. L., 1949. Red bed colouration. *J. Sediment. Petrol.*, 19: 99–103.

RUCHIN, L. B., 1958. *Grundzüge der Lithologie* (translated from Russian by A. Schüller). Akade-mie-Verlag, Berlin, 806 pp.

RUNCORN, S. K., 1961. Climatic change through geological time in the light of palaeomagnetic evidence for polar wandering and continental drift. *Quart. J. Roy. Meteorol. Soc.*, 87: 282–313.

RUNCORN, S. K., 1964. Palaeowind direction and palaeomagnetic latitudes. In: A. E. M. NAIRN (Editor), *Problems in Palaeoclimatology*. Interscience, New York, N.Y., pp.409–419.

RUSSEGGER, J., 1837. Kreide und Sandstein: Einfluss von Granit auf letzteren. *Neues Jahrb. Mineral.*, pp.665–669.

SANDFORD. K. S., 1937. Observations on the geology of northern central Africa. *Quart. J. Geol. Soc. London*, 93: 534–580.

SANDFORD, K. S., 1951. The stratigraphical position of the Nubian Series. *Intern. Geol. Congr., 18th, London*, 14:180.

SCHMALZ, R. F., 1968. Formation of red beds in modern and ancient deserts: Discussion. *Geol. Soc. Am. Bull.*, 79: 277–280.

SCHOCK, R. N., 1965. Note on the texture of some Pleistocene sands. *J. Sediment. Petrol.* 35 (2): 500–503.

SCHUMM, S. A., 1968. Speculations concerning paleohydrologic controls of terrestrial sedimen-tation. *Geol. Soc. Am. Bull.*, 79: 1573–1588.

SEGERSTROM, K., 1962. Deflated marine terrace as a source of dune chains, Atacama province, Chile. *U.S. Geol. Surv., Profess. Papers*, 450C: 91–93.

SENGUPTA, S. and VEENSTRA, H. J., 1968. On sieving and settling techniques for sand analysis. *Sedimentology*, 11: 83–98.

SHARP, R. P., 1963. Wind ripples. *J. Geol.* 71: 617–636.

SHAWA, M. S., 1969. "Nubian Sandstone": Discussion. *Bull. Am. Assoc. Petrol. Geologists*, 53 (1): 182.

SHEARMAN, D. J., 1963. Recent anhydrite, gypsum, dolomite and halite from the coastal flats of the Arabian shore of the Persian Gulf. *Proc. Geol. Soc. London*, 1607: 63–64.

SHEARMAN, D. J., 1966. Origin of marine evaporites by diagenesis. *Bull. Inst. Mining Met.*, 717: 208–215.

SHEPARD, F. P. and YOUNG, R., 1961. Distinguishing between beach and dune sands. *J. Sediment. Petrol.*, 31: 196–214.

SHERLOCK, R. L., 1947. *The Permo-Triassic formations. A World Review*. Hutchinsons, London, 367 pp.

SHOTTON, F. W., 1937. The Lower Bunter Sandstones of north Worcestershire and East Shrop-shire. *Geol. Mag.*, 74: 534–553.

SHOTTON, F. W., 1956. Some aspects of the New Red Desert in Britain. *Liverpool Manchester Geol. J.*, 1 (5): 450–465.

SHUKRI, N. M. and SAID, R., 1944. Contribution to the geology of the Nubian Sandstone, 1. Field observations and mechanical analysis. *Fouad 1 Univ. Cairo Bull., Fac. Sci.*, 25: 149–172.

SIMONS, D. B. and RICHARDSON, E. V., 1963. Form of bed roughness in alluvial channels. *Trans Am. Soc. Civil Engrs*, 128: 284–323.

SIMONS, D. B. and RICHARDSON, E. V., 1966. Resistance to flow in alluvial channels. *U.S. Geol. Surv., Profess. Papers*, 422-J: 61 pp.

SMALLEY, I. J. and VITA-FINZI, C., 1968. The formation of fine particles in sandy deserts and the nature of "desert" loess. *J. Sediment. Petrol.*, 38 (3): 766–774.

SMITH, H. T. U., 1965. Dune morphology and chronology in central and western Nebraska. *J. Geol.*, 73 (4): 557–578.

SMITH, T. E., 1967. A preliminary study of sandstone sedimentation in the Lower Carboniferous of the Tweed Basin. *Scot. J. Geol.*, 3 (2): 282–305.

SNEAD, R. E. and FRISHMAN, S. A., 1968. Origin of sands on the east side of the Las Bela Valley, West Pakistan. *Geol. Soc. Am. Bull.*, 79: 1671–1676.

SOUTENDAM, C. J. A., 1967. Some methods to study surface textures of sand grains. *Sedimentology*, 8: 281–290.

STIEGLITZ, R. D. and INDEN, R. F., 1969. Development of cavernous sediment in a non-beach environment. *J. Sediment. Petrol.*, 39 (1): 342–344.

STODDART, D. R., 1965. Nature and origin of beach rock. *J. Sediment. Petrol.*, 35 (1): 243–247.

STÖCKLIN, J., 1968. Salt deposits of the Middle East. In: R. B. MATTOX (Editor), *Saline Deposits— Geol. Soc. Am., Spec. Papers*, 88:157–181.

STOKES, W. L., 1961. Fluvial and eolian sandstone bodies in Colorado Plateau. In: J. A. PETERSON and J. C. OSMOND (Editors), *Geometry of Sandstone Bodies (A Symposium)*. Am. Assoc. Petrol. Geologists ,Tulsa, Okla, pp.151-178.

STONE, R. O., 1967. A desert glossary. *Earth-Sci. Rev.*, 3 (4): 211–268.

SUGDEN, W., 1964. Origin of facetted pebbles in some recent desert sediments of southern Iraq. *Sedimentology*, 3: 65–74.

SWINEFORD, A. and FRYE, J. C., 1945. A mechanical analysis of wind-blown dust compared with analyses of loess. *Am. J. Sci.*, 243: 249–255.

TANNER, W. F., 1956. Size and roundness in sediments: a discussion. *Bull. Geol. Soc. Am.*,67:535.

TANNER, W. F., 1965. Upper Jurassic paleogeography of the Four Corners region. *J. Sediment. Petrol.*, 35 (3): 564–574.

THESIGER, W., 1948. Across the empty quarter. *Geograph. J.*, 111 (5): 1–21.

THESIGER, W., 1959. *Arabian Sands*. Penguin Books, Harmondsworth, 347 pp.

TOMKINS, J. Q., 1965. Polygonal sandstone features in Boundary Butte Anticline Area, San Juan County, Utah. *Geol. Soc. Am. Bull.*, 76: 1075–1080.

TRICART, J. et MAINGUET, M., 1965. Charactéristiques granulométriques de quelques sables éoliens du désert péruvien. Aspects de la dynamique des barkanes. *Rev. Géomorphol. Dyn.*, 15 (7–9): 110–121.

TRICART, J., MICHEL, P. et VOGT, J., 1967. Oscillations climatiques quaternaires en Afriques Occidental. Résumé, V Congrès Internat. INQUA (Madrid-Barcelona), pp.187–188.

TROTTER, F. M., 1953. Reddened beds of Carboniferous age in N.W. England and their origin. *Proc. Yorkshire Geol. Soc.*, 29 (1): 1–20.

TROTTER, F. M., 1954. Reddened beds in the Coal Measures of S. Lancashire. *Bull. Geol. Surv. Gt. Brit.*, 5: 61–80.

VAN HOUTEN, F. B., 1961. Climatic significance of red beds. In: A. E. M. NAIRN (Editor), *Descriptive Palaeoclimatology*. Interscience, New York, N.Y., pp. 89–139.

VAN HOUTEN, F. B., 1964. Origin of red beds—some unsolved problems. In: A. E. M. NAIRN (Editor), *Problems in Palaeoclimatology*. Interscience, New York, N.Y., pp. 647–661.

VAN HOUTEN, F. B., 1968. Iron oxides in red beds. *Geol. Soc. Am. Bull.*, 79: 399–416.

VAN STRAATEN, L. M. J., 1961. Directional effect of winds, waves and currents along the Dutch North Sea coast. *Geol. Mijnbouw*, 40: 333–346.

VON ENGELN, P. D., 1942. *Geomorphology*. MacMillan, New York, N.Y., 655 pp.

WADIA, D. N., 1957. *Geology of India*, 3rd ed. Macmillan, London, 409 pp.

WAGNER, R. H., 1966. On the presence of probable Upper Stephanian beds in Ayrshire, Scotland. *Scot. J. Geol.*, 2 (1): 122.

WAHLSTROM, E. E., 1948. Pre-Fountain and recent weathering on Flagstaff Mountain near Boulder, Colorado. *Bull. Geol. Soc. Am.*, 59: 1173–1190.

WALKER, T. R., 1957. Frosting of quartz grains by carbonate replacement. *Bull. Geol. Soc. Am.* 68: 267–268.

WALKER, T. R., 1960. Carbonate replacement of detrital crystalline silicate minerals as a source of authigenic silica in sedimentary rocks. *Bull. Geol. Soc. Am.*, 71: 145–152.

WALKER, T. R., 1963. In situ formation of red beds in an arid to semi-arid climate (Abstract). *Geol. Soc. Am. Bull.*, Spec. Paper, 76: 174–175.

WALKER, T. R., 1967a. Formation of red beds in modern and ancient deserts. *Geol. Soc. Am. Bull.*, 78: 353–368.

WALKER, T. R., 1967b. Colour of Recent sediments in tropical Mexico: a contribution to the origin of red beds. *Geol. Soc. Am. Bull.*, 78: 917–920.

WALKER, T. R., 1968. Formation of red beds in modern and ancient deserts: Reply. *Geol. Soc. Am. Bull.*, 79: 281–282.

WALKER, T. R. and HONEA, R. M., 1969. Iron content of Modern deposits in the Sonoran Desert: a contribution to the origin of red beds. *Geol. Soc. Am. Bull.*, 80: 535–544.

WALKER, T. R., RIBBE, P. H. and HONEA, R. M., 1967. Geochemistry of hornblende alteration in Pliocene red beds, Baja California, Mexico. *Geol. Soc. Am. Bull.*, 78: 1055–1060.

WALLÉN, C. C., 1966. Arid zone meteorology. In: E. S. HILLS (Editor), *Arid Lands*. Methuen, London, pp.31–511.

WALTHER, J., 1888. Über Ergebnisse einer Forschungsreise auf der Sinaihalbinsel und in der arabischen Wüste. *Verhandl. Ges. Erdkunde*, 15: 244–255.

WALTHER, J., 1900. *Das Gesetz der Wüstenbildung in Gegenwart und Vorzeit.* Reimer, Berlin, 175 pp.

WATERSTON, C. D., 1965. The Old Red Sandstone. In: G. Y. CRAIG (Editor), *The Geology of Scotland*. Oliver and Boyd, Edinburgh, pp.270–304.

WAUGH, B., 1965. A preliminary electron microscope study of the development of authigenic silica in the Penrith Sandstone. *Proc. Yorkshire Geol. Soc.*, 35 (4): 59–69.

WEDMAN, E. J., 1964. Geohydrology of Sebkra Sedjoumi (Tunisia). *Intern. Assoc. Sci. Hydrol. Publ.*, 64: 50–67.

WELLMAN, H. T. and WILSON, A. T., 1965. Salt weathering, a neglected geological erosive agent in coastal and arid environments. *Nature*, 205 (4976): 1097–1098.

WELLS, A. J., 1962. Recent dolomite in the Persian Gulf. *Nature*, 194 (4825): 274–275.

WILLIAMS, G., 1964. Some aspects of aeolian saltation load. *Sedimentology*, 3: 257–287.

WOBBER, J. J., 1967. Space photography: a new analytical tool for the sedimentologist. *Sedimentology*, 9 (4): 265–317.

WOLFE, M. J., 1967. An electronmicroscope study of the surface textures of sandgrains from a basal conglomerate. *Sedimentology*, 8:239–248.

WRIGHT, H. E., 1956. Origin of the Chuska Sandstone, Arizona-New Mexico—A structural and petrographic study of a Tertiary aeolian sediment. *Bull. Geol. Soc. Am.*, 67: 413–434.

YAALON, D. H., 1967. Factors affecting the lithification of eolianite and interpretation of its environmental significance in the coastal plain of Israel. *J. Sediment. Petrol.*, 37 (4): 1189–1199.

YAALON, D. H. and GINZBOURG, D., 1966. Sedimentary characteristics and climatic analysis of easterly dust storms in the Negev (Israel). *Sedimentology*, 6: 315–332.

CROSS REFERENCES TO FIGURES, TABLES AND ENCLOSURES

Many of the figures in this book have been used to illustrate more than one aspect of a desert environment of sedimentation, sedimentary structure or other feature from which the existence of a former desert can be inferred. In many cases, they also suggest more than one means of sediment transport. The following list of pages, in which individual figures, tables and enclosures have been referred to, will assist the reader in making a more complete analysis of any particular figure.

Fig. no.	Page	Fig. no.	Page
Frontispiece	37, 90	36	11, 12, 48, 148
1	1, 4, 5, 93	37	12, 49, 52, 64
2	3,5	38	12, 49, 64
3	10,128	39	12, 49, 64
4	16, 28	40	12, 52, 64, 142
5	16, 33	41	12, 52, 53
6	11, 16, 121, 170	42	12, 54, 66
7	16	43	11, 12, 55, 150
8	16	44	11, 12, 48, 56
9	21	45	11, 12, 48, 53, 56, 148
10	22, 23, 84	46	11, 12, 48, 56
11	23, 24	47	11, 12, 48, 56
12	24	48	11, 12, 48, 56
13	24, 69, 74	49	39, 58, 64, 73, 134
14	26	50	58, 59, 60, 134
15	16, 20, 27	51	61
16	31, 32, 39, 121	52	61
17	32, 39, 121	53	63
18	12, 33, 40	54	64
19	24, 36, 183	55	64, 71, 73, 140
20	24, 36	56	12, 66, 143
21	37	57	12, 66, 143
22	39, 58	58	12, 66, 143
23	39, 58	59	12, 26, 69, 134
24	12, 39	60	12, 70, 73, 128, 134
25	12, 39	61	12, 64, 73, 131
26	12, 39, 41, 48, 80, 148	62	11, 12, 64, 70, 73, 128, 140
27	12, 42, 148	63	77, 81
28	12, 43	64	11, 21, 78
29	43, 148	65	11, 78
30	11, 12, 46	66	11, 16, 81, 145, 157, 170
31	11, 12, 47	67	82
32	11, 12, 47	68	82, 83, 92, 101, 106
33	11, 12, 33, 48	69	23, 84
34	11, 12, 48	70	23, 86, 88
35	11, 12, 47, 48	71	23, 87, 88

Fig. no.	Page
72	88, 98
73	90, 146
74	90, 92, 99, 106
75	92, 106, 148
76	95
77	96, 97
78	98, 99
79	11, 81, 101, 157, 188
80	81, 101
81	101, 157
82	101, 152
83	101
84	11, 101
85	101
86	103
87	11, 106
88	11, 106
89	11, 106
90	11, 106
91	11, 108, 110, 128
92	108, 128
93	110
94	12, 30, 110, 124
95	12, 30, 110, 124
96	116
97	116
98	32, 75, 121
99	122
100	124
101	70, 128
102	11, 128, 159
103	11, 133, 165
104	135
105	136
106	136
107	139
108	140
109	129, 136, 159
110	12, 141, 144
111	12, 141, 142
112	12, 141, 142, 144
113	12, 135, 141, 142, 143
114	144, 145
115	11, 144, 145, 146

Fig. no.	Page
116	42, 144, 147
117	11, 144, 148, 167
118	12, 144, 148
119	148, 167
120	11, 80, 144, 150, 167
121	11, 21, 80, 144, 150
122	11, 21, 144, 150, 153
123	150, 152, 153
124	11, 12, 144, 157
125	11, 144, 157
126	11, 144, 157
127	11, 127, 128, 159
128	11, 129, 159
129	11, 127, 159
130	133, 159
131	11, 12, 148, 165, 167
132	11, 12, 148, 165, 167, 170
133	11, 12, 165, 167, 170
134	11, 12, 145, 165, 167, 170
135	11, 12, 145, 165, 167, 170
136	11, 12, 16, 145, 165, 167, 170
137	12, 172
138	11, 12, 172
139	11, 12, 172
140	181
141	185
142	185, 189
143	185, 189
144	188, 189
145	185, 189
146	189

Table	Page
Table I	11, 141, 143
II	173, 176, 177, 180
III	177, 185, 191
IV	13, 191

Enclosure	Page
Enclosure 1	18, 29, 37, 61, 71, 86, 95, 96, 98, 115, 126, 127, 131, 141, 147, 184
2	37, 47, 74, 75, 94, 101, 102, 121, 124, 126, 127, 131, 141, 159, 184
3	61, 141
4	10, 39, 58, 84, 89, 126, 135, 141

INDEX

Abrasion, destroys desert varnish, 19
—, formation of ventifacts, 20
— and frosting, 167
—, loss of pigment by, 184, 190
—, rate of, 127
—, self-, during saltation, 165
— and weathering, 7, 15
— of wind-transported Foraminifera, 38
Abu Dhabi, Trucial States,
—, cemented dunes, 101
—, erosional highlands, 37
—, opposing wind directions, 88
—, Pliocene dune sands, 184
—, precipitation and evaporation rate, 1
—, prograding coastline, 126
—, quartz/carbonate ratio in dune sand, 127
—, tidal deltas, 124
Adhesion ripples, *see* Ripples
Adriatic Sea, 176
Afghanistan, 57
Africa, North, VII, 4, 18, 74, 113
—, South, 4, 5, 113
—, Southwest, 5, 83
—, West, 4, 92
Air-pressure systems, 3, 5, 6, 92, 94
Al Fugaha, Libya, 24, 26, 28, 69, 74
Algae, algal mat, 61, 69, 121, 127, 136, 156
Algeria, VII, 18, 61, 148
Algodones Dunes, California, 46
ALIMEN, H., VIII, 58, 131, 166
Alizarin red S, 144, 189
ALLEN, J. R. L., 30, 56, 95
Alluvial fan, in basins of inland drainage, 10
— —, braided channels, 31, 121
— —, cementation of sediments in, 34
— —, dissected, 32
— — and encroaching dune sands, 38
— —, flanking highlands, 37, 39, 122
— — and location of oases, 75, 121
— — in New Red Sandstone, 45
— — of Old Red Sandstone, 44
— — of Pleistocene, 32, 36
— —, source of dune sand, 8
ALMEIDA, F. F. M., 81
Alps, 118

America, North, VIII, 1, 60, 84, 89
—, South, 4, 81
Andes, 4, 5
ANDERSON, R. V., 28
Anhydrite, 121, 133, 134, 142, 143, 144, 156
Arabia, aeolian sand transport in northeast
   Arabia, 84
—, deserts of, VIII
—, deflation in Rub al Khali, 22
—, degrees of dune reddening, 184
—, dune sand and Pleistocene sea level, 92
—, loess in South Arabia, 118
—, 'Nubian Sandstone' of, 113
— and palaeowind directions, 83
—, source of Pleistocene aeolian sand, 127
—, Trade Wind desert, 4
—, use of qanats in, 74
Arabian Sea, 136, 140
Aragonite, 130, 131, 132
Aravalli Range, India, 5
ARCHER, A. A., 175, 183
Arizona, U.S.A., 81, 100, 136
ARNDT, H. H., 181
Arran, Scotland, 181
Asia, Central, 8, 10, 31, 118
Atacama Desert, South America, 5
Atlantic Ocean, Southern, 4
ATTIA, M. I., 113
AUDEN, J. B., 129
Australia, 4, 18, 83, 84, 92
Avalanche slope, slip face, 195, 197
— —, angle of repose for dry sand, 81, 82, 106
— — and palaeowind directions, 152, 153
— —, ripples on, 80
— — and uncommon wind directions, 88, 96,
   148

BAGNOLD, R. A., VIII
—, avalanche slopes, 81
—, saltation, 7
—, sand accumulation, 89
—, sand movement, 23, 92
—, sand movement by surface creep, 7, 21
—, sand ridges, 77
—, sand ripples, 79, 80, 108

BAGNOLD, R. A. *(continued)*
—, seif dune formation, 89
—, sheet sand formation, 106
—, threshold velocities, 24
—, transverse instability of sand, 89
Bahr, 58, 195
Bahrein Island, Persian Gulf, 126
BAILEY, E. B., 174, 181
Baja California, Mexico, 86, 96, 179, 180
BALL, J., 26
BALL, M. M., 122
Baluchistan, 5
Bar, longshore, 69, 73, 121, 126
BARBOUR, G. B., 118
Barik, Oman, 82
BARREL, J., 44, 174, 177
Barren Red Measures, Gt. Britain, 181, 183, 193
Base level, 10, 32
Basins of inland drainage, 8, 10, 18, 28, 57, 134
Batinah Coast, Oman, 71, 94, 128
Batlaq-e-Gav Khunt, Iran, 57
Beach, beach sands, 8, 12, 31, 46, 122, 130, 145
Beach rock, 130
Beauce Limestone, Oligocene, France, 131
BEAUMONT, P., 17
Benguela Current, South Atlantic, 5
Bermuda, 100, 122
BERNER, R. A., 180, 191
BEYDOUN, Z. R., 95, 118, 148
BIGARELLA, J. J., 20, 100, 110, 122
Bima Sandstone, Cretaceous, Nigeria, 181
Biotite, 179
Bir Zelten, Libya, 10
Biswas, S., IX
BLACKWELDER, E., 15, 29
BLISSENBACH, E., 30
BLOOMFIELD, C., 190
BLUCK, B. J., 29, 44
BLUNDELL, C. R. K., 175, 182, 183
BOBEK, H., 16, 20, 61, 84, 136
Bocana de Virrila, Peru, 134
BOND, G., 94
BORCHERT, H., 176
Boron, 58
Botucatú Sandstone (Early Mesozoic), Brazil, 20, 100
Boulders, boulder lag, 8, 16, 18, 32
—, formed in situ, 16, 23, 33
—, in mud-flow conglomerate, 29
BOURCART, J., 174, 179
BOWMAN, T. S., 113
Braided streams, 31, 33, 44, 45, 195
Braiding of wadi sediments, 27
BRAMER, H., 167

BREDEHOEFT, I. D., 61
Britain, 45, 110, 133
Bryozoa, 124, 128, 159
Brockram, Permian, Britain, 110
BRUCK, P. M., 45
BRÜCKNER, W. D., 15
BRYAN, K., 118
BUHSE, F. A., 66
Buntsandstein, Triassic, Germany, 49
Buraimi Oasis, Arabia, 74, 127, 184
BUROLLET, P. F., 113
Burrows, plant-root, *see* Dikaka
BUSSON, G., 112
BUTLER, G. P., 122, 124, 134
BUTZER, K. W., 95

CAILLEUX, A., 172
Calcite cement, 12, 45, 117, 126, 188, 189, 192
— —, high-magnesian, 131, 132
— —, low-magnesian, 131, 132
Caliche, 24, 45, 195
California, U.S.A., 8, 46
Calcrete, 112, 195
Cambrian deserts, VII, 113
— salt, 57, 58, 134
CAMPBELL, R. L., 157
Cape Ranges, South Africa, 4
Capillarity, 19, 63, 64, 71, 121, 150, 156, 183
CAPOT-REY, R., VIII
Carboniferous, 177, 181–183, 185, 188
Carmel Formation, Jurassic, U.S.A., 66
CARTER, H. J., 159
Caspian Sea, 133, 134
Catskill Formation, Devonian, Pennsylvania, 181
Catskill Mountains, U.S.A., 179
Cementation of aeolian sands, 43, 59, 131, 132
— of wadi sediments, 33, 34, 36, 43, 45
CHAPMAN, F., 159
Chemical weathering, 7, 15, 16
Chile, 130
China, loess of, 118
CHOUBERT, G., 174, 179
Chuska Sandstone, Tertiary, Arizona/New Mexico, 100
Clay, authigenic, 11, 144, 190, 192
— drapes and films, 6, 12, 39, 52, 53, 55, 58, 144
— in dune sands, 11, 53, 58
— flakes, curled and cracked, 12, 41, 42, 47, 48, 52, 53, 56 58, 112, 141, 144
—, fluvial, 10
—, gypsiferous, 69, 70
—, illite, 35, 178
— in suspension in air, 7, 24
—, kaolinite, 157, 178, 185, 188, 192

—, lateritic, 182
—, marine, 31
—, montmorillonite, 179
— pebbles, 6, 12, 44, 49, 53, 55, 56, 68, 112, 144
— polygons, 49, 52, 55, 58, 64, 66, 68
—, resistance to deflation, 24
—, semi-permeable, 27, 60
Coal, replacement by dolomite, 181
Coal Measures, Carboniferous, Britain, 181, 182, 183
Coastal plain, 10, 31, 39, 121, 122, 131
Coastlines, desert, 1, 84, 86, 115, 121, 126
Coast Ranges, U.S.A., 5
Coconino Sandstone, Permian, Arizona, 81, 110
Coffinier, A.A.E.A., 60, 61, 182
Colorado, U.S.A., 39, 179
Colorado River, 46, 124
Congo, 94
Continental basin, 5, 8, 118, 188, 189, 190, 193
— shelf, 126, 130, 159
Convection of wind, 3, 5, 37, 86, 89, 94, 148
Cooke, R. U., 17
Cooper, W. S., 84, 96, 122
Coque, R., 61
Coriolis force, 3
Cox, A. H., 183
Cox, D. C., 130
Creep, surface (by aeolian action), 7, 21, 77, 78, 80, 92
Crest, of dune, 82, 88, 90, 101, 102, 153
—, of sand ridge, 77
—, of ripple, 79, 80
Cretaceous, 10, 110, 113, 115, 181
Curray, J. R., 100
Cyrenaica, Libya, 10, 132

Dahna, Saudi Arabia, 84
Daryacheh-ye-Namak, Iran, 57
Dasht, 16
Davilar, R. R. J., ix
Davis, W. M., 10
Deflated marine terrace, 130
Deflation, of coastal sebkhas, 122, 134, 136, 139
—, differential, 23, 24, 34, 117
—, hollow, 20, 24, 26, 27, 28, 69, 74
—, inhibited by moisture, 26, 69, 73, 122
— lag, 18, 20, 22, 41, 48, 77, 78
— of fluvial sediments, 12, 27, 31, 32, 42, 118
— of inland sebkhas, 63, 68, 73
— of interdune areas, 22, 167
— plain, 77, 81, 167
— surface, 16, 18, 19, 20, 29, 170, 183
Delta, fluvial, 31, 46, 124

— oolite, 124
—, temporary, 31, 112, 124
Desert, coasts, 5, 121, 124, 134
— (defined), 1, 195
— erosion, 7, 24
—, monsoon, 5
—, polar, 6
—, rainshadow, 4, 5
—, Trade-Wind, 4, 5, 177
— varnish, 19, 20, 21, 36, 183
Devon, England, clay flakes and clay polygons, 49, 54
—, —, palaeowind directions, 100, 148
—, —, Permian wadi sediments, 42, 43, 188
—, —, Permian sand dykes, 66, 68
—, —, pigmented aeolian sands, 188
—, —, wadi conglomerates, 42, 43
De Lapparent, G., 174, 179
De Sitter, L. U., 60
Devonian, 45, 113, 178, 179
Dew, 15, 21, 115, 190
Diagenesis, 11, 112, 121, 133, 159, 167, 189
Di Cesare, F., 24, 112
Dickey, P. A., 133, 134
Dikaka, 48, 74, 113–117, 118, 150, 195
Djofra Graben, Libya, 39, 58
Doeglas, D. J., 31
Dolomite, in coastal sebkhas, 122, 136
—, encrusting quartz grains, 189, 192
— as indication of desert environment, 112
— of Magnesian Limestone, 133, 165, 188
— and source of quartz dune sand in Qatar, 86
—, stable mineral, 131
Donahue, J., 167, 172
Dorsey, G. E., 173, 174
Downing, R. A., 175, 182, 183
Drakensberg Mts., South Africa, 4
Dubai, Trucial States, 102, 159, 182
Dubief, J., 90
Dumfriesshire, Scotland, 81
Dune sands, preserved beneath transgression, 10, 92, 93
Dunes, barchan, bedding of, 11, 82, 106, 113, 150
—, —, conversion to other dune types, 86, 87, 89, 99
—, —, formation of, 81, 83, 88, 92, 95, 96
—, —, migration of, 82, 84, 98, 104
—, —, and palaeowind directions, 100, 101, 103, 152
—, carbonate, cemented, 10, 128, 132
—, —, formation of, 31, 126
—, —, Permian, 133
—, —, Pleistocene, 130
—, —, and source of sediment, 31, 124, 127
—, cemented, 10, 38, 83, 92, 101, 103, 112, 128

Dunes *(continued)*
—, coastal, as barrier to transgression, 10, 69, 70, 71, 73, 128
—, —, bedding of, 122, 124
—, —, cemented, 128, 131
—, —, and contorted bedding, 108
—, —, and dikaka, 115, 124
—, —, erosion of, 121
—, —, formation of, 122
—, —, and marine faunas, 127, 130
—, —, preservation by coastal transport and sebkhas, 122
—, drowned, 58
—, gypsum, 83, 110, 136
—, gypsum cemented, 70, 83, 98, 101, 131, 144
—, height of, 88, 95
—, linear, 11, 89, 98, 124, 147
—, migration of, migratory, 10, 82, 84, 115
—, orientation of bedding, barchan, 100, 101, 104, 106
—, —, seif, 100, 101, 103, 104, 106
—, —, transverse, 95, 96
—, peri-glacial, 6, 94
—, seif, bedding of, 11, 92, 106, 108, 151
—, —, conversion to/from other dune types, 89, 92, 98, 99, 104
—, —, formation of, 89, 90, 95, 96, 154
—, —, and palaeowind directions, 100, 101, 102, 103, 150, 151
—, —, Permian, 101, 110
—, —, Pleistocene, 38, 90, 92, 93, 94, 96, 99
—, stabilised, 92, 115, 122, 123, 191
—, stellate, pyramidal, 86, 87, 88
—, transverse, 95, 99, 106, 122
Dune sands, ancient, 10, 12,
—, sources of, 7, 8, 12, 26, 39, 86, 96
DUNBAR, C.O., 174, 176, 179
DUNHAM, K. C., 174, 176, 177
Durham, England, 81, 101
Dust, 21, 24, 26, 69, 118
Dust storm, 6, 59, 118, 119

Eberbach, Germany, 52
EDMUNDS, F. H., 183
Egypt, 26, 113
Electron microscope, 166, 172
Elgin, Scotland, 188
EMERY, K. O., 130
ENGEL, C. G., 19, 183
England, Permian desert sediments of, 148
—, —, mud polygons and clay flakes, 49, 54
—, Permo-Triassic dune sands of, 100, 101, 110
—, red sediments of, 181, 182, 183, 185
Environment, aeolian, 165, 167
—, arid continental, 113, 179
—, coastal sebkha, 60, 121

—, continental, 172, 176
—, desert, 13, 15, 30, 112, 141–143, 157, 172, 179
—, diagenetic, 61, 189
—, estuarine, 66
—, evaporitic, 142
—, fluvial, 44, 66, 165, 167, 172
—, glacial, 167
—, inland sebkha, 60, 64, 143
—, interstitial, 180
—, lagoonal, 124
—, marine, 127–130, 159, 165, 172, 176
—, oxidising, 172, 177
Eocene, 22, 57
Eolianite, 100, 131, 195
Equinox, 4
Erosion, desert, 7, 24, 34, 39, 69
—, fluvial, 32, 34, 37, 39, 40, 49, 58
—, marine, 121, 126, 128
—, wind, 83, 101
Europe, New Red Sandstone oil and gas reservoirs, VII, 36
—, Permian evaporite basin of, 135
—, Permo-Triassic deserts of, VIII, 13
—, Permo-Triassic mud-polygons, 49
—, Pleistocene loess of, 119
—, Triassic evaporitic clays of, 140
EVAMY, B. D., IX, 88, 114, 127, 131, 144, 184 189
EVANS, G., IX, 121, 124
EVANS, J. W., 129, 130, 159
Evaporites, 121, 133–136, 143
— and red beds, 179
Evaporation and bedded evaporites, 133
— and calcite cementation, 24, 45, 132
— of desert rainfall, 6
— encouraged by lack of vegetation, 10
— and formation of salt crust, 121
— and gypsum-cemented dune sands, 131
—, halite and gypsum deposition, 26, 61, 134, 140
—, rate of, 1, 34, 57, 134
— from surface of terminal lake, 8
Exfoliation, 7, 15, 16, 20, 32

Fahud, Oman, 16, 27, 28, 69
FAIRBRIDGE, R. W., 92, 94, 126, 132
Falaj, 74, 196
FEDDEN, F., 129
Feidj, 29, 101, 102, 147, 148, 196
Feldspars, alkali, 157
—, alteration to kaolinite, 185, 188, 189
—, authigenic overgrowths, 190, 192
—, plagioclase, 189
—, potash, 136
Ferromagnesian silicates, 178

FENET, D., VIII
Fezzan, Libya, 74, 110, 112
FINKEL, H. J., 83
FLINT, R. F., 5, 94
Flood plain, 12, 44, 45
Flow regimes, fluvial, lower, 12
—, —, upper, 12, 30, 39, 108
Florida, U.S.A., 117, 122
Flute casts, 52
Foggara, 74, 196
FOLK, R. L., 174, 180
Fontainbleau Sandstone, Oligocene, France, 131, 132
Foraminifera, abrasion of, 38
— of coastal lagoons, 124
— in dune sands, 8, 46, 71, 108, 127, 128, 139, 156, 159
— in inland sebkhas, 71
—, surface polish of, 159
— in wadi sediments, 156
Foresets, accretion, fluvial, 12, 30, 39, 48
—, —, aeolian, 11, 33, 41, 42, 88, 96, 106, 133, 145, 148
Fossils, marine, VII, 110, 113, 159
France, 31
FRIEDMAN, G. M., 92, 130, 131
FRIEND, P. F., 175, 178, 179, 181
FRISHMAN, S. A., 122, 132, 167
Frosting, 11, 156, 165–167, 170, 172, 192, 196
— and micro-chemical corrosion, 165
FRYE, L. C., 119
FUNNEL, B. M., 167, 172

Ganges Plain, 5, 145
GAUTIER, E. F., VIII
Gatelawbridge Quarry, Dumfriesshire, 58
GERMANOV, A. I., 182
Germany, Cretaceous land plants, 115
—, "New Red" deserts, 45, 188
—, peri-glacial dunes, 6
—, Permian sand dykes, 68
—, Recent adhesion ripples, 73, 142
—, Triassic aeolian sands, 36
GERSTER, G., VII
GÈZE, B., 173, 174
Gibber Plain, 18, 196
GIBBONS, S. G., 21
GILL, W. D., 181
GILREATH, J. A., 157
GINSBURG, R. N., 130
GINZBOURG, D., 118
Glacial moraines and loess, 118
GLENNIE, K. W., 57, 88, 114, 127, 184
Gobi Desert, Asia, VIII, 5, 8, 118
GODDARD, E. N., 176, 181
Goethite, 188

Gravel, fluvial, 10, 29, 31, 39
—, lag, 24, 32, 41
—, foresetted, 12, 48
—, marine, 31
Great Divide, Australia, 4
Great Eastern Erg, Algeria, 61
Great Kawir, Iran, 8, 57, 74, 84, 136
Great Plains, U.S.A., 119
GREEN, R., 133
Guinea Coast, West Africa, 4
Gulf of Kara Bogaz, Caspian Sea, 133, 134
— Kutch, India, 159
— Oman, 71, 94
— Sirte, Libya, 126
— Salwa, Persian Gulf, 86
Gypsum, cemented dikaka, 117, 144
—, cemented dunes, 73, 98, 101, 131
— in coastal sebkhas, 121, 134, 135, 136
—, cross-laminated, 136
— in deflation hollows, 26, 28
— dunes, 83, 110, 136
— estuarine, 134, 140
— grains in dunes, 139
— in inland sebkhas, 61, 64, 71
— in marine sediments, 133
— weathering agent, 18

Hadramaut, Arabia, 118, 147, 148
Haematite, cement, 144
—, coating, 172, 176–178
—, pigment, 179, 180
HALL, A., 189
Halite, 26, 121, 133, 134–136, 139
Halophytes, 117
Hamada al Hamra, Libya, 84
HAMILTON, N., 82
Hamoun-i-Helmond, Iran/Afghanistan, 57
Hamun-e-Jaz Murian, Iran, 57
HARE, F. K., 4, 92
Harmattan, 4
HARMS, J. C., 68
HARSHBARGER, J. W., 66
Harug el Hasued, Libya, 84
HASTENRATH, S. L., 83
Hausmannia, 115
HIGGINS, C. G., 20
HILLS, E. S., 83
Hilton Beck, Vale of Eden, 110
HINZE, C., 176
HOBBS, W. H., 15, 66
HOFFMEISTER, J. E., 117
Hoggar Mountains, Algeria, 182
HOLM, D. A., VIII, 60, 84, 88, 159, 195
HOLMES, A., VII, 1, 20, 132, 133, 195
HONEA, R. M., 180
Hornblende, 179

HÖRNER, N. G., 10, 31, 118
Horse Latitudes, 3, 4, 6
HOUBOLT, J. J. H. C., 90
Houghton-le-Spring, Co. Durham, 81
Hughes-Clarke, M. W., 127
Humboldt Current (Southern Pacific Ocean), 5
Hydrohaematite, 180

Igma anticline, Algeria, 61
Illinois Basin, U.S.A., 61
Imbrication, of aeolian sand grains, 82
—, of pebbles and boulders, 33, 43, 110
India, Pleistocene dune sands, 130, 159, 184
—, Ranns of Kutch, 136
—, Rajasthan Desert, 88
—, effect on Southwest Monsoon, 5
Indian Ocean, 5
INDEN, R. F., 43
Indus, River, 124
— Delta, 140
IMMAN, D. L., 165
Insolation, 7, 15, 16, 20, 21, 167, 196
Interdune, aeolian sands, 38, 184
— deflation plains, 22, 23, 77, 127, 148, 170
— depth to water table, 182
— fluvial gravels, 29
—, inland sebkhas, 61, 96, 97
— sand ridges, 78
— spacing and wind velocity, 95
— temporary lakes, 58, 59
— "wind cells", 90
Iran, basins of inland drainage, 8, 57
—, dunes of Great Kawir, 84
—, qanats, 74
—, salt polygons, 61, 136
—, split pebbles of the "dasht", 16
Isfahan, Iran, 74
Istria, Yugoslavia, 176
Israel, 118, 131

Jabal Uaddan, Libya, 23
JAUZEIN, A., 61
Jaz Murian, Iran, 57
Jebel Baraka, Trucial States, 115
— Hafit, Arabia, 37, 74, 98
JONES, G. P., 181
JOPLING, A. V., 30
Jordi, R., 10
Jurassic aeolian sands, 81, 110, 136

KAISER, E., 15, 83
Kalahari Desert, South Africa, 4, 83
Kansas, U.S.A., 119
Kara Bogaz, Gulf of, 133, 134
Karroo Series, South Africa, 113

KASSAS, M., 114
Kathiawar, India, 159
Kavir-e-Namak, Iran, 57
Kelso Dunes, California, 80
KENDALL, C. G. ST. C., 1, 93, 121
Keuper, Triassic, 140
Kharga Oasis, Egypt, 74
KIERSCH, G. A., 81, 101, 110
Kinetic energy of saltating sand grains, 7, 165
KRINSLEY, D. H., 167, 172
KRYNINE, P. D., 173, 174
KUENEN, PH. H., 15, 127, 165, 170
Kutch, India, 129, 159

Lagoon, 10, 121, 124, 126, 135, 136
Lake Bakhtegan, Iran, 57
"Lake Cahuilla", California, 46
Lake Chad, N. Central Africa, 58
"Lake Lucero", New Mexico, 136
Lake Neyriz, Iran, 57
Lakes, temporary, desert, 39, 57, 58, 59, 64, 69, 74, 112, 136
—, terminal, 8, 10
—, wandering, 31
LAMB, H. H., 92
Laminae, horizontal, aeolian, 11, 39, 41, 42, 56, 106, 108, 145, 146, 156
—, —, fluvial, 12, 30, 39
— in dikaka, 115, 116
—, wavy, contorted, convolute bedding, 39, 64, 108, 128, 135, 139, 142
LAMING, D. J. C., VIII, 33, 43, 68, 100, 177
Laterite, 174
LAWRENCE, T. E., VII
Ledstone Quarry, Yorkshire, 110
Leeds, Yorkshire, 110
Libya, coastal lagoon, 135, 136
—, deflation plains, 18, 84
—, desert, VIII
—, differential deflation, 23, 24
—, dune sands, 106, 108, 128, 132
—, falaj, 74
—, fluvial deltas, 124
—, inland sebkhas, 64
—, "Nubian Sandstone", 110
—, prograding coast, 126
—, sandstorm, 21
—, temporary lakes, 39, 58
—, thickness of desert sediments, 10
Limonite, 176
Liwa Sand Sea, Trucial States, 88, 96
Locharbriggs Quarry, Dumfriesshire, 81
Loess, 7, 24, 118, 119, 196
LOGAN, R. F., 5
Longshore currents, marine, 31, 121, 122, 124
Lop Nor, Central Asia, 31

LOTZE, F., 134
LYONS, H. G., 113

MACKENZIE, F. T., 100, 122
MADIGAN, C. T., 84, 90
MÄGDEFRAU, K., 115
Magnesian Limestone, Permian, England, 133, 188
Mahotra, R., IX
Maidencombe Bay, Devon, 43
MAINGUET, M., VIII
Mamlahah, 60, 196
MANDERSCHEID, G., 113
Mauchline Basin, Scotland, 181
MARICELLI, J. J., 157
Marine sedimentary iron ores, 176
Masira Island, Oman, 127
Mastodon (Tetralophodon), 115, 184
MATTHEWS, R. K., 131
MAXSON, J. H., 21
MCBURNEY, C. B. M., 132
McCOY, F. W., 45
MCGEE, W. J., 6
MCKEE, E. D., IX
—, ancient sand ripples, 81
—, climbing ripples, 56
—, contorted dune bedding, 110
—, dune bedding, 83, 92
—, flood deposits, 30, 39, 108
—, gypsum dunes, 83, 110, 136
—, horizontally-bedded aeolian sands, 108
—, "Nubian Sandstone", 110, 113
—, palaeoclimates, 191
—, pyramidal dunes, 88
—, recumbent folds in sediments, 30, 110
—, seif dune formation, 89
—, stereographic polar nets, 101
—, transverse dunes, 96
Mediterranean Sea, coast of, 10, 95, 108, 112, 124, 126
MEIGS, P., VII
MEISCHNER, D., 176
MERRIAM, R., 46
Messak Sandstone, Cretaceous, Libya, 113
Mexico, 5, 46, 86, 93, 96, 177, 179
Mica, 12
MIDDLETON, G. V., 30
Miliolids, 127, 130, 159
Miliolite, 159
MILLER, D, N., 174, 180
MILLOT, G., 45, 175, 177, 178, 185, 191, 192
Mindel Glaciation, 132
Minerals, heavy, 47, 167
Miocene, 184
Mist, 5
Misurata, Libya, 126, 136

Moenkopi Formation, Triassic, Arizona, 110, 136
Mojave Desert, California, 5, 8, 80
Monsoon, Northeast, 5, 58
—, Southwest, 5, 37, 38, 88, 90, 92, 136, 196
MOORE, L. R., 175, 182, 183
MOORE, W. G., 74, 196
Morocco, 74, 132
Morris, F. K., 15
MORRIS, R. C., 134
Moulds, plant-root, *see* Dikaka
Mud cracks, 12, 44, 49, 66, 112, 144
Mudflow conglomerates, 12, 29, 31, 44, 144, 148
MULTER, H. G., 117
Murzuk Sand Sea, Libya, 84
Musandam Peninsula, Arabia, 126
MYKURA, W., 175, 177, 181, 185

NAGTEGAAL, P. J. C., 45
Namib Desert, Southwest Africa, 5, 83
Namurian, Carboniferous, 188
Nathorstiana, 115
Navajo Sandstone, Jurassic, Utah, 81, 110
NEAL, J. T., 49
Nebraska, U.S.A,, 94
Neckar, River, Germany, 52
Negev, Israel, 118
Netherlands, The, VII, 6, 84, 89, 136
New Mexico, U.S.A., 100, 110, 136
New Red Sandstone, Permo-Triassic, 43, 45, 177, 178, 181
NEWTON, R. B., 113
Niger Delta, 172
Nigeria, northern, 181
Nile, River, 124
North Sea, formation of submarine sand ridges, 90
— —, peri-glacial sands, 172
NORRIS, K. S., 45, 180
NORRIS, R. M., 45, 180, 184
NOTA, D. J. G., 176
Nubian Sandstone, 26, 74, 110, 112, 113

OAKLEY, K. P., 183
Oasis, 26, 73, 74, 75
OBRUCHEV, V. A., 118
Old Red Sandstone, Devonian, 44, 45, 177, 180, 181, 183
Oligocene, dune sands, 131
Oman, ancient wadi sediments, 36
—, dune sands, 82, 90, 128
—, Fahud Anticline, 16, 27
—, falaj, 74
—, inland sebkhas, 61, 63, 64, 71
—, wind and water-laid sediments, 37, 41, 52

Oman Mountains, alluvial fans and wadi sediments, 31, 32, 36, 37, 75, 121, 127
— —, cemented wadi sediments, 34, 74
— —, and convection winds, 80, 95
Oolith, oolite, 8, 124, 131, 132, 159
OOMKENS, E., IX, 64, 66, 68, 141, 142
OPDYKE, N. D., 19, 105, 183, 191
Organic matter, 176, 178
Orinoco River, South America, 176

Pachham Island, Great Rann of Kutch, 139
Pacific, North American coast of, 84, 122
—, Southern, 4
Pakistan, 122, 132
Paignton, Devon, 42, 68
Palaeoclimates, 105
—, criteria for recognition of, 177, 178, 188, 191, 192
Palaeogeography, 121, 129, 147, 190
Palaeo-winds, see Winds, palaeo
Palaeozoic formations, 10, 45, 179
— ice caps, 105
Paris Basin, France, 58, 131
Patagonia, South America, 5
Pebble, pebbly, 39, 41, 116
— in aeolian sands, 42, 48, 148
—, clay, 6, 12, 44, 49, 53, 56, 66, 112, 144
— in sheet sands, 106, 108
—, imbrication of, 33, 43, 110
—, lag, 8, 16, 18, 41, 77
—, movement by wind, 7, 24
—, wind abrasion of, 20
Pennsylvania, U.S.A., 181
Penrith Sandstone, Permian, England, 110
Peranera Formation, Permian, Spain, 45
PERDOK, W. G., 15, 165, 170
Permeable, semi-, 156
Permeability barriers, 59, 135, 156
— — in aeolian sands, 116, 150, 156, 188
— — in wadi sediments, 36
Permian adhesion ripples, 73
— aeolian sediments, 81, 145
— alluvium, 179
— clay flakes, 54, 55
— continental basins, 45, 188
— desert conditions, 183
— desert sediments, 148
— dune sands, 58, 100, 101, 110, 157, 183, 185, 188, 190
— evaporites, 134
— glaciation, 105
— plants, 115
— red beds, 185
— sand dykes, 66, 68
— slumped dune sands, 110
— soil formation, 177

— volcanics, 181, 185
— wadi sediments, 42, 43, 110, 185
Permo-Trias deserts, VII, VIII, 13, 177, 182
— — dune sands, 83, 100, 181
— — mud cracks, 49
Persian Gulf, coastal dune sands, 21, 159
— —, coast of, 31, 121, 127, 140
— —, evaporites, 117, 134
— —, on-shore convection winds, 86
— —, Qatar, 84
— —, rate of evaporation over, 1
PETERSON, G. L., 68
Peru, 83, 134
PILGRIM, G. E., 159
Pisida, Libya, 135
PLANKEEL, F. H., 148
Plants, in desert, 1, 74, 114, 115, 191
Plattensandstein, Triassic, Germany, 52
Playa, 49, 60, 136
Pleistocene climatic changes, 134
— coastal carbonate dunes, 122, 130
— deserts, 105
— dune formation, 38, 90, 92, 96, 99, 100, 102, 115, 127, 129, 130, 166, 184
— glaciations, 31, 38, 86, 92, 94, 96, 127, 130, 159
— loess, 118, 119
— rain ("pluvials"), 29, 31, 32, 94, 95, 115
— sea level changes, 31, 126, 129, 130, 134, 159
— wadi sediments, 31, 34, 147
— winds, 6, 38, 90, 99, 101, 127
Pliocene, 83, 116, 118, 127, 131, 179, 184
Poikilitic crystals, 122, 131
Polignac, Algeria, 61
POMEYROL, R., 113
Pontian, Pliocene, dune sands, 115
POOLE, F. G., 100, 105
Porbander Limestone, Pleistocene, India, 159
Porosity, 36, 59, 131
PORRENGA, D. H., 58, 192
Potassium ferricyanide, 144, 189
POWERS, R. W., 60, 114, 196
PRAMANIK, S. K., 5
PRICE, W. A., 180
Privett, D. W., 1
Prograding desert coasts, 126
Pyrenees, 45
Pyrite, 172, 178, 188, 191

Qanat, 74, 196
Qatar, 84, 86, 126
Qattara Depression, Egypt, 26, 28, 69
Quaternary, dunes and continental sediments, 70, 113, 117, 126, 128

Quartz grains, authigenic overgrowths, 167, 189, 190, 192
—, calcite corrosion of, 156, 166
—, frosting of, 156, 165, 166
—, rate of abrasion, 8, 127
Quicksand, 66

Raasay, Scotland, 45
Rain, 4, 5, 10, 32, 36, 39, 45, 57, 94, 108, 110, 136
—, desert, 6, 29, 64
—, frequency in deserts, 6, 38, 64
—, sporadic, 1, 19, 20, 28, 115
Rainshadow, 1, 4, 5
Raindrop pits, 49
Rajasthan Desert, IX, 5, 88, 94, 115, 184, 190
RAMANATHAN, K. R., 5
Rann of Kutch, Great, 136
Ranns of Kutch, India, IX, 136, 140
Ras al Khaimah, Trucial Coast, 32, 75, 121, 122, 126
Ra's Ghanadah, Trucial Coast, 124
RAYMOND, P. E., 173, 174
Recumbent folds in aquatic sediments, 12, 30, 110, 112, 113
— — in aeolian sediments, 108, 110, 113, 128
Red Sea, 134
REES, A. I., 82
Reg, 18, 196
REICHE, P., 100
REINECK, H. E., 71, 73, 142, 195
Rhone, River, 31
RICHARDSON, E. V., 30, 39, 108
RIGASSI, D. A., 113
Ripples, adhesion, 71, 73, 140, 142, 144, 195
—, aeolian, 46, 78, 79, 80, 95, 108, 144, 197
—, assymetry of, 80
—, climbing, 30, 40, 56, 150
—, fluvial, 12, 30, 39, 52, 108
—, granule, 78, 80
— index, 80
—, wavelength of, 80
Riss, glaciation, 132
Rivers, 30, 49, 57, 124
—, glacial, 6, 118
—, seasonal, 10, 30, 52, 53, 142
—, water velocity of, 29, 39, 40
ROBB, G. L., 174, 180
ROGERS, J., 174, 176, 179
Rootlets, plant roots and root casts, 1, 113, 114, 115, 118, 124, 128
Roundham Head, Devon, 42, 68
Roundness, pebbles and boulders, 16, 22, 33, 43
—, sand grains, 11, 16, 21, 144, 156, 159, 167, 170

Rub al Khali, interdune outcrop, 22
—, loess, 118
—, sand dunes, 37, 86, 94, 95, 96, 190
—, wadi sediments, 29, 31, 147
RUCHIN, L. B., 33
RUNCORN, S. K., 100, 105
RUSSEGGER, J., 113

Sabkha el Kourzia, Tunisia, 61
Sabratha, Libya, 132
Sahara Desert, 4, 18, 58, 90, 118, 172, 182
SAID, R., 113
SALAMUMI, R. S., 20, 100
Salina, 60
Salinity, saline, 8, 26, 27, 117, 133, 134
Salt cementation, 59
— concentrations, 1, 8, 57
— crust, 27, 57, 60, 61, 66, 69, 121, 134, 136
— plugs, 57
— polygons, 61, 64, 136
— preserved in clay, 63
— rock, halite, 26, 61, 62, 133, 136, 140
— in sebkhas, 60, 61, 63, 64, 69, 71, 88, 121, 134, 135, 136
— as weathering agent, 16
Salton Sea, California, 45
Sand, aeolian, supply of, 84, 95, 96, 97
—, carbonate, 8, 38, 73, 108, 122, 124, 126, 127, 128, 130, 159
— drift, 8, 22, 114, 115, 197
—, sandstone dyke, 12, 55, 64, 68, 143, 144
— movement by saltation, 7, 21, 24, 77, 78, 80, 82, 92, 108, 165
— movement by surface creep, 7, 21, 77, 78, 80, 82, 92, 108
— ridge, aeolian, 77, 78
— — marine, 90, 95
— ripples, 78, 79, 80
— sea, 1, 8, 78, 89, 146, 197
—, silicified, 112
— transverse instability in strong winds, 89
SANDFORD, K. S., 113
Saudi Arabia, 84, 86, 126
Scalpay, Scotland, 45
Scarcliffe, Derbyshire, 133
SCHMALZ, R. F., 190
SCHOCK, R. N., 145
SCHUMM, S. A., 45
Scotland, Old Red Sandstone of, 44, 177, 180
—, New Red Sandstone of, 45   4
—, Permian dune sands of, 58, 101
—, Permian desert sediments of, 181, 185, 188, 190
Sea level, 10, 32, 64, 86, 92, 124, 126, 127, 128, 129, 136, 159
Sebha, Libya, 89

Sebkha, coastal, 32, 61, 75, 101 121, 122, 124, 126, 127, 130, 134, 135, 140, 197
—, inland, 60, 61, 64, 66, 69, 70, 73, 75, 128, 131, 140, 148, 182, 197
—, interdune, 61, 69, 95, 96, 97, 98
Sebkha Matti, Trucial Coast, 73, 115, 126, 127, 131, 184
Sebkra Sedjoumi, Tunisia, 139
Sediment transport, aeolian, 12, 16, 172, 184
— — fluvial, 6, 29, 30, 170, 172
Sediment transport directions, aeolian, 43, 84, 89, 145, 150
— — —, fluvial, 43, 145, 147
— — —, contrasting aeolian/fluvial, 147, 148
SEGERSTROM, K., 130
SENGUPTA, S., 148
Serir, 18, 197
Shamal, 73, 84, 96, 122, 197
Sharjah, Trucial Coast, 102
SHARP, R. P., 19, 78, 79, 80, 183
SHAWA, M. S., 113
Sheet floods, 12, 44, 45
Sheet sands, 106, 108
SHEARMAN, D. J., 60, 121, 133, 134
SHEPARD, F. P., 144
SHERLOCK, R. L., VIII
Shiraz, Iran, 57
SHOTTON, F. W., VIII, 100, 180, 183
SHUKRI, N. M., 113
Siderite, 176
Silcrete, 112, 197
Silicified wood, 112
Sind, Pakistan, 159
SIMONS, D. B., 30, 39, 108
Simpson Desert, Australia, 84, 90
Siwalik Hills, India and Nepal, 145
Siwaliks, Tertiary, 180, 181
SKIPWITH, P. A. D'E, 1, 93, 121
Slip face, see Avalanche slope
Slumps, contorted bedding in dune sands, 108, 110, 112, 113, 128
SMALLEY, I. J., 17, 118
SMITH, H. T. U., 6, 94
SMITH, T. E., 45
SNEAD, R. E., 122, 132, 167
Soils, desert, 6, 117, 148, 167, 180
—, lateritic, 173, 178
—, tropical, 173, 177
Sonoran Desert, Mexico, 5, 46, 179, 184
Sorting in aeolian sands, 11, 16, 56, 81, 108, 148, 156, 157
— in fluvial sands, 12, 56
SOUTENDAM, C. J. A., 167
Southeast Trade Winds, 4, 5
Spit, sand, 122, 124
SQUIRRELL, H. C., 175, 183

Stampian, Oligocene, dune sands, France, 58
Stephanian (Carboniferous), 177, 183, 185
Steppe, 118
STIEGLITZ, R. D., 43
STÖCKLIN, J., 58
STODDART, D. R., 130
STOKES, W. L., 34
STONE, R. O., 195
Stereographic polar net, 83, 100, 101, 103, 104, 106
Strait of Hormuz, 134
Stream-flow sediments, 11, 12, 29, 30, 39, 42, 148
Sub-aerial exposure of water-laid sediments, 11–13, 45, 49, 52, 55, 56, 112, 141
Sudan, 94
SUGDEN, W., 15, 20
Suspension, aeolian, 7, 21, 24, 26, 118
—, colloidal, 175, 177
—, fluvial, 29
Swineford, A., 119

TANNER, W. F., 136, 165
Tarif, Abu Dhabi, 1
Tertiary deserts, formations, VIII, 27, 58, 64, 100, 115, 165
— Siwaliks, 180
— salt, 134
THESIGER, W., VII, 184, 190
Thornhill, Dumfriesshire, 58
Threshold velocity, 24
TIBBETS, G. C., 10, 89, 92, 108
Tides, high, 121, 140
—, storm, 126, 135, 136, 140
Tienshan Range, Central Asia, 118
Tigris–Euphrates, River, 124
Todilto Formation, Jurassic, New Mexico, 136
TOMKINS, J. Q., 66
Trade Winds, 4, 5, 6, 94
Trade Wind deserts, 4, 5
Transgression, marine, 10, 110, 113, 126, 128, 189, 190, 193
Triassic aeolian sandstones, 36, 49, 81, 110, 136, 148, 183
— evaporitic sediments, 140
— wadi sediments, 49
TRICART, J., VIII, 93
Tripoli, Libya, 73, 128
TROTTER, F. M., 174, 182
Trucial Coast (Trucial States), Persian Gulf, adhesion ripples, 73
— —, cemented dune sands, 131
— —, changing wind directions, 88, 94, 101
— —, coastal sebkhas, 134
— —, dikaka, 115, 117
— —, fluctuating water table, 182

— —, mud cracks, 49, 55
— —, source of aeolian sands, 46, 84, 184
— —, wind and water-laid sediments, 55
Tunisia, 61, 126, 135, 139
Tweed Basin, Scotland, 45

Ubari Sand Sea, Libya, 58, 64, 74, 84, 89, 95, 106
Umm as Samim, Oman, 18, 61, 63, 64, 75, 87, 88
Umm Said, Qatar, 86
United States of America, VII, 5, 6, 49, 119
Uruguay, 100
Uruq al Mu'taridah, Arabia, 95, 96
Utah, U.S.A., 66, 81, 110

Vadose cementation, 126
Vale of Eden, England, 110, 181, 185, 188, 190
VAN DER BENT, E. TH., 61
VAN DEVENTER, H., 63
VAN HOUTEN, F. B., 175, 176, 177, 180
VAN STRAATEN, L. M. J. U., 84
VEENSTRA, H. J., 148
Vegetation, desert, 6, 8, 10, 57, 115
—, other terrestrial, 45, 58, 73, 119, 122, 124
Ventifacts, 15, 20, 21, 112
VITA-FINZI, C., 118
Volpriehausen Sandstone, Triassic, Germany, 49
VON ENGELN, O. D., 60
Vosges, France, 45, 177

Wadi, 198
— and aeolian sediments, 8, 10, 29, 36, 37, 39, 42, 46, 47, 48, 52, 55, 145
— and alluvial fans, 8, 29, 43, 198
— and dikaka, 115
— braided channels, 29, 30, 34, 42, 43, 121, 198
— cemented sediments, 34, 36, 74, 144
— channels, 29, 31, 34, 39, 43, 70
— in flood, flood water, 30, 31, 34, 38, 40, 61, 110, 112
— gravel, 33, 39, 40, 41, 74, 95
— as source of aeolian sand, 45, 46, 47, 127, 198
— sporadic watercourse, 6, 198
— and temporary deltas, 31, 110, 124
— and transport of sediment, 39, 56
Wadi Al Ayn, Oman, 41, 80
— Amayri, Oman, 52
— Batha, Oman, 38, 90, 99
— Dhaid, Trucial States, 46, 48, 49, 55,
— Hadramaut, Arabia, 118
— Tareglat, Libya, 70
WADIA, D. N., 159
WAGNER, R. H., 177

Wahiba Sands, Oman, colour of dune sands, 184, 190
— — and convection winds, 37
— — and dikaka, 115
— — and modified seif dunes, 99, 106
— — and palaeowind directions, 103
— —, Pleistocene seif dunes, 38, 90, 96, 126
— —, relationship with wadi sands, 38
— — and secondary wind directions, 92
— —, seifs formed by strong winds, 95
WAHLSTROM, E. E., 173, 174
Walchia filiciformis, 115
— piniformis, 115
Wales, South, 181, 182, 183
WALKER, T. R., alteration of iron-bearing minerals, 180
—, calcite corrosion of quartz, 166
—, oxygenated ground water, 182
—, red beds in deserts, 175, 179, 180, 181, 184, 190, 191, 193
—, red tropical soils, 177
WALLÉN, C. C., 5
WALTHER, J., VII, 20, 113, 173, 174, 179
Water, ground and cementation, 24, 34, 131
— and deflation hollows, 26–28
— and desert lakes, 59
— and dikaka, 117
— in inland sebkhas, 64, 71, 75, 97, 98, 131, 156
— and oases, 74
— and occurrence of red beds, 180, 182, 188, 189, 190, 193
—, salinity of, 26, 60, 61, 63, 74, 75
Water table and cementation, 45, 98, 112, 131
— — in coastal sebkhas, 122, 135
— — and deflation, 69, 73, 97, 122
— — and desert lakes, 59
— — fluctuating, 182, 191, 193
— — and formation of mud polygons, 49
— — in inland sebkhas, 60, 98
— — and occurrence of red beds, 178, 183
— — perched, 190
WATERSTON, C. D., 44, 45
WAUGH, B., 167
WEDMAN, E. J., 139
Weichselia, 115
WELLMAN, H. T., 15
WELLS, A. J., 122
Westerlies, 4, 5, 118
Westphalian, Carboniferous, 181, 188
White Sands National Park, U.S.A., 110, 136
WILLIAMS, G., 21
WILSON, A. T., 15
"Wind cell", 90
Wind, dominant, prevailing, 1, 37, 77, 80, 88, 94, 96, 101, 102, 122, 145, 147, 148, 153

Wind *(continued)*
— erosion, 15, 23, 26, 78
—, off-shore, 1
—, on-shore, 1, 5, 71, 84, 86, 122, 126, 128, 130
—, palaeo-, 83, 99, 100, 101, 147, 150, 156
— sorting of sediments, 47
—, strong, 26, 78, 80, 92, 119, 127, 154, 184
—, transport of sediment and abrasion, 127, 165, 167
— — — to dunes, 23, 130
— — — during deflation, 28, 31, 32, 42
— — — from highlands, 39
— — — of low sphericity, 21
— — — by on-shore winds, 71, 159
— — — to place of deposition, 84
— — — by strong winds, 92, 96
— — — of suitable grainsize, 45
— — — in suspension, 22, 26
— velocity and dune formation, 84, 89, 95, 96, 99, 104, 124
— — and formation of sheet sands, 108
— — gradient, 24, 86
— — and ripple formation, 79, 80, 108

— — and sediment transport, 21, 77, 92, 118
— — at surface, 8, 124
WOBBER, J. J., 57
WOLF, K. H., ix
WOLFE, M. J., 167
WRIGHT, H. E., 100
Würm Glaciation, 226, 132
— pluvial, 95

Xerophytic plants, 1
X-ray diffraction, 131, 133, 144, 188

YAALON, D. H., 21, 118, 131, 132
"Yellow Sands", Permian, England, 101, 110, 188, 189
Yorkshire, England, 110
YOUNG, R., 144
Yucatan Peninsula, Mexico, 93

Zagros Mountains, Iran, 57
Zechstein, Permian, 177, 188
Zechstein Sea, 110, 133, 189
ZIEGLER, M. A., 57